HIGH ENERGY LASER (HEL)

Tomorrow's Weapon
in Directed Energy Weapons

Volume I

BAHMAN ZOHURI

Order this book online at www.trafford.com
or email orders@trafford.com

Most Trafford titles are also available at major online book retailers.

Printed in the United States of America.

ISBN: 978-1-4907-5136-8 (sc)
ISBN: 978-1-4907-5138-2 (hc)
ISBN: 978-1-4907-5137-5 (e)

Library of Congress Control Number: 2014920899

Trafford rev. 11/22/2014

 www.trafford.com
North America & international
toll-free: 1 888 232 4444 (USA & Canada)
fax: 812 355 4082

CONTENTS

This book is dedicated to my mother and
father Marzieh and Akbar Zohuri
Without their encouragements, this book
would not have been written

ABOUT THE AUTHOR

Dr. Bahman Zohuri is currently at the Galaxy Advanced Engineering a consulting company that he stared himself in 1991 when he left both semiconductor and defense industries after many years working as a chief scientist. After graduating from University of Illinois in field of Physics and Applied Mathematics, he joined Westinghouse Electric Corporation where he performed thermal hydraulic analysis and natural circulation for Inherent Shutdown Heat Removal System (ISHRS) in the core of a Liquid Metal Fast Breeder Reactor (LMFBR) as a secondary fully inherent shut system for secondary loop heat exchange. All these designs were used for Nuclear Safety and Reliability Engineering for Self-Actuated Shutdown System. He designed the Mercury Heat Pipe and Electromagnetic Pumps for Large Pool Concepts of LMFBR for heat rejection purpose for this reactor around 1978 where he received a patent for it. He later on was transferred to defense division of Westinghouse where he was responsible for the dynamic analysis and method of launch and handling of MX missile out of canister. The results are applied to MX launch seal performance and muzzle blast phenomena analysis (i.e. missile vibration and hydrodynamic shock formation). He also was involved in analytical calculation and computation in the study of Nonlinear Ion Wave in Rarefying Plasma. The results are applied to the propagation of "Soliton Wave" and the resulting charge collector traces, in the rarefactions characteristic of the corona of the a laser irradiated target pellet. As part of his graduate research work at Argonne National Laboratory he performed computation and programming of multi-exchange integral in surface physics and solid state physics. He holds different patent in areas such as diffusion processes and design of diffusion furnace while he was senior process engineer working for different semiconductor industries such as Intel, Varian and National Semiconductor corporations. Later on he joined Lockheed Missile and Aerospace Corporation as

Senior Chief Scientist and was responsible for Senior in R&D and the study of vulnerability, survivability and both radiation and laser hardening of different components of payload (i.e. IR Sensor) for Defense Support Program (DSP), Boost Surveillance and Tracking Satellite (BSTS) and Space Surveillance and Tracking Satellite (SSTS) against laser or nuclear threat. While in there he also studied and performed the analysis of characteristics of laser beam and nuclear radiation interaction with materials, Transient Radiation Effects in Electronics (TREE), Electromagnetic Pulse (EMP), System Generated Electromagnetic Pulse (SGEMP), Single-Event Upset (SEU), Blast and, Thermo-mechanical, hardness assurance, maintenance, device technology.

He did few years of consulting under his company Galaxy Advanced Engineering with Sandia National Laboratories (SNL), where he was supporting development of operational hazard assessments for the Air Force Safety Center (AFSC) in concert with other interest parties. Intended use of the results was their eventual inclusion in Air Force Instructions (AFIs) specifically issued for Directed Energy Weapons (DEW) operational safety. He completed the first version of a comprehensive library of detailed laser tools for Airborne Laser (ABL), Advanced Tactical Laser (ATL), Tactical High Energy Laser (THEL), Mobile/Tactical High Energy Laser (M-THEL), etc.

He also was responsible on SDI computer programs involved with Battle Management C^3 and Artificial Intelligence (AI), and autonomous system. He is author few publications and holds various patents such as Laser Activated Radioactive Decay and Results of Thru-Bulkhead Initiation.

PREFACE

Directed Energy Weapons is nothing new to mankind, historically the origination of such weapons falls in centuries ago when first time the famous Greek mathematician, physicist, engineer, inventor, and astronomer, **Archimedes of Syracuse** where he used different mirrors to collect sun beams and focusing them on Roman's fleet in order to destroy enemy ships with fire. This is known as **The Archimedes Heat Ray**. Archimedes may have used mirrors acting collectively as a parabolic reflector to burn ships attacking Syracuse. The device was used to focus sunlight onto approaching ships, causing them to catch fire. Off course the myth or reality of Archimedes Heat Ray still is questionable story, but certain experiments with help of group of students from Massachusetts Institute of Technology that was carried out with 127 one-foot (30 cm) square mirror tiles in October of 2005 that was focused on a mock-up wooden ship at a range of around 100 feet (30 m). The flames broke out on a patch of the ship, but only after the sky had been cloudless and the ship had remained stationary for around ten minutes. It was concluded the device was a feasible weapon under these conditions.

Battelle of tomorrows will be fought with different weapons that have more lethal effects and faster delivery systems. One of mankind's greatest achievements in the twenties century is the ability to destroy his entire race several times over. At this time of intensive arms buildup, as more and more dollars and rubles are invested in the next generation of weapons, it is in the best interest of every citizen to be aware and be able to make an informed judgment on the best possible direction for the arm race. Offensive or defensive weapons are a cruel reality that nevertheless must be reckoned with on both sides of the Iron Curtain.

The scientific work during the 1950s that led to the invention of the laser was followed closely by work in military research institutes and organizations all over the world and this opened a new door to the Archimedes Heat Ray and his invention. Laser have found many military applications, not as a new weapons, but rather as the supporting technology to enhance the performance of other weapons such as laser guided bomb, etc. Our fascination and appreciation of modern weaponry is at an all-time high. It was not until 1970s that the possibility of laser weapons again captured the imagination of military planners. High-energy and other Directed Energy Weapons finally became a reality, and the possibility of using them in battlefields of tomorrows has been investigated vigorously ever since.

The development of laser weapon and other directed energy weapons technology conjures up the Heat Ray of Archimedes and Flash Gordon-like images of vaporizing enemies, demolishing buildings, and burning through metal. In this book the author has tried to introduce such weaponry to different readers of different technical background as well as introducing the certain technical approach to such research and to help better understanding of such weapons utilizing various technical and research resources.

The next ten years will see the emergence of high energy lasers as an operational capability in US service. These weapons will have the unique capability to attack targets at the speed of light and are likely to significantly impair the effectiveness of many weapon types, especially ballistic weapons. Constrained by propagation physics, these weapons will not provide all weather capabilities, and will perform best in clear sky dry air conditions.

The book under its laser section talks about the interaction between high-power laser beams and matter while other sections touched upon Particle and High-Power Radar beams as a weapon of tomorrows. Laser-Beam Interactions with Materials treats, from a physicist's point of view, the wide variety of processes that lasers can induced in materials. Physical phenomena ranging from optics to shock waves are discussed. The approach is taken emphasizes of the fundamental ideas both from a new comer or research worker point of view to provide both important background for material science, mathematics, optics, etc or most critical up-to-date review of the field.

A directed-energy weapon (DEW) emits energy in an aimed direction without the means of a projectile. It transfers energy to a target for a desired effect. Some such weapons are real or in development; others are at present only science fiction.

The energy can come in various forms:

- Electromagnetic radiation (typically lasers or masers).
- Particles with mass (particle beam weapons).
- Sound (sonic weaponry).
- Fire (flamethrowers).
- High-Power Laser Weapons.

Some lethal directed-energy weapons are under active research and development, but most examples appear in science fiction, non-functional toys, film props or animation.

In science fiction, these weapons are sometimes known as death rays or ray-guns and are usually portrayed as projecting energy at a person or object to kill or destroy. Many modern examples of science fiction have more specific names for directed energy weapons, due to research advances.

For those readers that need to deep dive into the technologies behind such research short course in various topics of mathematics and physics have been offered in the appendices in order for them to brush up these topics and be able to understand different solutions and mathematical modeling that are offered how to solve for example heat diffusion equation for different boundary and initial conditions. I case of application of laser as a weapon, author has attempt to serve both scientists interested in the physical phenomena of laser effects and engineers interested in practical applications of laser effects in industry. Thus, several sections are devoted to reviewing and dealing with solution of diffusion equation utilizing the aid of the integral transforms techniques. In the opinion of the author, among several different approaches that are available for the solution of boundary value problems for heat conduction, the integral transform technique offers the most straight forward and elegant way, provided that the transforms, the inversions, and the kernels are readily available.

Some appendices at the end of the book are devoted to systematic mathematics and physics of heat conduction solution and its boundary value problems. As result the transforms, the inversions, complex variables and their examples are presented and the kernels are tabulated, and the Laplace and Fourier transforms are also have been introduced. Appendix on Introduction to Ordinary and Partial Differential is also presented to help the reader to understand the solution techniques that are used to solve the heat conduction problem for various boundary values. Appendices on optics and electromagnetic field help also better understanding behavior of physics and mathematics of these weapons.

Note: In most of appendices of different topics either the references mentioned at the end of each appendix have been used and quoted directly or indirectly or it is up to each reader for more knowledge and information to refer to them separately. Most of these materials are covered in Volume 2 of this series. I encourage the researches and readers interested in any of these subjects presented in the appendices for each mathematical subject either refer to classical text book or purchase the second volume of this book where all topics are summarized and presented.

It is important that readers to have some advanced knowledge of conduction of heat transfer and methods of solving Partial Differential Equations either steady or none steady states with their given boundary and initial conditions. Some knowledge of Optic Physics and understanding of Electromagnetism properties and associated problems are also very much encouraged and it become very handy.

ACKNOWLEDGMENT

I am indebted to the many people who aided me, encouraged me and the people whom supported me beyond the expectation. Some of those who are not around to see end result of their encouragement in production of this book, yet I hope they can see this acknowledgment. I especially want to thank Nancy Reis and Patrick McDaniel of Sandia National Laboratory who both put the idea in me to start the book based on some work that I was contracted to do for them. Dr. McDaniel, whom I am deeply indebted, has extensively helped me developing and modifying new computer codes and continuously is giving his support with no hesitation. My thank goes to Joe Rogers of NASA, one of my best friend who helped with most of the computer codes that are presented in this book to bring them to its present status from their legacy stages.

My another best friend William Kemp of Air Force Weapon Laboratory at Albuquerque New Mexico who is really a true friend and remains to be one. Finally, I am indebted to many people and the individuals and organizations that granted permission to reproduce copyrights materials and published figures.

Above all, I offer very special thanks to my mother, father while they were alive, wife and children. They provided constant interest and encouragement, without which this book would not have been written.

Their patience with my many absences from home and long hours in front of computer during preparation of this manuscript is especially appreciated.

CHAPTER ONE: DIRECTED ENERGY WEAPONS

Will the United States develop laser and beam weaponry for a strong nuclear defense to replace the policy of Mutually Assured Destruction? Has the .Soviet Union violated treaties by using "yellow rain" in Afghanistan and Indochina? What future lies is store for the clean neutron bomb? What kinds of super missiles are being tested for the future? What new biological and chemical weapons has the United States been cooking up?

1.0 Introduction

The idea of using an omnipotent "death ray" on the battlefield is not a new concept. Ancient literature credits the Greek mathematician Archimedes as the first to conceive the idea of using light as a defensive weapon. Hippocrates, commander of the Greek force, applied Archimedes' concept by focusing the energy of sunlight through a series of mirrors to produce a beam that set fire to the sails of the Roman fleet under Consul Marcus Claudius Marcellus during the siege of Syracuse in 212 B.C. [1]

Laser weapon projects have been shrouded by very tight security. In spite of this, it is possible to follow the general lines, at least, of the High-Energy Laser (HEL) weapon research field through the open literature.

Our fascination and appreciation of modern weaponry is at an all-time high. With the wonders and horrors of the Persian Gulf war and event of 911 fresh in our minds, the development of laser weapon technology conjures up Flash Gordon-like images of vaporizing enemies, demolishing building, and burning through metals.[2]

Armed forces in many countries are already using a great number of laser devices, and the inexorable pace of progress in developing

1

special laser weapons indicates that they will ultimately revolutionize the modern battlefield. Practically invisible when fired, silent, capable of pinpoint accuracy, and traveling at the speed of light, laser weapons would seem to offer unparalleled advantages over conventional weapons.

This paper examines the effects of lasers -- one of the first exotic Directed Energy Weapons (DEW) to capture public attention and our focus in particular is on Airborne Laser (ABL).

While this may be true, once unleashed, this awesome power can trigger other devastating consequences as well. Anti-eye laser weapons are currently being developed that can result in the mass blinding of soldiers, pilots, and tank crews.

Laser experts Anderberg and Wolbarsht [2] describe the staggering medical, social, and psychological ramifications that the use of laser weapons will entail and becomes as part of our study for Laser Safety Range Tool, which is subject of this project. Furthermore, we explore the historical development of these weapons and briefly touch the fact that how far other countries, including France, England, and Russia, have progressed in their technology. We also try to serve the purpose of an introduction to the language of Direct Energy Weapon (DEW) for military planners and non-technical persons who need them to understand the fundamental of what the engineers and scientists involved in their development are talking about by basically touching some physics and mathematics involved in this field. Describe all the difficulties these folks are dealing with and how to overcome these obstacles in order to produce the right tool and technologies that will induce the proper DEW for our defense of our country. A better weapon in hands of our arm force to carry on such defensive task. Any employee found to have violated these policies and procedures may be subject to disciplinary action, up to and including termination of employment.

We have put collection of software and computer codes that are developed by our engineers and scientist around the nation within national laboratories and defense companies under one umbrella and developed the Windows/PC version of these codes as a source of repository of such capabilities. Most of these codes were developed on main and macro frame computing system and under this project we managed to migrate them to micro-frame environment for simplicity of running these codes for the purpose of further enhancement and development of LSRT and DEW in ABL area. In some cases, we further enhanced the technical capability of these legacy codes in order to serve the purpose of today's technology toward development of the directed energy weapons. Table one is good representation of these codes

Folks who are interested to obtain these codes for the purpose of their work toward field of DEW should contact either principal of this report or original source that is mentioned in Table-1 and Table-2. in this chapter Although we tried to gather all existing unclassified computer code together yet they are still consider critical military information that requires proper paper work to obtain these computer codes from our data bank and some cases it might require licensing query of third party software.

To obtain most of these codes you are required to have some direct and related U.S. government contract from appropriate office or agency with government. Then the offices that are in charge of these codes will arrange for release of these codes.

For example most of codes that are released from Sandia National Laboratory such as CHT or codes such as DYNA3D and other related codes from Lawrence Livermore National Laboratory fall in these categories

Although the author of this book has most of these codes in most cases we have to follow the Federal Government guide lines for release of these codes as well minus few exceptions. Please get in touch with the author for further discussion of these codes as well as consulting his web site at www.gaeinc.com for availability of some of these codes through his company.

Bahman Zohuri

We welcome any comment and correction by expert in this field to correct and enhance our assumption on these codes or recommend better computational analysis and software tools.

Next few sections in this chapter we introduce unclassified computer codes that may be obtainable form the source that is known to this author. Some of these codes although not classified but restricted and are available to US government agencies or their contractors.

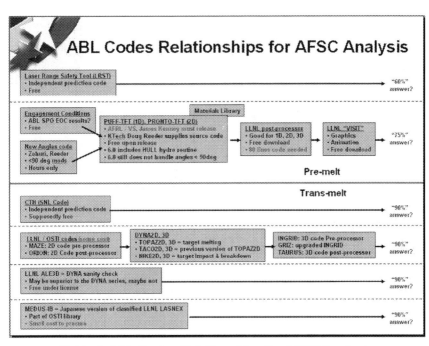

Table 1: ABL Codes Relationships for AFSC Analysis

ABL Codes Relationships for AFSC Analysis

- PUFF-TFT, PRONTO-TFT
  - Both these codes are looking at laser interaction with target up to the point the frequency of laser is not equal to frequency of Plasma due to melt down of target material during the engagement time. These two codes take under consideration the Reflectivity, and BRDF issues based on target material and looks at index of refraction of the beam extinction coefficient and skin depth of materials used on by target. When we both our own number for the materials of the target then the code might get classified.

- PUFF-TFT = 1D analysis
- PRONTO-TFT = 2D per KTECH web site + Hilland ... Reeder says he has no idea who in KTECH handles it
- Mr. Kenney, AFRL/VS, probably handles PRONTO-TFT
- PUFF-TFT 6.0 + PRONTO-TFT + LLNL VisiT = 1-D and 2-D modeling to feed the LRST
- Both codes should be free of the charge to us

- Similar error in PRONTO-TFT (2-D)? Won't know until source code is in hand
- There should be no cost associated with fixing the <90 deg angle of incident in PUFF-TFT
- Improving angle of incidence problem in in PUFF-TFT may give us leverage with AFRL

- Material library comes with both codes
- Materials data = generic, but may be critical info → Military Technical Data Agreement → Galaxy = valid through Nov 2009

- We already have the post-processor VisiT -- binary and source code downloaded from LLNL

- LLNL DYNA series:
  - TOPAZ code = melting
  - NIKE = impact and breakdown of target
  - Pre and post-processors come with each

- CTH (SNL) = LLNL DYNA series of codes

- If we want to study beyond the capability of above two codes where the melting of the target take place then there is the LASNEX (LASNEX models in two dimensions by assuming axial symmetry. It represents the spatial variation of its many physical quantities, such as temperature, density or pressure, on a two-dimensional (2-D), axially symmetric mesh composed of arbitrarily shaped quadrilaterals. LASNEX evolves the hydrodynamics and follows the electron, ion, and radiation heat conduction, and the coupling among these energy fields. There are many possible sources and boundary conditions that can be imposed on a LASNEX simulation, which can vary both in time and space.) code developed by LLNL and that code is classified and can not be released to us under normal circumstances

Table 2: Comments on ABL Codes Relationships for AFSC Analysis

1.2 PUFF74, A Material Response Computer Code

The **PUFF74** code is a computer code, which calculates stress wave formation and propagation by numerical integration of the conservation equations in a one-dimensional Lagrangian coordinate system. The code has been under development since 1961 and has evolved from a simple hydrodynamics code to a flexible material response code, which includes the effects of material strength, porosity, and fracture for both homogeneous and composite materials.

The code at present version (Version 4.0) is capable of handling the following physical models:

1. A framework for calculating the material response in composite materials,
2. A pressure-volume-energy equation of state model for homogeneous materials or constituents of a composite material,
3. A pore-compaction model for porous homogeneous materials or constituents of a composite materials,
4. A one-dimensional viscoplastic model for geometric dispersion effects in composite materials.

The latest model development for the **PUFF74** code has been accomplished under the CADRE Program. As part of this program studies have been made to determine the dynamic material properties, which govern the response of composite materials to rapid energy deposition.

To facilitate the input procedures for radiation deposition calculations, an automatic initial zoning model was added to the PUFF 66 code in extensive use of the code. Reference 3 presents the description of the automatic zoning model.1969 by Cooper. The guidelines used to develop this model evolved through

The next addition to the PUFF code was the framework for introducing a free surface into the sample mesh a t a location where material fracture is detected. The logic for introducing free surfaces, calculating the response of free surfaces as a function of time and recombining fractured segments was developed model in the original coding. Since the coding was written in a modular form, more sophisticated fracture models could be substituted with a minimum of effort.

As model development and calculations of experimental tests continued, a graphics package was added to the PUFF code to allow the user to produce on-1ine plots and externally-produced plots and data storage (Calcomp or microfilm). GAE has used the Universal Graphics Products know as UGL to replace the CA-DISSPLA and produce all the following graphics out and show the power of UGL for its CA-DISSPLA Compatibilities. The plot package added t o the code made extensive use of the general graphic data display programs developed at the Air Force Weapons Laboratory (AFWL) display program existing a t ARIL at the time the plot package was added to PUFF. Modifications to the AFWL data display program and to the graphics package in the PUFF code have been made on a continuing basis t o improve the efficiency of the plotting procedures.

Following is random selection of graphics output of PUFF74/UGL combined.

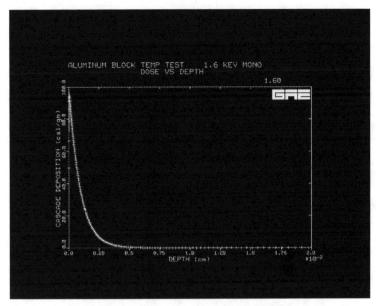

Figure 1-1a: Sample output of PUFF74 using
Universal Graphics Library form GAE.

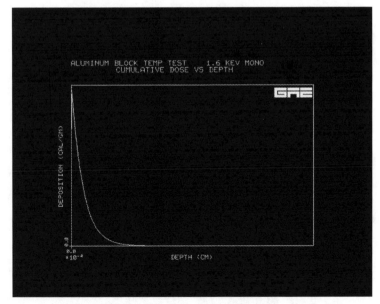

Figure 1-1b: Sample output of PUFF74 using
Universal Graphics Library form GAE.

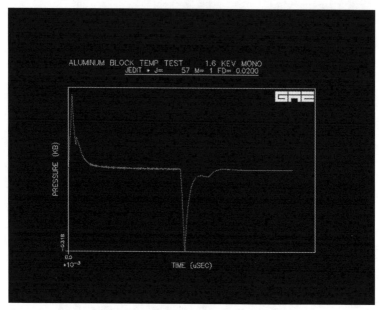

Figure 1-1c: Sample output of PUFF74 using
Universal Graphics Library form GAE.

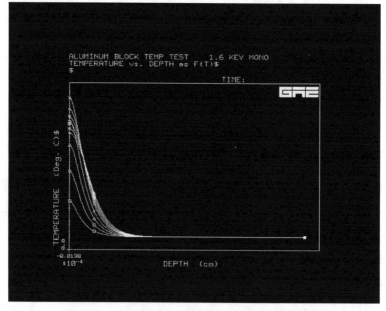

Figure 1-1d: Sample output of PUFF74 using
Universal Graphics Library form GAE.

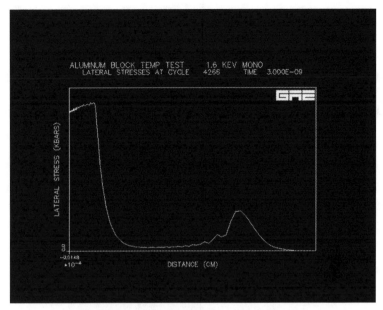

Figure 1-1e: Sample output of PUFF74 using
Universal Graphics Library form GAE.

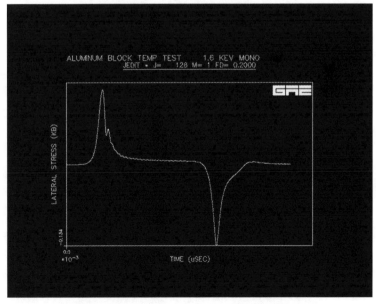

Figure 1-1f: Sample output of PUFF74 using
Universal Graphics Library form GAE.

1.2.1 Availability of PUFF74 Computer Code

The Window/PC version of this code is available from Galaxy Advanced Engineering, Inc. for purchase price. This version has been modified from its original version that used to run on VAX/VMS computer and users need to obtain their own copy form this company. Contact the Galaxy Advanced Engineering, Inc. for its Window/ PC version. To our knowledge the code is no longer available from government agencies or its contractors. You can find more detail how to obtain and purchase by referring to the following URL;

https://www.gaeinc.com

1.3 PUFF-TFT, A Material Response Computer Code

The PUFF-TFT code has now been updated (Version 5.0) to allow modeling of sample responses to sudden energy loading (e.g., X rays or Lasers) for arbitrary starting temperatures. Problems can be run for any initial temperature, both elevated and, most importantly, for cryogenic conditions. Updates have also been made in the stress response for the "thermal-only" mode, especially for the cooldown stresses after plastic flow. Likewise, the code tracks material properties (yielding, shear module, spall strengths) for cryogenic conditions.

The code amendments have been done in a "transparent" manner for the user, requiring the minimum of input parameter changes. To active this, the code maintains the existing convention of:

$$\text{Enthalpy} = 0.0 \text{ cal/g at temperature} = 25 \text{ C}$$

and temperature continues to be in degrees centigrade. Consequently, for that equal to 25 °C, the code will start with a non-zero enthalpy. For T > 25 °C, this initial enthalpy will be positive, whereas for T < 25 °C, the enthalpy is negative.

The previous code version did not distinguish between "dose" (the added energy due to X rays, thermal flow, etc.) and "enthalpy." This was appropriate, since both terms initialized with a common value of zero. The new code makes the distinction, since dose still starts from zero enthalpy.

The "transparent" amendments are such that the user continues to use the existing database for such parameters as melt energy, vapor energy, and latent heats. Likewise, for T > 25 ^{0}C, the existing polynomial coefficients to describe specific heats, enthalpies, and conductivities are maintained.

The code was written for the Air Force Weapon Laboratory (AFWL) primarily to allow evaluation of thin-layer stack response to X-ray deposition resulting in one dimensional (1-D) strain stress response. The code takes into account the X-ray generation of secondary cascade particles (photoelectrons, Auger electrons and fluorescent photons) using a cascade routine, and incorporates a thermal condition routine allowing the effects of rapid thermal diffusivity to be included.

The output of the X-ray/cascade/thermal routine is used as input to an updated version of the PUFF74 hydrodynamic code, which includes hydrodynamic, elasto-plastic, porous and dispersive material responses in a fully-coupled manner, and also accounts for simple phase changes.

The formulation of differential equations follows either Eulerian or Lagrangian descriptions. The Eulerian description is a spatial description; while the Lagrangian is a material description. In an Eulerian framework, all grid points, and consequently cell boundaries, remain fixed with time. Mass, momentum, and energy flow across cell boundaries. In a Lagrangian description, the grid points are attached to the material and move with the material. In this formulation, mass within a cell is invariant, but the volume of the cell may change with time because of expansion or compression, of the materials.

The PUFF-TFT code calculates stress wave formation and propagation by numerical integration of the conservation equations in a one-dimensional Lagrangian coordinate system. The TFT package accounts for the effects of dose enhancement due to the transport of secondary particles with ranges comparable to the thickness of the thin material layers and thermal conduction between thin material layers. These two modifications (among others) more accurately portray the degree of energy sharing between thin layers, thereby modifying the expected energy depositions based on normal x-ray interactions and possibly altering the anticipated thermo-mechanical response of the medium.

The PUFF74 code, originally developed in the mid-sixties, has undergone a number of revisions to become a flexible material response code that includes the effects of material strength, porosity, and fracture for both homogeneous and composite materials. The code calculates stress wave formation and propagation by numerical integration of the conservation equations in a one-dimensional Lagrangian coordinate system. In addition to the hydrodynamic equation of state, which is required for all materials, the code contains an elastic-plastic model for strength effects, a P-Alpha porosity model for treating irreversible compaction, and four models for treating strain-rate dependent or dispersive effects.

Below you can see some graphic output sample of PUFF-TFT code

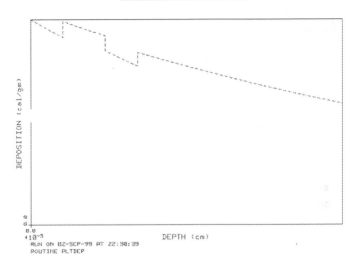

**Figure 1-1g: Sample output of PUFF-TFT using
Universal Graphics Library form GAE**

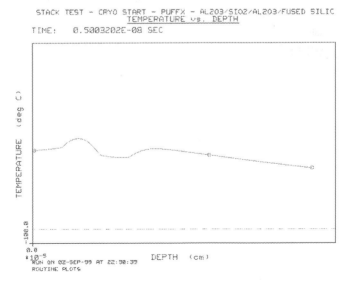

**Figure 1-1h: Sample output of PUFF-TFT using
Universal Graphics Library form GAE**

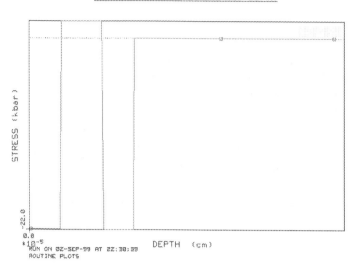

Figure 1-1i: Sample output of PUFF-TFT using
Universal Graphics Library form GAE

1.3.1 Availability of PUFF-TFT Computer Code

The Window/PC version of this code is available from Galaxy Advanced Engineering, Inc. for purchase price. This version has been modified from its original version that used to run on CDC computer and users need to obtain their own copy by applying to Oak Ridge National Laboratory technology transfer office or contact the Galaxy Advanced Engineering, Inc. for its Window/PC version. You can find more detail how to obtain and purchase by referring to the following URL;

https://www.gaeinc.com

1.4 SANDYL, A Monte Carlo Three-Dimensional Computer Code

SANDYL is a FORTRAN code for computing, photon-electron transport and deposition in complex systems by the Monte Carlo method. In this computation, a large number of possible particle trajectories are generated one at a time and, as the particle proceeds through the material of the system, contributions to the quantities making up the desired information are tallied. After a number of trajectories, the averages of these quantities are statistical approximations, to the solution. All histories of source Andy secondary particles with energies in the 1-keV to 1000-MeV ranges are followed through the system.

The problem geometry is divided into zones, of homogeneous atomic composition bounded, by sections of planes and quadrics. Thus the material of each zone, is a, specified element or combination of elements.

For a photon history, the trajectory is generated by following the photon from scattering to scattering using then various probability distributions to find distances between collisions, types of collisions, types of secondary's, and their energies and scattering angles. The photon interactions are photo, electric absorption (atomic ionization), coherent scattering, incoherent scattering, and pair production. The secondary photons which are followed include bremsstrahlung, fluorescence photons, and $e^+ - e^-$ annihilation radiation.

The condensed-history Monte Carlo method is used for the electron transport. In a history, the spatial steps taken by an electron are pre-computed and may include the effects of a number of collisions. The corresponding scattering angle, and energy loss in the step are found from the multiple scattering distributions for these quantities, Atomic ionization and secondary particles are generated within the step according to the probabilities for their occurrence.

Electron energy loss is through inelastic electron-electron collisions, bremsstrahlung generation, and polarization of the medium (density effect). Included in the loss is the fluctuation due to the variation in the number of energy-loss collisions in a given Monte Carl step (straggling). Scattering angular distributions are determined from elastic nuclear-collision cross sections corrected for electron-electron interactions. The secondary electrons which are followed include knock-on, pair, Auger (through atomic ionizations), Compton, and photoelectric electrons.

SANDYL is a Monte Carlo Three-Dimensional Code for Calculating Combined Photon-Electron Transport in Complex Systems. SANDYL incorporates material from the SORS photon and ETRAN photon-electron codes. Major additions and modifications occur in the atomic ionization and relaxation routines and in the general geometry multiple-material aspects of the electron transport.

SANDYL uses the Monte Carlo as a method of method. In its computations, a large number of possible particle trajectories are generated one at a time and, as the particle proceeds through the material of the system, contributions to the quantities making up the desired information are tallied. After a number of trajectories, the averages of these quantities are statistical approximations to the solution.

The problem geometry is divided into zones of homogeneous atomic composition bounded by sections of planes and quadrics. Thus, the material of each zone is a specified element or combination of elements. For a photon history, the trajectory is generated by following the photon from scattering to scattering using the various probability distributions to find distances between collisions, types of collisions, types of secondary, and their energies and scattering angles. The condensed-history Monte Carlo method is used for the electron transport.

The code does time and space dependent transport calculations of the photon-electron cascade in complex systems. All generations of particles in the 1-keV to 1000-MeV energy range are followed.

1.4.1 Availability of SANDYL Computer Code

The Window/PC version of this code is available from Galaxy Advanced Engineering, Inc. for purchase price. This version has been modified from its original version that used to run on CDC computer and users need to obtain their own copy by applying to Oak Ridge National Laboratory technology transfer office or contact the Galaxy Advanced Engineering, Inc. for its Window/PC version. You can find more detail how to obtain and purchase by referring to the following URL;

https://www.gaeinc.com

1.5 ASTHMA88 (Axi-Symmetric Transient Heating and Materials Ablation) Code

The ASTHMA88 program has been developed for computing the 2-D -Symmetric transient thermo-chemical response of decomposing materials subject to hyper-thermal convective and radiative environments. The ASTHMA88 code employs an implicit/explicit, finite-difference computational procedure with a fixed two-dimensional grid whose layout is independent of the physical axes. The numerical modeling includes equations for mass and energy conservation and material decomposition; the flow of pyrolysis gas through the porous, decomposing solid; the calculation of material properties as a function of temperature and material state; general ablating surface and back wall/side wall boundary conditions, and a comprehensive surface energy balance which accounts for convection and radiation absorption, re-radiation, in-depth condition, surface ablation, pyrolysis gas flow, transpiration effects, and thin-layer mechanical removal or surface melting. Validation studies demonstrate excellent agreement with other standard thermo-chemical analysis codes i.e. CMA (1-D, decomposing) and ASTHMA81 (2-D, non-decomposing]).

The **ASTHMA88** code can handle multiple decomposing and non-decomposing, anisotropic materials in simple or complex two-dimensional Axi-Symmetric configurations. Surface boundary conditions may be described in three options:

1. Simple specified temperature and recession
2. Specified heat flux with no recession

General thermo-chemical model is incorporating both equilibrium and non-equilibrium computations, for any material exposed to any convective and/or radiative environment.

1.5.1 Availability of ASTHMA88 Computer Code

The Window/PC version of this code is available from Galaxy Advanced Engineering, Inc. for purchase price. This version has been modified from its original version that used to run on VAX/VMS computer and users need to obtain their own copy form this company. Contact the Galaxy Advanced Engineering, Inc. for its Window/ PC version. To our knowledge the code is no longer available from government agencies or its contractors. You can find more detail how to obtain and purchase by referring to the following URL;

https://www.gaeinc.com

1.6 ALE3D (Arbitrary Lagrangian/Eulerian Multi-Physics 3D) Computer Code

Composite materials are used in many advanced application systems and structures at Lawrence Livermore National Laboratory (LLNL). We have previously enhanced our ability to simulate structural response and progressive failure of composite systems in ALE3D (an Arbitrary Lagrange/Eulerian multi-physics code developed at LLNL) by porting an existing composite constitutive model (Model 22, the Fiber Composite with Damage Model) from DYNA3D (a nonlinear, explicit, 3-D FEM code for solid and structural mechanics). This year, a more advanced model (DYNA3D Model 62, the Uni-Directional Elasto-Plastic Composite Model) has been implemented. Experiments were conducted to validate the elastic response of the model and to give insights and data needed for the addition of a failure algorithm into the model.

They implemented the Uni-Directional Elasto-Plastic Composite Model into ALE3D. This included implementing the ability to input orthotropic orientation data into prescribed local volume elements. Another modeling goal was to enhance the model by incorporating a failure algorithm that includes matrix delaminating, fiber tensile, and fiber compressive failure. Several experiments were conducted to provide data for the verification and validation of the model's implementation in ALE3D.

The improved fiber composite material models can be used in simulations (to failure) in the many LLNL programs, such as those for composite munitions, armor penetration, pressure vessels, and rocket motors. This project has been beneficial in supporting the composite modeling efforts within the DoD Joint Munitions Program and the Focused Lethality Munitions Program. This study supports LLNL's engineering core competency in high-rate mechanical deformation simulations of large complex structures by providing an enhanced capability to model composite structures with ALE3D.

The implementation of the Fiber Composite with Damage model into ALE3D, which was completed in the first year of this project, was verified with several code-to-code comparisons. The hoop stresses in pressurized cylinders from simulations run with DYNA3D, with the new Fiber Composite model in ALE3D, and with an existing anisotropic ALE3D model, all agreed within 1%. This included both explicit and implicit ALE3D runs.

The Uni-Directional Elasto-Plastic Composite model was implemented into ALE3D. An important part of this task was creating an algorithm to initialize and update material directions at the ply and element levels. The model was validated using the same pressurized-cylinder simulations described above, and the results were found to closely match the DYNA3D predictions.

Composite failure mechanisms can be divided into two types: intra-ply failure mechanisms, such as fiber breakage, matrix failure (cracking/crushing), and fiber buckling; and inter-ply failure mechanisms involving ply delaminating.

Intra-ply failure can be applied at the ply level and so fits in well with this model's "unit cell" approach. Inter-ply failure that includes crack opening between plies and plies sliding relative to each other affect all layers simultaneously, and so is more difficult to implement. All the relevant mathematical expressions necessary for these functionalities have been derived, and the corresponding changes to the existing code have outlined. Implementation will be undertaken next year.

A series of compression tests to failure were conducted on eight different composite cylinder specimens with different fiber, fiber orientations, and resins. The data collected on the stiffness, Poisson's ratio, and ultimate strength of each specimen provide model validation data for the newly implemented models 22 and 62. The data also provide an expanded source of failure data for upcoming failure model validation in ALE3D.

Figure.1-2: Fiber composite compression cylinder with 1.0-in.-diameter pin.

Strain concentration factors in fiber composite cylinders with holes and bonded pins were measured using the Aramis video strain measurement system. The basic fiber composite cylinder with pin configuration is shown in Figure.3-62. The Figure 3-63 shows a comparison for the case of no pin (open hole) between the measured experimental data and the simulated response from ALE3D. The results appear to be very similar.

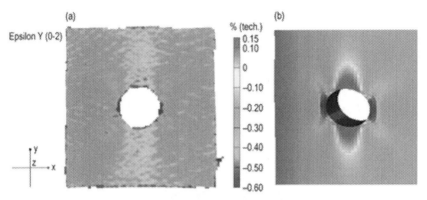

Figure.1-3: (a) Aramis axial stain results for fiber composite compression cylinder with no pin at 300,000 lbs of load. (b) The ALE3D simulation.

Strain concentration factors due to focused shear in composites were measured using the specimen shown in Figure 1-3. This sample was loaded in compression to produce a concentrated shear band in the composite sample. The Aramis load strain curve is shown in Figure.3-65.

Figure 1-4: Composite Shear Specimen from section of a MK82

In a proposed follow-on project, we will continue to improve fiber composite modeling in ALE3D, with an emphasis on local bending response and progressive damage. We plan to implement ply-level capabilities and damage algorithms taken from a specialized LLNL ply-level composite code known as ORTHO3D, and verify their implementation experimentally.

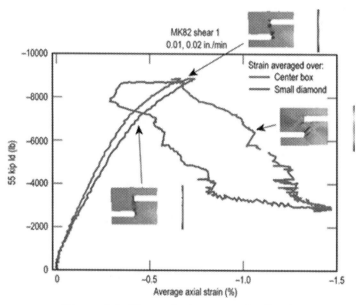

Figure 1-5: Shear strain concentration in composite Mk82 shear specimen.

1.6.1 ALE3D Program Availability

This code is available from Lawrence Livermore National Laboratory and users need to obtain their own copy by applying to LLNL technology transfer office or contact the author of the code Andrew Anderson (925) 423-9634 or refer to the site of this code at the following URL;

https://www-eng.llnl.gov/mod_sim/mod_sim_tools.html

1.7 CTH Computer Code

CTH is a multi-material, large deformation, strong shock wave, solid mechanics code that runs on most UNIX workstations and MPP supercomputers. CTH is one of the most heavily used computational structural mechanics codes on DoD High Performance Computing (HPC) platforms. While CTH includes some internal graphics capabilities, it is preferable to take advantage of widely used scientific visualization packages like EnSight and ParaView to analyze the results of calculations. A new method has been devised that extends the capabilities of CTH to allow three dimensional polygonal models to be written directly from a running calculation in a format compatible to both EnSight and ParaView. Additionally, an interpreter for the scripting language Python has been embedded into CTH, and it's post-processor Spymaster. Embedded Python allows for almost limitless, parallel capabilities to be added that do not require a recompilation or re-linking of the CTH executable. Examples of these capabilities include one and two way code coupling, and Behind Armor Debris (BAD) applications.

The latest version of the widely used shock wave physics computer code, CTH, developed by Sandia National Laboratories, will soon be available to customers nationwide. The code simulates high-speed impact and penetration phenomena involving a variety of materials.

Interest in the new version of the software is particularly high among customers like the Department of Energy (DOE) and Department of Defense (DOD), which use the software for studying weapon effects, armor/anti-armor interactions, warhead design, high-explosive initiation physics, and weapon safety issues. Major users include the national laboratories, the Army, Navy, and Air Force laboratories, and their subcontractors. At Sandia, a DOE laboratory, the code is used in national missile defense, hazardous material dispersal by explosive detonation, weapon components design, and reactive materials research.

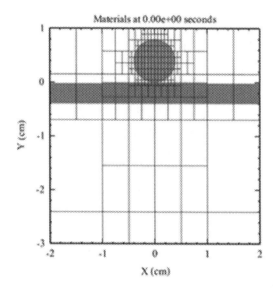

Figure 1-6a: CTH Run time for t=0.00e+00 seconds

For armor/anti-armor design — of interest to DOD — the software allows users to determine which types of bullets or projectiles can best penetrate armor. It also provides information about how to design an improved penetration protection mechanism.

"This new version is really exciting because it offers a computational capability never before available in this type of code, an adaptive mesh refinement model [AMR]," says Paul Taylor, head of the CTH project at Sandia. "AMR gives the software the ability to increase resolution and accuracy in those regions of a simulation where it is needed and reduce resolution in those regions where it is not. For example, in the simulation of a projectile penetrating a target material, greater resolution can be achieved in the region surrounding the impact interface between the two materials where large distortions and high strain rates are occurring."

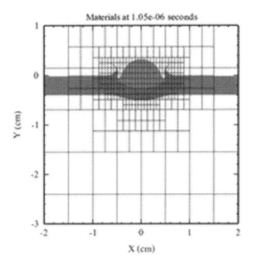

Figure 1-6b: CTH Run time for t=1.05e+06 seconds

The medical community is also paying attention to Sandia's CTH software. Taylor currently has a small collaborative research effort underway with the University Of New Mexico School Of Medicine, which is interested in using the shock physics code to better understand brain injury caused by physical trauma, such as a person's head hitting a car windshield. Using the magnetic resonance image (MRI) of an individual's head to construct a CTH model, simulations can be performed showing how shock waves travel through the head and cause brain damage.

The software breaks down the penetration simulation into millions of grid-like "cells." As the modeled projectile (such as a copper ball impacting a steel plate) impacts and penetrates the target, progressively smaller blocks of cells are placed around the projectile, each showing in detail the deformation and breakup of the ball and target plate.

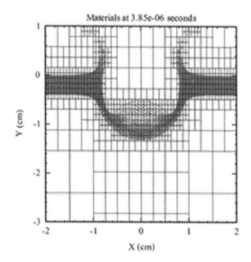

Figure 1-6c: CTH Run time for t=3.85e+06 seconds

CTH with the AMR enhancement also offers the ability to analyze problems involving sophisticated materials with greater accuracy. With the addition of new material models, it can simulate a wider variety of materials, including metals, ceramics, plastics, composites, high explosives, rocket propellants, and gases.

Sandia developed the early precursor to CTH in the 1970s for one-dimensional problems, expanding it to simulate problems in two and three dimensions in the 1980s.

The Labs began licensing the shockwave physics code in the early 1990s to DOE, DOD, their contractors, and some private US companies with interests in shock physics.

An updated version of the software, which is export controlled, is distributed to customers about every 18 months. Currently 259 licenses have been issued.

DOD, DOE, and their contractors receive use licenses for a small distribution fee. Commercial companies can purchase licenses for $25,000. The updated software will be distributed on CDs at a cost of $400 for each noncommercial, licensed customer.

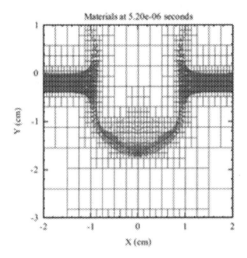

Figure 1-6d: CTH Run time for t=5.20e+06 seconds

One of the most appealing aspects of CTH for users is that it can run on almost any computer platform. Taylor offers CTH classes at Sandia several times a year to users from all over the country.

1.7.1 Availability of CTH Computer Code

This code is available from Sandia National Laboratory. Sandia is a multi-program laboratory operated by Sandia Corporation, a Lockheed Martin Company, for the United States Department of Energy under contract DE-AC04-94AL85000. With main facilities in Albuquerque, N.M., and Livermore, Calif., Sandia has major research and development responsibilities in national security, energy and environmental technologies, and economic competitiveness.

Media contact:
Chris Burroughs, coburro@sandia.gov, (505) 844-0948

Technical contact:
Paul Taylor, pataylo@sandia.gov (505) 844-1960

1.8 HYPUF, Stress Wave Response Computer Code

HYPUF is a stress wave response code that has the ability to calculate ionization effects in high temperature, high-density plasmas. As such, HYPUF/PC is a derivative of the PUFF-66 code. HYPUF is also a code for any defense contractor having a need to calculate the response of materials to radiation induced stress waves.

The modification to present **HYPUF** code available in PC program is part of a continuing program to provide a code suitable for analysis of material interaction with X-ray lasers and other high intensity radiation sources. Previous version of this code included automatic zoning, rezoning and spall (fracture) capabilities. The modifications in the present code include elastic-viscoseplastic,

Maxwell dispersion and Bade geometric dispersion material response models are implemented, restructuring of the code to facilitate future modifications and numerous minor corrections to the equation of state and ionization equation of state subroutines. All above three models are incorporated as closely as possible to the way they were implemented in PUFF74 code. The only differences between the implementation in the two codes was that imposed by the fact that HYPUF/PC is a temperature based rather than energy based code and that **HYPUF/PC** has its equation of state package completely separate from the HYDRO routine.

The elastic-viscoplastic model is an extension of the elastic-plastic model, which is used to calculate stress deviators in solid materials. In the elastic-viscoplastic model, the stress deviator can overshoot the yield surface value. The stress deviator is computed incrementally from the differential equation.

1.8.1 Availability of HYPUF, Stress Wave Response Computer Code

The Window/PC version of this code is available from Galaxy Advanced Engineering, Inc. for purchase price. This version has been modified from its original version that used to run on VAX/VMS computer and users need to obtain their own copy form this company. Contact the Galaxy Advanced Engineering, Inc. for its Window/ PC version. To our knowledge the code is no longer available from government agencies or its contractors. You can find more detail how to obtain and purchase by referring to the following URL;

https://www.gaeinc.com

1.9 DYNA2D and DYNA3D Computer Codes Series

There series of computer codes that were released by Lawrence Livermore National Laboratory such as DYNA2D, DYNA3D, as Lagrangian Finite Element methods of analysis. DYNA2D and DYNA3D are an explicit finite element code for analyzing the transient dynamic response of three dimensional solids and structures. The element formulations available include one-dimensional truss and beam elements, two-dimensional quadrilateral and triangular shell elements, two-dimensional delamination and cohesive interface elements, and three-dimensional continuum elements.

Many material models are available to represent a wide range of material behavior, including elasticity, plasticity, composites, thermal effects, and rate dependence. In addition, DYNA2D and DYNA3D have a sophisticated contact interface capability, including frictional sliding and single surface contact, to handle arbitrary mechanical interactions between independent bodies or between two portions of one body. Also, all element types support rigid materials for modeling rigid body dynamics or for accurately representing the geometry and mass distribution of a complex body at minimum cost. A material model driver with interactive graphics display is integrated into DYNA2D and DYNA3D to allow computation of the stress response to any prescribed strain history without inertial effects. This feature allows accurate assessment of the representation of complex material behavior by the numerical constitutive model in DYNA2D and DYNA3D.

The 3D version of these codes, DYNA3D is an explicit, three-dimensional, finite element program for analyzing the large deformation dynamic response of inelastic solids and structures. DYNA3D contain 30 material models and 10 equations of state (EOS) to cover a wide range of material behavior. The material models implemented are: elastic, orthotropic elastic, kinematic/isotropic plasticity, thermoelastoplastic, soil and crushable foam, linear viscoelastic, Blatz-Ko rubber, high explosive burn, hydrodynamic without deviatory stresses, elastoplastic hydrodynamic, temperature dependent elastoplastic, isotropic elastoplastic, isotropic elastoplastic with failure, soil and crushable foam with failure, Johnson/Cook plasticity model, pseudo TENSOR geological model, elastoplastic with fracture, power law isotropic plasticity, strain rate dependent plasticity, rigid, thermal orthotropic, composite damage model, thermal orthotropic with 12 curves, piecewise linear isotropic plasticity, and inviscid two invariant geologic cap, orthotropic crushable model, Moonsy-Rivlin rubber, resultant plasticity, closed form update shell plasticity, and Frazer-Nash rubber model. The IBM 3090 version does not contain the last two models mentioned.

The hydrodynamic material models determine only the deviatoric stresses. Pressure is determined by one of ten equations of state including linear polynomial, JWL high explosive, Sack "Tuesday" high explosive, Gruneisen, ratio of polynomials, linear polynomial with energy deposition, ignition and growth of reaction in HE, tabulated compaction, tabulated, and TENSOR pore collapse. DYNA3D generates three binary output databases. One contains information for complete states at infrequent intervals; 50 to 100 states are typical. The second contains information for a subset of nodes and elements at frequent intervals; 1,000 to 10,000 states are typical. The last contains interfaces data for contact surfaces.

Method of solution is based on a contact-impact algorithm permits gaps and sliding along material interfaces with friction. All versions except for the IBM3090 include an interface type defining one-way treatment of sliding with voids and friction. By a specialization of this algorithm, such interfaces can be rigidly tied to admit variable zoning with no need for transition regions. Spatial discretazation is achieved by implementation of Hughes-Liu rectangular beams and shells, Belytschko-Tsay shells and beams, triangular shell elements based on work by Belytschko and colleagues, and 8-node solid-shell elements. All element classes can be included as parts of a rigid body. Three-dimensional plane stress constitutive subroutines update the stress tensor for the shell elements such that the stress component normal to the shell mid-surface is zero. One constitutive evaluation is made for each integration point through the shell thickness. The 8-node solid element uses either one point integration or the Flanagan and Belytschko constant stress formulation with exact volume integration. Zero energy modes in the shell and solid elements are controlled by either an hourglass viscosity of stiffness. The equations of motion are integrated in time by the central difference method. A Jaumann stress rate formulation is used with the exception of the orthotropic elastic and the rubber material subroutines which use Green-St.Venant strains to compute second Piola-Kirchoff stresses which transform to Cauchy stresses.

1.9.1 Availability of DYNA2D and DYNA 3D Computer Codes

Both these code are available from the following site but has no technical support nor is up-to-date with any present computing operating system and codes have a lot of logical errors that need to be fixed and based this author experience working with these codes for long time, they are not easy to fix unless you are willing to spend hours and hours of debugging.

This package is distributed by:
Energy Science and Technology Software Center
P.O. Box 62
1 Science.Gov Way
Oak Ridge, TN 37831
(865) 576-2606 TEL
(865) 576-6436 FAX
E-mail: ESTSC@osti.gov

The Window/PC versions of these codes are available from Galaxy Advanced Engineering, Inc. Just refer to www.gaeinc.com

1.10 NIKE2D and NIKE3D Computer Codes Series

NIKE2D is an implicit finite element code for analyzing the finite deformation, quasistatic, and dynamic response of two-dimensional, axisymmetric, plane-strain, and plane-stress solids. The finite element formulation accounts for both material and geometric nonlinearities. A number of material models are incorporated to simulate a wide range of material behavior including elasto-plasticity, anisotropy, creep, thermal effects, and rate dependence. Arbitrary contact between independent bodies is handled by a variety of slide-line algorithms. These algorithms model gaps and sliding along material interfaces, including interface friction and single-surface contact. Interactive graphics and rezoning are included for analyses with large mesh distortions. NIKE2D is no longer funded for active development by LLNL or direct user support and is made available on an "as-is" basis. Select hardware projects have chosen to fund limited development or maintenance activities.

NIKE3D is a fully implicit, three-dimensional finite element code for analyzing the finite strain static and dynamic response of inelastic solids, shells, and beams. Spatial discretization is achieved by the use of eight-node solid elements, two-node truss and beam elements, and four-node membrane and shell elements. Over 20 constitutive models are available for representing a wide range of elastic, plastic, viscous, and thermally dependent material behavior. Contact-impact algorithms permit gaps, frictional sliding, and mesh discontinuities along material interfaces. Several nonlinear solution strategies are available, including full-, modified-, and quasi-Newton methods. The resulting system of simultaneous linear equations is either solved iteratively by an element-by-element method, or directly by a factorization method, for which case bandwidth minimization is optional. Data may be stored either in or out of core memory to allow for large analyses.

1.10.1 Availability NIKE2D and NIKE3D Computer Codes Series

Both these code are available from the following site but has no technical support nor is up-to-date with any present computing operating system and codes have a lot of logical errors that need to be fixed and based this author experience working with these codes for long time, they are not easy to fix unless you are willing to spend hours and hours of debugging.

This package is distributed by:
Energy Science and Technology Software Center
P.O. Box 62
1 Science.Gov Way
Oak Ridge, TN 37831
(865) 576-2606 TEL
(865) 576-6436 FAX
E-mail: ESTSC@osti.gov

The Window/PC versions of these codes are available from Galaxy Advanced Engineering, Inc. Just refer to www.gaeinc.com

1.11 TOPAZ2D and TOPAZ3D Computer Codes Series

TOPAZ2D is a two-dimensional, implicit, finite element computer code for heat transfer analysis. It can be used to solve for the steady-state or transient temperature field on two-dimensional geometries. TOPAZ2D is no longer funded for active development or direct user support and is made available on an "as-is" basis. Select hardware projects have chosen to fund limited development or maintenance activities.

TOPAZ3D is a three-dimensional, implicit, finite element computer code for heat transfer analysis. It can be used to solve for the steady-state or transient temperature field on three-dimensional geometries. Material properties may be temperature-dependent and either isotropic or orthotropic. A variety of time- and temperature-dependent boundary conditions can be specified, including temperature, flux, convection, and radiation. By implementing the user subroutine feature, users can model chemical reaction kinetics and allow for any type of functional representation of boundary conditions and internal heat generation. TOPAZ3D can solve problems of diffuse and specular band radiation in an enclosure coupled with conduction in the material surrounding the enclosure. Additional features include thermal contact resistance across an interface, bulk fluids, phase change, and energy balances. Thermal stresses can be calculated using the solid mechanics code NIKE3D, which reads the temperature state data calculated by TOPAZ3D.

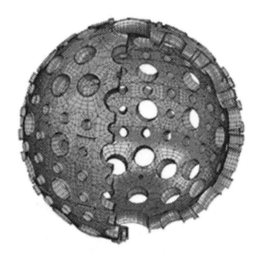

Figure 1-7: TOPAZ3D and NIKE3D OUTPUT

The TOPAZ3D and NIKE3D codes are used to analyze the expansion of the National Ignition Facility's laser target chamber resulting from the heat of a laser shot and its contraction to equilibrium in the cool-down period

1.11.1 Availability TOPAZ2D and TOPAZ3D Computer Codes Series

Both these code are available from the following site but has no technical support nor is up-to-date with any present computing operating system and codes have a lot of logical errors that need to be fixed and based this author experience working with these codes for long time, they are not easy to fix unless you are willing to spend hours and hours of debugging.

This package is distributed by:
Energy Science and Technology Software Center
P.O. Box 62
1 Science.Gov Way
Oak Ridge, TN 37831
(865) 576-2606 TEL
(865) 576-6436 FAX
E-mail: ESTSC@osti.gov

The Window/PC versions of these codes are available from Galaxy Advanced Engineering, Inc. Just refer to www.gaeinc.com

CHAPTER TWO: LASER TECHNOLOGY

The development of lasers has been an exciting chapter in the history of science and engineering. It has produced a new device with potential for applications in an extraordinary variety of fields. Einstein developed the concept of stimulated emission on theoretical grounds. Stimulated emission is the phenomenon that is utilized in lasers. Stimulated emission produces amplification of light so that buildup of high-intensity light in the laser can occur. Einstein described the fundamental nature of the stimulated emission process theoretically.

This characterization of stimulated emission did not lead immediately to the laser. Additional preliminary work on optical spectroscopy was done in the 1930s. Most of the atomic and molecular energy levels that are used in lasers were studied and investigated during those decades.

2.1 Basic Principles

The word laser is an acronym for light amplification by stimulated emission of radiation, although common usage today is to use the word as a noun -- laser -- rather than as an acronym -- LASER.

A laser is a device that creates and amplifies a narrow, intense beam of coherent light.

Atoms emit radiation. We see it every day when the "excited" neon atoms in a neon sign emit light. Normally, they radiate their light in random directions at random times. The result is incoherent light -- a technical term for what you would consider a jumble of photons going in all directions.

The trick in generating coherent light -- of a single or just a few frequencies going in one precise direction -- is to find the right atoms with the right internal storage mechanisms and create an environment in which they can all cooperate -- to give up their light at the right time and all in the same direction.

In a laser, the atoms or molecules of a crystal, such as ruby or garnet -- or of a gas, liquid, or other substance -- are excited in what is called the *laser cavity* so that more of them are at higher energy levels than are at lower energy levels. Reflective surfaces at both ends of the cavity permit energy to reflect back and forth, building up in each passage.

Only three basic components are necessary for laser action: a lasing medium, a pumping system that supplies energy to the lasing medium, and a resonant optional cavity. Lenses, mirrors, shutters, saturable absorbers, and other accessories may be added to the system to obtain more power, shorter pulses, or special beam shapes.

2.2 Overall Theme

This report deals with the effects of directed energy weapons, treating such diverse types of weaponry in particular laser and in our case Air Born Laser (ABL). Although when we talk about directed energy weapon, we can consider such weapon as particle beams, microwaves [3] and even bullets as part of Directed Energy Weapon (DEW) system. In order to understand these weapons and their effects, it is necessary first to develop a common framework for their analysis and in our particular case, we expand our concentration on just laser as DEW in particular ABL under scope of this project and related issues of Laser Safety Range Tool (LSRT).

It is a thesis of this report that all laser weapons (Continuous or Pulse) may be understood as devices which deposit energy in targets, and that the energy which must be deposited to achieve a given level of damage is relatively intensive to the type of laser weapon employed, type of engagement environment, dual time on target and type of targets these weapons are engaged.

Of course, energy cannot be deposited in a target unless it has first delivered there. Therefore, an important element in understanding laser weapons is knowledge of how they deliver (or "propagate") their energy. Some loss of energy is invariably associated with this propagation, whether it is the atmospheric effect such as a known phenomenon as thermal blooming [4] or delivery system as well as other related technical and obstacle issues. A laser weapon must therefore produce more energy than needed to damage a target, since some of its energy will be lost in propagation. As result, weapon design depends upon two factors. First, the anticipated target, which determines the energy required for damage. Secondly, the anticipated scenario (range, engagement time, etc.) which determines how much energy should be produced to insure that an adequate amount is delivered in the time available and dual time on target.

2.3 A Word about Units

Since our goal is to reduce the jargon associated with different types of laser weaponry to common units, the choice for these common units is obviously of interest. For the most part, we will use metric units of MKS, where length is in Meter, mass is in Kilograms, and time in seconds. In these units, energy is expressed as *Joules*.

2.4 Developing Damage Criteria

If we are to determine how much energy a weapon must produce to damage a target, we need to know two things;

  i.   How much energy it takes to damage a target
  ii. What fraction if the energy generated will be lost in propagation to it.

These will be developed in detail for different weapon types in subsequent sections. For the moment, we will consider some of the fundamental issues, which affect damage, and propagation of laser weapon independent of its type (CW or Pulse).

2.5 The Energy Required for Damage

In order to be quantitative about the amount of energy necessary for damage, we must first define what we mean by damage. For a military system, this could be anything from an upset in a target's computer (in case of Microwave Weapon) and preventing it from operating, or to total vaporization (in case of laser Weapon). These two extremes are usually referred to as "Soft" and "Hard" damage or kill, respectively. Study of soft damage clearly is beyond scope of this project and is much more sensitive to specific details of the target system and its shielding as well as related countermeasure under attack than hard damage. Few good references are published and are available for soft kill or damage study [5].

Without knowing the details of a computer, its circuitry designs, and the hardness of its chips and electronic components, we will not know if it has been upset until we see it in operation, whereas vaporizing it produces immediate feedback on the effectiveness of an attack of an attack and it is subject of this project. On the other hand, vaporizing a target will require more energy than degrading its performance. We will concentrate in this book on hard or catastrophic damage for two reasons: it avoids target-specific details, which are often classified, and it provides a useful first cut at separating weapon parameters, which will almost certainly result in damage from those for which the likelihood of damage is questionable, or for which more detailed analysis is required.

As a simple example of the kind of energies necessary to achieve damage, let us first consider what it takes to vaporize a given target using laser techniques employed in effects of high-power laser radiation [6] or Effect of Laser Radiation on Absorbing Condensed Matter [7].

2.6 The Laser Beam

The laser beam has many unique qualities, which can be manipulated in many ways by the use of different accessories that are added to the basic laser. The beam is characterized by its collimation, coherence, monochromaticity, speed, and intensity[2]. The laser beam is the source of light that can have all above properties while the other source light may possess of these properties but not all at same time.

Collimation in a laser can be very high, which means that the radiation emitted by most lasers is confined to a very narrow beam, which slowly diverges as the beam moves away from the laser source, a phenomena that is known as diffraction.

Diffraction refers to the spreading, or divergence, of light which emerges from an aperture of given diameter, as shown in Figure 2-1 [8].

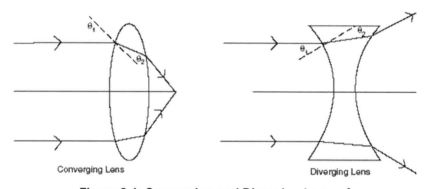

Converging Lens   Diverging Lens

Figure 2-1: Converging and Diverging Lenses[9]

In this figure, a beam of light of essentially infinite beam width is passed through an aperture of Diameter D. Calculating the beam divergence or diffraction is a matter of elementary geometry analysis and it can be shown that the angle of divergence θ is related to D and the wavelength, λ, of the beam by relationship $\theta \approx \lambda / D$ [9]. The divergence of the beam is normally a small enough angle so that the approximation holds that the sin and tangent of the divergence angle have same value, with the angle itself expressed in milliradian's (a milliradian divergence would mean that a beam would be 1 yard wide at 1,000 yards range, 2 yards wide at 2,000 yards, and so forth) [2]. Due to nature of wave light, it is impossible to make a laser weapon that is 100% collimated beam and has no divergence at all (See Figure 2-2). However, the angle of divergence of a laser beam can be forced to be as small as possible by usage of a converging lens that is placed in path of the beam. Such approach reduces the effect of divergence to achieve a longer effective beam as illustrated in Figure 2-3.

These lenses serve as an apparatus to bend the laser beam inward, focusing it to a spot of radius W. The width of the focal spot depends upon the focal length, f, of lens For shorter length of f the beam focuses to smaller spot, and will diverge rapidly beyond that spot and for longer, f, the light diverge as it leaves the source of the light at the aperture.

The best optimum focal length at which beam has the best optimum collimation for greatest distance is known as the *Rayleigh Range*[10], Z_r. The beam radius at the Rayleigh Range is $W=D/3\sqrt{2}$, and the Rayleigh Range is given by $Z_r = \pi W^2 / \lambda$. Therefore, in practical application, laser light can be used as a collimated beam over a distance of about twice the Rayleigh Range or about D^2 / λ, where D is the aperture from which the light emerges from the weapon, and λ the wavelength of the light. If the laser designer wants this laser beam to be focused as much as possible on small spot at long distances, the reciprocal relationship between divergence and the size of the output optics is used (See Figure 2-4). When a beam with a very small divergence is required, large lenses must be used on the output of laser aperture. Beyond this distance, divergence and diffraction at an angle of about λ / D must be taken into account in evaluating the energy density on target. With ordinary lenses, the focal spot may not be smaller than a few times the wavelength of light. For most military purpose, this is certainly more than sufficient. In some High-Energy Laser (HEL) weapon systems, a concave mirror is used to focus as much energy on the target as possible.

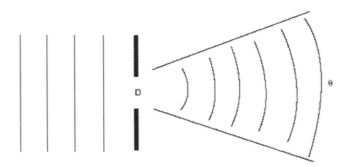

Figure 2-2: Diffraction of Light Passing through an Aperture

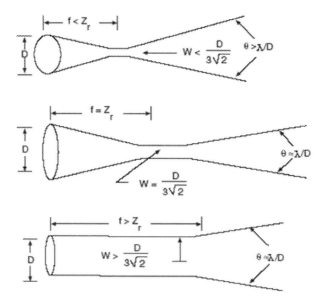

Figure 2-3: Focusing of a Beam of Light and the Rayleigh Range

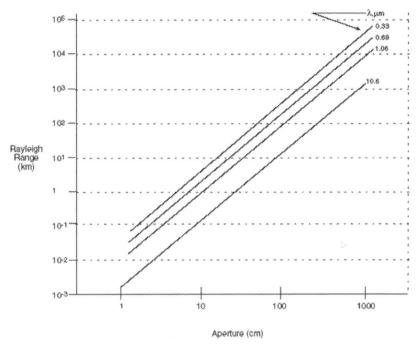

Figure 2-4: Rayleigh Range vs. Aperture and Laser Wavelength

Note: Propagation within Rayleigh Range is known as "Near Filed" propagation, and a greater distance as "Far Filed" propagation.

Laser can operate in the Continuous-Wave (CW) or the pulsed mode. The mode of operation depends on whether the pump energy is CW or pulsed. A CW mode laser emits light steadily as long as it is turned on. A pulsed mode laser can have either one single pulse or repeated pulses, possibly on a regular basis in a train. The Pulse Repetition Frequency (PRF) is the number of pulses a laser produces in a given time. The duration of the pulse (or pulse width) and the PRF may vary immensely between different lasers. Lasers are available with a PRF as high as several hundreds of thousands or millions of pulses per second. In a visible beam band, the human eye will not see such a pulsation, and the beam will appear to be CW [2].

One of the most important factors to a designer and user of laser weapons is the energy level delivered by laser beam. Energy is the power emitted by a laser within a given time. The following equation can be used to calculate the intensity of the beam:

$$E = P \cdot t$$

Where E is the energy in joules, P is power in watts, and t is time in seconds. The energy of repetitively pulsed lasers is calculated using the average power level emitted over a standard interval, which is usually one second.

A high-energy laser weapon designed to down aircraft, missile from several miles away may have several megawatts of power, while a low-energy helium-neon laser such as is used in a lecture hall pointer or a supermarket scanner usually has only a mille-watt or less of average CW power, although the CW power of a helium-neon laser can be as much as 50 mill watts[2].

2.7 Summary

Present-day laser technology is very extensive and diversified, and, within certain limits, it allows for many civilian as well as military applications. Military staff, defense researcher institutes, and defense industries are constantly looking for new laser concept that are suitable for military application and that will fulfill the very tough but realistic battlefield requirements. Many new military laser systems will most certainly be designed to back up their military needs. Thus, if and when realistic battlefield laser weapons concepts pass through the research and development phase, there will be a strong laser industry already in existence to mass-produce these weapons[2].

CHAPTER THREE: LASER SAFETY

It seems inevitable that the battlefield laser threat will markedly increase in the coming years. This will be because of not only the development and implementation of laser weapons but also the increasing number of other helpful laser-powered devices such as range finders and target designators. Therefore, it will be necessary for armies to protect their sensors and personnel by introducing passive as well as active countermeasures for laser technology. The primary laser threat will come from laser weapons, although conventional weapons guided to their targets by lasers will also constitute an indirect laser threat, as will be demonstrated later in this chapter.

Protection and countermeasures against laser weapons are difficult problems, which so far have remained unsolved despite years of research. A simple and cheap eye protection against anti-eye laser weapons still does not exist; consequently, protection of personnel involves many complicated factors ranging from filters to defensive battlefield behavior. This chapter will mainly deal with what we can do to protect personnel, sensors, and combat units against the laser beams from low-energy laser (LEL) weapons. Protective measure required to counter high-energy laser (HEL) weapons will only be described briefly.

3.1 Laser Safety

The laser has become a common tool of civilian and soldiers all over the world. Many lasers, perhaps most of them, are in some way dangerous to people. For several reasons, it is our eyesight that is most threatened, but there are many other dangers to deal with as well. Laser safety is very complex problem.

3.2 Laser Hazards

The use of lasers almost always carries with it some kind of danger, either at the laser site itself or wherever there is a direct, reflected, or scattered laser beam. At the laser site, it is not only the actual laser beam, which can be dangerous, but electrical, chemical, and other hazards exist as well. Most laser power supplies can cause server electrical shocks, possibly even electrocution. Furthermore, many highly explosive and toxic substances are used in solid, liquid, or gas from to power laser cooling systems. For many reasons, it is useful to divide the hazards from laser beam into two main groups: Those to the eye and those to the skin. The eyes may be severely damaged, and even permanently blinded by rather low energy laser beams, while the skin is not nearly as sensitive. To get severe skin burns in the visible and infrared part of the spectrum, it is normally necessary to use a very high-energy laser beam, which delivers, at least, several watts per second square centimeter (W/cm^2) to the target. Safety threshold limits both for the skin and eyes are well defined and have resulted in very strict safety regulation.

3.2.1 Laser Hazards to the Eye

To understand laser hazards to the eye fully, with their implications for laser safety requirements and the possibilities of anti-eye laser weapons, will be discussed in this part briefly. It is necessary to understand the anatomy of the eye, which is beyond the scope of this report, but detail aspect of such discussion can be found in reference 2.

The hazardous effects of a laser beam that is transmitted through the eye are, in the vast majority of cases, limited to the retina. The effect upon the retina may range in severity from a temporary reaction without residual pathological changes to permanent blindness. A soldier using magnifying optics may not only be much easier to blind but may also be a more valuable target than a soldier with a naked eye. Tank gunners, artillery fire controller, forward observer, missile operators, commanders, and others all use magnifying optics in critical moments on the battlefield, and their optical systems may then be detected and identified by the characteristic reflections and exposed to laser radiation. For example at the microscopic scale, light reflects off locally flat incremental areas of the target skin according to a Bidirectional Reflectivity Distribution Function (BRDF) effects, which must be measured and exist inside the materials database[11]. The detail at the scale of target components, the primitive shapes account for local variations of the surface normal, surface areas, local material assignments, and self-shadowing effects can be found in reference 12. Within that, that reference author will resolve all geometry effects at this scale through standard ray tracing techniques as part of Laser Range Safety Tools (LRST)[12].

The smallest observable reaction may be a whitening of the retina. However, as the retinal irradiance is increased, lesions occur which progress in severity from swelling (edema) to burning (coagulation) and then bleeding (hemorrhage) as well as additional tissue reaction around the lesion. Very high retinal irradiance will causes gas bubbles to form near the site of absorption.

The retina itself is not much more sensitive to laser damage than any other parts of the body. The level of energy that may cause severe damage to any part of the body is between 50 and 500 mill joules per square centimeter for a short pulse. It is only the optical concentration of the energy by the optics of the eye that makes a low-powered laser capable of damaging the retina specifically rather than the rest of the eye or body.

The most important part of the eye for vision is the macular area and, in particular, the fovea centralize, which is densely packed with cones. If the laser beam causes a retinal burn of any size in this area, the result is permanent loss of fine-detail vision sufficient to cause legal blindness, and no treatment is possible. Of course, much vision is still present but not enough to read rapidly, drive an automobile, or do any visually demanding task [2].

When discussing laser safety and the eye, it is necessary to differentiate between the effects inside the eye within the retinal hazard region (400-1,400 nanometers) and the effects on the outside of the eye from those laser beams that do not reach the retina [2].

The retinal hazard region covers the spectrum from 400 to 1,400 nanometers and includes the visible and near-infrared parts of the spectrum. The shorter wavelengths in the near ultraviolet are absorbed mainly in the lens, and the even shorter far-ultraviolet wavelengths are absorbed mainly in the cornea. Longer wavelengths in the mid-infrared region are also absorbed in the cornea. Thus, there can be harmful effects to the eye from laser exposures even in the parts of the optical spectrum outside the retinal hazard region [2].

The excessive absorption of intermediate ultraviolet radiation by the cornea causes ultraviolet photokeratitis. This is a very painful but temporary injury, often called snow blindness or welder's flash [2].

However, as most of these effects require that the eye be subjected to high levels of laser radiation for a comparatively long time, half a minute or more, it seems unlikely that these effects in the ultraviolet part of the spectrum could form the basis for a laser weapon.

In the mid-and far-infrared region, the possibility for absorption in the cornea, especially for wavelengths longer than 2,000 nanometers, is very high. Therefore, the cornea is very susceptible to damaging heat during exposure to mid-infrared radiation. If the energy level of the beam is high enough to cause corneal heating, this will produces immediate and severe pain and automatically trigger the blink reflex. The cornea is quite sensitive, and an elevation of only 20 $^\circ$F in temperature will cause a pain response [2]. The question is whether sufficient thermal energy would be absorbed in the cornea to cause injury in the short time before the blink reflex is activated. The lids are much less sensitive to damage because the circulation blood carries away the heat and a large amount of the laser beam is reflected.

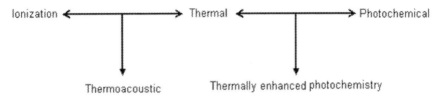

Figure 3.1: Types of interaction of laser energy with the eye and other biological tissues. Only the thermal and thermo acoustic modes of interaction are important with present-day antipersonnel laser weapons [2]

The infrared lasers that may be used to injure the cornea are CO^2, Hydrogen Fluoride (HF), Deuterium Fluoride (DF), and CO. Such lasers with an output power of more than 10 watts per square centimeter could deliver at least 0.5 to 10 joules per square centimeter to the cornea before the blink reflex gives any protection, as shown in Figure 3.2. Existing infrared lasers can certainly damage the cornea before any head movement can occur. Research has shown that thermal injury to the cornea produces a white spot or an opacification of the surface. The injury is extremely painful and needs immediate and well-qualified medical care. The severity of corneal burn injuries from laser exposure can be compared to that of burns and injuries resulting from ignition or explosion of flammable objects.

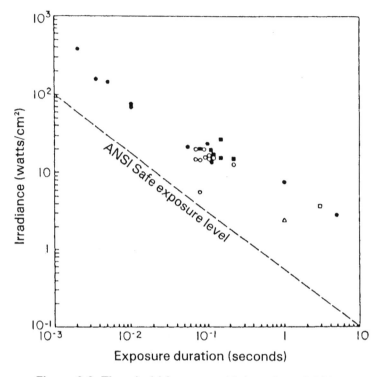

Figure 3.2: Threshold for corneal injury from CO_2 laser radiation. The differences between data points at the same exposure duration are largely to the use of different corneal image sizes. The data points are from several laboratories and fit a thermal heat flow damage model quite well [2]

3.2.2 Laser Hazards to the Skin

Laser can have several important effects on the skin. The thermal effect is the most significant one. Burn injuries are divided into three basic groups. A first-degree burn is a very superficial reddening of the skin, a second –degree burn produces blistering, and a third-degree burn, the most server kind, destroys the entire outer layer of the skin. The irradiance necessary to cause a first-degree burn is 12 watts per square centimeter; for second- and third-degree burns, the necessary irradiation is 24 and 34 watts per square centimeter, respectively. If the exposure is shortened, the irradiance required to give a third-degree burn is significantly increased. Laser injury threshold for the skin are dependent on the wavelength of the laser as well as on the pigmentation of the skin. Dark skins absorb more and thus get hotter for the same laser energy. For long exposures, the energy levels necessary to produce injury are highly dependent upon exposure duration. It is possible for high-energy lasers to produce significant burns within an exposure period of less than one second [2].

A soldier on the battlefield, aware of the threat from laser exposure, will be rather well protected as long as his uniform or the immediate environment is not set on fire. However, it has to be recognized that, even in a protected state, burn injuries to the eyes will probably still be a problem. In far-infrared and ultraviolet regions of the spectrum, where the laser energy does not reach the retina, corneal injury thresholds are approximately the same as for skin injury. Therefore, laser burns to both the exterior of the eye and skin are possible, but these do not seem to be important threats at the moment [2].

3.3 Safety Regulations

There are a variety of laser safety standards including Federal and state regulations, and non-regulatory standards. The most important and most often quoted is the American National Standards Institute's Z136 series of laser safety standards. These standards are the foundation of laser safety programs in industry, medicine, research, and government. The ANSI Z136 series of laser safety standards are referenced by the Occupational Safety and Health Administration (OSHA) and many U.S. states as the basis of evaluating laser-related occupational safety issues.

ANSI Z136.1 Safe Use of Lasers, the parent document in the Z136 series, provides information on how to classify lasers for safety, laser safety calculations and measurements, laser hazard control measures, and recommendations for Laser Safety Officers and Laser Safety Committees in all types of laser facilities. It is designed to provide the laser user with the information needed to properly develop a comprehensive laser safety program.

For manufacturers of laser products, the standard of principal importance is the regulation of the Center for Devices and Radiological Health (CDRH), Food and Drug Administration (FDA), which regulates product performance. All laser products sold in the USA since August 1976 must be certified by the manufacturer as meeting certain product performance (safety) standards, and each laser must bear a label indicating compliance with the standard and denoting the laser hazard classification.

The establishment of the threshold levels for different laser injuries is basic to the whole question of laser safety. The threshold level is an exposure value below which adverse changes have a low probability of occurrence and no significant risk exists. There is always some question about what the actual value of the threshold is, because it varies with the wavelength and exposure duration but also with the individual.

The value of the threshold may be set by using a statistical analysis to determine a certain damage probability (usually 50%) and then setting the safety level at a selected level of probability below this, usually the 0.01 or 0.001% level. This energy/power level is often a factor of 10 below that for the 50% damage point. In order to calculate a correct threshold level, it is also necessary to try to simulate some kind of worst-case scenario—when the eye is hit in its most sensitive part and takes in as much laser light from the laser in question as is possible under the circumstances.

3.4 Laser Hazard Classification

Research studies, along with an understanding of the hazards of sunlight and conventional, man-made light sources have permitted scientists to establish safe exposure limits for nearly all types of laser radiation. These limits are generally referred to as Maximum Permissible Exposures (MPE's) by laser safety professionals. In many cases, it is unnecessary to make use of MPE's directly. The experience gained in millions of hours of laser use in the laboratory and industry has permitted the development of a system of laser hazard categories or classifications. The manufacturer of lasers and laser products is required to certify that the laser is designated as one of four general classes, or risk categories, and label it accordingly. This allows the use of standardized safety measures to reduce or eliminate accidents depending on the class of the laser or laser system being used. The following is a brief description of the four primary categories of lasers:

Class 1

A Class 1 laser is considered safe based upon current medical knowledge. This class includes all lasers or laser systems which cannot emit levels of optical radiation above the exposure limits for the eye under any exposure conditions inherent in the design of the laser product. There may be a more hazardous laser embedded in the enclosure of a Class 1 product, but no harmful radiation can escape the enclosure.

Class 2

A Class 2 laser or laser system must emit a visible laser beam. Because of its brightness, Class 2 laser light will be too dazzling to stare into for extended periods. Momentary viewing is not considered hazardous since the upper radiant power limit on this type of device is less than the MPE (Maximum Permissible Exposure) for momentary exposure of 0.25 second or less. Intentional extended viewing, however, is considered hazardous.

Class 3

A Class 3 laser or laser system can emit any wavelength, but it cannot produce a diffuse (not mirror-like) reflection hazard unless focused or viewed for extended periods at close range. It is also not considered a fire hazard or serious skin hazard. Any continuous wave (CW) laser that is not Class 1 or Class 2 is a Class 3 device if its output power is 0.5 W or less. Since the output beam of such a laser is definitely hazardous for intra-beam viewing, control measures center on eliminating this possibility.

Class 4

A Class 4 laser or laser system is any that exceeds the output limits (Accessible Emission Limits, AEL's) of a Class 3 device. As would be expected, these lasers may be either a fire or skin hazard or a diffuse reflection hazard. Very stringent control measures are required for a Class 4 laser or laser system.

3.5 Laser Range Safety Tool (LRST) Physics

It may be of interest to consider what the safe distances are for current military laser devices. This will give an indication of the size of the hazardous area around each device. Each specific laser has a safety distance of its own based upon its output properties. The acronym used to describe this distance; in the U.S. regulations at least, is Nominal Ocular Hazard Distance (NOHD) that stands for Nominal Ocular Hazard Distance. The basic definition of NOHD is, the axial beam distance from the laser where the exposure or irradiance falls below the applicable exposure limit. The NOHD is calculated to determine at what distance an unprotected person can stand directly in the beam and be exposed momentarily without being injured. The use of magnifying optics must be taken into account, because they will markedly increase the NOHD. A 6-mile NOHD may be increased to 50 miles if an individual looks into the laser with optics that magnify 13 times. It should be remembered that the laser may be hazardous to the eye even beyond the NOHD if the laser is viewed or stared at for a prolonged time. The NOHD is calculated based on momentary viewing only. It is also necessary to take into account the problem of accuracy in aiming the laser. Also, the possibility of reflection is caused by mirrolike surfaces such as windows, optical surfaces, greenhouse, still ponds, or road signs covered with reflective coating. However, for some lasers, there may be a Hazardous Diffuse Reflection Area (HDRA), which is typically less than 10 yards from the reflecting surface. An example of a laser danger zone is shown in Figure 3.3.

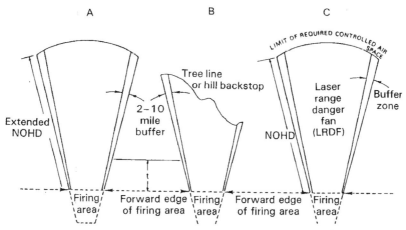

**Figure 3.3: Laser range safety fans. Laser range safety fans
are used the U.S. Army to indicate the nominal ocular hazard
distance (NOHD). The NOHD is normally terminated by a backstop.
The un-terminated NOHD depends on beam expansion and
atmospheric attenuation. In case A, the NOHD is a line-of-sight
fan parallel to the ground and would only be used when there
is no backstop. Case B is the more usual situation where a
backstop is established by a hill or tree line. In case C, the fan is
perpendicular to the ground and is applied to airspace hazards [2]**

The laser beam is decreased or attenuated by some atmospheric
conditions, and this is a factor that should be considered when the
NOHD is longer than a few kilometers. Atmospheric attenuation is
mainly dependent on the sum of three following different effects:

- Large particle scattering
- Molecular scattering, and
- Absorption by gas molecules (Thermal Blooming)

Each of these effects is defined briefly in the following paragraphs.

Large particle, or Mie, scattering is the dominant factor in the visible
and the near-infrared part of the spectrum, where the particle size of
the atmospheric contaminates larger than the wavelength of the laser
light.

Molecular or Rayleigh scattering by oxygen, nitrogen, and other molecular constituent, and, in these cases, the molecular size is much less than wavelength of laser beams.

The contribution of absorption by gas molecules and other particles to attenuation is most important in the infrared region of the spectrum.

The molecular scattering of the laser beam increases at shorter wavelengths. However, this effect is not substantial over short distances. A normal and clean atmosphere is relatively transparent to the argon laser beam (blue), the ruby laser beam (red), and the Nd:YAG beam (near infrared). If NOHD calculated for vacuum transmission is known and compared to the NOHD compensated for the ambient atmosphere (see Figure 3.4), it may be concluded that, for low-energy lasers, the atmosphere even at battlefield distance up to 10 miles, at least, it is not a big problem. A ruby laser beam might be attenuated as little as 10% at 6 miles [2].

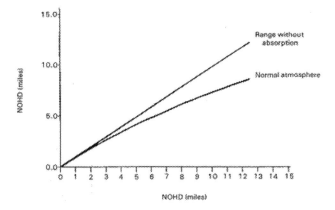

Figure 3.4: The effects of clear atmosphere on the nominal ocular hazard distance (NOHD). This figure shows the theoretical distance in a vacuum and the actual distance in a clear atmosphere. The straight line is for a laser beam at a wavelength (1064 nm) not absorbed heavily by the atmosphere. The curved line shows effects of a normal atmosphere. Including that even in the clearest atmosphere there is a considerable attenuation. As the distances are large, this attenuation will not affect the use of lasers within a typical battlefield but will modify the effects of lasers from aircraft or in an antiaircraft situation [2]

High Energy Laser (HEL) beams are much more heavily dependent on the weather conditions, especially rain, snow, dust, clouds and smoke. This will be discussed further in section 4. However, what may be concluded from laser safety calculations is that most military concluded from laser safety calculations is that most military lasers are not very dependent on the atmosphere when the air is fairly clean and the laser is used at battlefield distances.

Therefore LRST of target reflectivity know as BRDF (Bi-directional Reflectivity Distribution Function) database should be reviewed and updated for the target that laser weapon is engaging. Continuous testing for LRST should be conducted and desired results for each test condition must be studied considering the following criteria;

- LRST vs. hand calculation radiometry
- Check of ANSI Maximum Permissible Exposure (MPE)
- LRST hazard zone vs. hand calculation hazard zone

The American National Standards Institute (ANSI) initiated the first work on a comprehensive standard for the safe use of lasers. Initial hypothetical Scenario for LRST should be assumed and test results should be compared with those which are hand calculated using various related computer codes and we hope to be at least within optimum design range or at least well within uncertainties built into ANSI standard.

A safety analysis of the outdoor use of current military range finders and target designators against the eye of the human being such as soldiers. However, so far as is publicly known, only one country has made such a use part of its military practice. This is the case of the use by the British of low-energy lasers to flash blind Argentinean pilots in the Falklands conflict. At present, there are no known unclassified tactical manuals which cover the deliberate use of lasers against the eyes of soldiers as a weapon of warfare or reflection of a beam in term of BRDF from a target engagement. What the military will do in future conflicts, which will certainly involve a mass use of lasers, remain to be seen.

The underlying requirements of the Laser Range Safety Tool (LRST) and its written code[12] will be to generate an accurate time history of intensity at potential positions where humans might be exposed to reflected laser beam light from a target missile being irradiated in case of Airborne Laser (ABL)[12].

There are about eight basic algorithmic steps necessary to evaluate eye hazards in LRST. Figure 3.5 shows a simple diagram of this process.

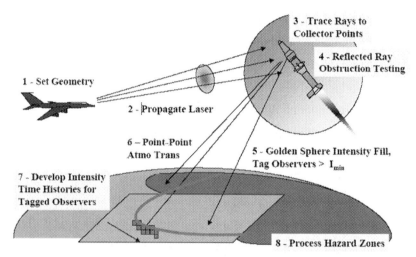

Figure 3.5 Eight Basic Algorithmic Steps to Evaluate Hazards

Certain conditions, pre-engagement, and dual on target time of laser beam scenario and its geometry with target in battlefield must be calculated. Such thing as the position of and velocity of ABL an incoming threat also should come under consideration as well as environmental condition has to be part of the parameter of engagement equation.

The incoming threat such as in flight missile position and velocity should be derived from database table of pre-simulated position is imported into code as part of solution to LRST consideration. All the vector position of missile in relative to itself and ABL that is known and referred to as Golden Sphere has been considered in the LRST code simualtions[12].

Overall the LRST is a software tool for calculating reflected energy hazards under the role of BRDF in the context of test range development of the Airborne Laser (ABL) system. The LRST software package consists of a suite of programs that provide facilitates for describing and simulating test scenarios, including the range, the ABL, aircraft laser complement, the target, and the observers. What is missing from this software the effects of BRDF on friendly troops on the ground and pre-engagement warning that ABL will be in tangle with incoming missile threat. The other missing link of the LRST is consideration of falling debris due to physical destructive ABL impact on target and dual-time on target. But the LRST software does an excellent job of providing a detailed description of physical basis of the simulation and the computational algorithms utilized to calculate the radiometry and hazards.

CHAPTER FOUR: LASER WEAPONS

Laser technology is only 30 years old, but it is much diversified. There are already varieties of military applications, although there are many limitations restricting the use of lasers. Today, the armed forces in most countries routinely use a wide range of laser devices such as laser range finders and designators. In some countries, work is proceeding on more imaginative laser weapon concepts that will eventually fulfill realistic, yet very precise, military requirements. The design of a specific laser weapon is heavily influenced by the characteristics of the intended target. If the desired effect of the weapon is to neutralize aircraft, helicopters, or missiles by burning holes through them or tanks by putting many miniature cracks (crazing) in the glass vision blocks to make them appear to be frosted, a very high energy laser has to be used with a power output on the order of several megawatts (MW). Such a laser would be a true anti-material weapon. However, if the target is a sensitive electro-optical system or some other type of sensor system, which has to be jammed or destroyed by a laser operating in a countermeasure mode, the choice will be a low-energy laser operating within the frequency bandwidth of the target sensor. This use of a laser can also be considered anti-material. If the target is a soldier, there is one part of his body that is extremely sensitive to laser radiation—his eyes. It is sufficient to use a low-energy laser operating in the visible or near-infrared (near-IR) part of the spectrum to damage the soldier's eyes and, in effect, cause blindness. If the laser is to cause burn injuries to the soldier's skin or to set fire to his uniform, a high-energy laser is required. In either case, if the purpose of the laser is to blind or burn the soldier, it will obviously be antipersonnel.

4.1 Laser as a Weapon

Even before the laser was invented, science fiction writers told of incredible weapons and machines that emitted a bright saber of light, a death ray that disintegrated everything in its path. Even today, science fiction movies and books place high emphasis on weapons that use light instead of bullets. The laser beam is popularly thought of as a very powerful death ray which can be fired from a hand-held laser gun to vaporize soldiers, demolish building, and burn through target armors. In reality, the laser is a suitable tool for many military applications and can be turned into a deadly weapon but there are definitely limitations to what a laser can do. The laser really is a ray weapon, and its light rays can damage some targets in a way that appeals to the most vivid imagination. It is important to take these somewhat speculative factors into consideration when studying the psychological effects of the use of laser weapons on the battlefield. Otherwise, it will not be possible to get a complete and realistic picture of what using a laser really means to the combatants.

4.2 Possible Targets

A discussion of laser weapon applications outlining what laser weapons can really do must start with the destination of the laser beam—the target. The desire effect on the target ultimately decides what is needed from the laser. To a large extent, the interaction between the laser beam that is selected and the target also determines which cost-effective weapons are developed, produced, and deployed into battlefield.

The sensitivity of the target to laser light determines whether a low-energy or high-energy laser is required. If the target is sufficiently sensitive to low levels of energy within a comparatively broad band of the spectrum, a cheap and cost-effective laser weapon can be designed and amass-produced. If high energy is required, the possibility of designing a usable and affordable laser weapon decreases drastically.

4.3 Energy Level at the Target

One of the basic questions facing the laser weapon designer is what energy level must be absorbed by the target in order to get the desired result. The absorbed energy (E) is some fraction (A) of the product of the power density or intensity (I) present in the laser beam and the emission duration (t). E is measured in energy units, joules (J) or watt seconds per area, usually expressed in square centimeters, I in power units, watts (W) per square centimeter, and the time in seconds in the following equation:

$$E = A(I \times t)$$

This means that if the emission duration is required to be short, as it would be in the engagement of multiple targets, the power density has to be as high as possible. The power density is calculated as the beam power divided by the size of the "beamed" area, which means that a high beam power and a small surface area will give a high power density. How much of the laser power will finally be absorbed by the target in the affected surface area will determine what destructive effect will be achieved. The laser power goes from the laser to the target, suffers transmission losses in the optical system and the atmosphere, and has a further loss when some of the power is reflected from the target surface. The absorbed power is normally no more than 20-60% of the original emitted laser power.

One parameter that is useful in determining the effectiveness of a Gaussian laser beam is the beam irradiance at the target. For a beam with output power P_0 and cross-sectional A at the target, the peak irradiance I_p at the target is

$$I_p = \frac{P_0 \tau}{A}$$

where τ is the atmospheric transmittance[17].

The effectiveness of a laser beam in causing mechanical damage is, thus, dependent on beam power, pulse duration, wavelength, air pressure, the material, and the finish of the target surface. For example, a painted area has considerably increased energy absorption when compared to an unpainted aluminum plate. The absorption varies widely between different materials and at different wavelengths. The absorption of a ruby laser at 694 nanometers is 11% for aluminum, 35% for light-colored human skin and 20% for white paint. The corresponding figures for a CO_2 laser at 10,600 nanometers are 1.9, 95, and 90%. This also indicates that one way to counter a HEL weapon is to choose a very reflective material for the target surface. On the other hand, longer wavelengths emitted by the laser can reduce the effects of highly reflective materials and increase the absorption. Every factor in this very difficult pattern combines to determine the degree of target destruction as well as the final energy level that will be needed to produce the desired effect.

It is obvious that the level of energy required to destroy a target varies considerably depending on the circumstances. Therefore, it is not surprising that the required energy level figures quoted in the open literature also show rather large variations. In spite of this, some numbers may be given which indicate the general range of energy levels.

An aircraft, helicopter, or missile could be hit with an HEL weapon in many different ways that in the end would nullify it. Fuel tanks could be ruptured, or the fuel itself could be caused to explode. Windshields could be shattered, and parts of the control surfaces such as elevators or rudders could be destroyed or disturbed enough to make it impossible to continue fighting. The rotor head of a helicopter or the wing of an airplane or missile could be made to fail, resulting in a crash. Sensors, radars, and other navigation aids could be destroyed; if this destruction occurs during a sensitive and crucial moment in the last phase of an attack, it could result in a crash or an aborted mission. Also, in some situations, an HEL weapon could even explode the ammunition carried by an airborne attacker.

To punch through the metal skin of an airplane requires about 700 joules per square centimeter, although it should be noted that a hole burned in the skin of an airplane may not be sufficient to destroy it in the air or even to make it crash. A more realistic energy level to disable an aircraft may be five to ten times higher, which means that a successful HEL weapon will have to be able to deliver at least 5,000-10,000 joules per square centimeter on the target.

Optical sensors and radomes (plastic radar domes) are much easier to damage; no more than 10 joules per square centimeter needs to be delivered directly on the target. Furthermore, if the laser wavelength is within the sensitive wavelength region of the sensor in question, the energy needed could be extremely low. If the HEL weapon is used as an antipersonnel weapon, that is, as a long-range flamethrower, the energy necessary to burn exposed skin is merely 15 joules per square centimeter, and damage to the cornea, the clear window into the eye, requires only 1 joule per square centimeter.

4.4 Absorption and Scattering

The Earth's atmosphere is acting like an absorbing medium[13]. Absorption occurs when a photon of radiation is absorbed by a gaseous molecule of the atmosphere that converts the photon into the molecule's kinetic energy. Hence, absorption is a way and procedure by which the atmosphere is heated and it is a strong function of laser or radiation of wavelength. For example propagation of radiation essentially gets eliminated at a wavelength below 0.2 μm due to absorption by O^2 and O^3, while there is very little absorption at the visible wavelengths (0.4 to 0.7 μm).

Scattering of electromagnetic waves in the visible and IR wavelengths occurs when the radiation propagates through certain air molecules and particles. Light scattering is strongly wavelength dependent, but there is no loss of energy like in absorption. The physical size of the scatters determines the type of scattering.

Rayleigh Scattering – This is named after Lord Rayleigh caused by air molecules and haze that are small in comparison with the wavelength λ of the radiation (see Figure 4.1 below). Rayleigh scattering, also called *molecular scattering*, applies only to very clear atmosphere.

The scattering coefficient is proportional to λ^{-4}, a relation known as the *Rayleigh law*. For these small air molecules, scattering is eligible at wavelengths greater than roughly 3 μm. At wavelengths below 1 μm, Rayleigh scattering produces the blue color of the sky as a consequence that blue light is scattered much more than other visible wavelengths.

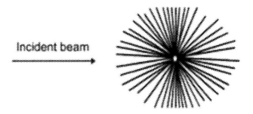

Figure 4.1: Rayleigh Scattering

Mie Scattering – (named after Gustav Mie) scattering by particles comparable in size to the radiation wavelength (also called *aerosol scattering*). Unlike Rayleigh scattering, scattering by particles comparable in size to or greater than the radiation wavelength is concentrated in the forward direction (see Figure 4.2) Scattering losses decreases rapidly with increasing wavelength, eventually approaching the Rayleigh scattering case. Mie scattering is the reason why sunset appear red.

Figure 4.2: Mie Scattering

A term that is sometimes used to describe atmospheric "visibility is the visual range, which corresponds to the range at which radiation at 0.55 μm is attenuated to 0.02 time is transmitted level. Rayleigh scattering by molecules implies a visual range of approximately 340 km (or 213 miles)[18].

Absorption and scattering are often grouped together under the topic of *extinction*, defined as the reduction or attenuation in the amount of radiation passing through the atmosphere. The *transmittance* (also called *atmospheric transmission*) of laser radiation that has propagated a distance L is related to extinction as described by Beer's law, which can be written as [17,18].

$$\tau = \exp[-\alpha(\lambda)L] \qquad \text{unit less}$$

Where $\alpha(\lambda)$ the extinction coefficient18 and the product are $\alpha(\lambda)L$ is called the *optical depth*. The extinction coefficient is composed of two parts:

$$\alpha(\lambda) = A_a + S_a \qquad [m^{-1}]$$

Where A_a is the absorption coefficient and S_a is the scattering coefficient. Absorption and scattering are deterministic effects that are fairly well known.

Software packages like LOWTRAN, FASCODE, MODTRAN, HITRAN, and PCLNWIN (most of these codes are available from Galaxy Advanced Engineering) are commonly used by both government and private industry to predict transmittance (attenuation) effects as a function of wavelength λ, based on a variety of conditions—meteorological range, latitude (tropical, mid, arctic), altitude, etc[19]. A typical output from MODTRAN for rural aerosols with meteorological range of 23 km is shown in (figure 4.3) as a function of wavelength over 1 to 10 μm.

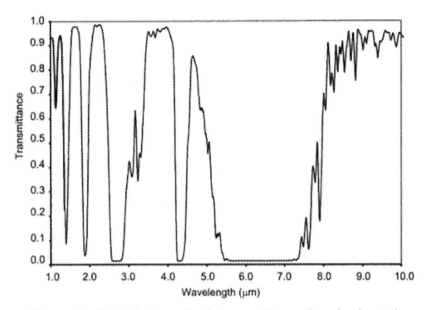

Figure 4.3: Typical atmospheric transmittance for a horizontal 1-km path. Height above ground is 3 m with no rain or clouds

4.5 Atmospheric Structure with Altitude

The atmosphere is a gaseous envelope that surrounds the Earth and extends to several hundred kilometers above the surface. Over 98% of the atmosphere by volume is comprised of the elements nitrogen and oxygen. The major constituents of the atmosphere are water vapor, carbon dioxide, nitrous oxide, carbon monoxide, and ozone. Based mostly on temperature variations, the Earth's atmosphere is divided into four primary layers (Figure 4-4):

Troposphere—extends up to 11 km and contains roughly 75% of the Earth's atmospheric mass. Maximum air temperature occurs near the surface of the Earth, but decreases with altitude t0 -55°C. The *tropopause* is and isothermal layer extending 9 km above the troposphere where air temperature remains constant at -55°C. The tropopause and troposphere together are known as the *lower atmosphere*.

Stratosphere—layer above the tropopause, which extends from 20 km up to 48 km altitude. The air temperature is roughly constant in the very lowest part of the stratosphere but then increases with altitude because the ozone gas in this layer absorbs ultra violate sunlight, thereby creating heat energy. The ozone layer, which protects life from harmful ultraviolet radiation, is concentrated between 10 and 50 km. Separating the stratosphere from the mesosphere is the stratopause, another isothermal layer at approximately -3°C.

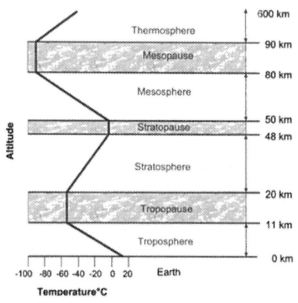

Figure 4.4: Diagram depicting various atmospheric layers and air temperature

Mesosphere—extends from the stratopause to roughly 80 km. Temperature here generally decreases at a constant rate down to -90°C, which is the coldest temperature in the atmosphere. The *mesopause* is the third isothermal layer, separating the mesosphere, along with the stratopause and mesopause, constitute what is commonly called the *middle atmosphere*.

Thermosphere—extends from the mesopause to roughly 600 km. Air temperature in the thermosphere increases quite strongly above 90 km due to the Sun's energy. Most of the *ionosphere* and the *exosphere* are included in the thermosphere. The ionosphere starts around 70 or 80 km up to an indefinite height (~1000 km) and is so named because it is sufficiently ionized by solar ultraviolet radiation that the concentration of free electrons in this layer affects the propagation of radio waves.

4.6 The Major Laser Weapon Concepts

There is generally more than one laser weapon alternative for each proposed laser weapon mission on the battlefield. It is quite possible to vary the laser properties and energy level, the tracking system, and the fire control equipment according to the military requirements for each specific mission. Environmental influences will also have a very strong impact on the final choice of laser weapon applications. For example, Hydrogen Fluoride (HF) laser is not the best choice for long-range use within the atmosphere, because its wavelength is strongly absorbed by the atmosphere. Every laser weapon that is designed to operate within the atmosphere over any great range, whether ground- (GBL), sea- (SBL) or air-based (ABL), must use wavelengths at which the atmosphere absorption and scattering are as small as possible [2].

To be effective, the wavelength of a laser weapon must be short, at least in the visible band, but preferably in the ultraviolet or x-ray band. The greatest difficulty in designing short-wavelength lasers is power— the shorter the wavelength, the more energy that is required. Optical (visible or ultraviolet) lasers work by heating the skin of the target. The beam must remain at the same spot for several seconds until the skin is hot enough to do internal damage to the target. This is tough because the typical ballistic missile travels in excess of 6 miles per second. Imagine focusing on the same 2' or 3' spot over a distance of 50,000 feet and you have an idea how accurate such a laser weapon must be [14].

In addition to the problems of accuracy, laser weapons of any power tend to be monstrous and there are many technical obstacles that designer should overcome. The SBL is using rely mirrors to direct the beam to the target. ABL lasers are using turbine-powered chemical jets and they are placed aboard of aircraft, but the wavelength of the light is long—6 to 10 micrometers—far in the infrared region. This makes laser relatively inefficient at destroying their targets unless certain atmospheric and environmental condition met for target engagements.

X-ray lasers, still wrapped in secrecy, emit an extremely high-powered beam that can literally destroy a missile in mid-flight. X-rays can't be deflected by mirrors, however, which means that the weapon must be easily aimed and in a direct line of sight to the target. Fortunately, x-ray lasers can be built small, expert say, making them suitable for space-based operation. The biggest disadvantage to x-ray lasers is that they use an internal nuclear explosion to work, so they are essentially one short-device.

A relative newcomer to this laser weapon scene is the free-electron laser, which is being developed at the several national laboratories and universities. The Free Electron Laser (FEL) uses a stream of electrons that is made to emit photons of light after being oscillated by giant electromagnetic. Free-electron lasers (FELs) have been built and they do work. However, if put into production, an actual anti-ballistic missile FEL would take up a huge field such as football field or more. Obviously, such a device would be useful only as a stationary ground-based laser (GBL) weapon with its present technology.

Laser weapons may be used within an army's air defense against aircraft, helicopters, and missiles. The desired effect on the target may either be to burn holes or destroy key structures, to blind or trick the sensors, or blind the crews temporally or permanently. The high-energy air defense laser may use all three effects at the same time if the target is within reach of the main effects of the laser. At longer distances, only the anti-sensor and ant-eye capability will be possible. The low-energy air defense laser will use enough energy to be effective against sensors and eyes. It also possible to field a laser with the main purpose of blinding or flash blinding the crews. Flash blinding will be most effective in the dark when the eye is dark adapted and much more sensitive to overload by bright flashes [2].

4.7 Small-Scale Weapons Using Lab-Type Lasers

So far part of this report has covered high-energy weapons, designed to counter a major military conflicts and attack. Laser guns in the movies are often hand-held devices, or at most, small enough to prop on a vehicle. Lasers powerful enough to inflict damage, but small enough to be carried, have developed, but they are not used in any current military application. It's relatively easy, for example, to build a hand-held ruby laser that puts out bursts of large amounts of light energy. When focused to a point, the light from a ruby laser can cut through paper, cloth, skin, or even thin metal [13].

Ruby crystal are poor conductors of heat, so ruby lasers emit only short pulses of light to allow the crystal to cool between firings. Nd:YAG lasers operate in a similar fashion as ruby lasers, but they can produce a continuous beam. Making a hand-held Nd:YAG laser is no easy feat, however. The Nd:YAG crystal must be optically pumped by another high-powered laser or by an extremely bright flash lamp or light source. Though the power output of an Nd:YAG laser is extremely high, considering the current state-of-art, a hand-held model is impractical. However, such a weapon could be built as a "laser canon," transported on an armored vehicle or on a towed trailer [13].

CO_2 lasers are often used in industry as cutting tools. This type of laser is known for its efficiency—30% or more compared to the 1 to 2% of most gas and crystal lasers. A pistol-sized CO_2 laser would probably be difficult to design and manufacture because the CO_2 gas mixture (which includes helium and nitrogen) must be constantly circulated through the tube. What's more, the laser requires a hefty electrical power supply. Still, such apron could be built in an enclosure about the same size as a personal rocket launcher. These are designed to be slung over a shoulder and fired when standing in an upright position [13].

4.8 High-Energy Lasers as Weapons

An air defense HEL weapon designed to shoot down airplanes, helicopters, and missiles successfully must have the ability to keep a very powerful beam at one point on the target for a long enough time to deliver at least 5,000 joules per square centimeter. This requires a laser in the megawatt range. If the shot is to be successful, it must be directed to a certain part of the target that is limited in size and very sensitive and then kept there until the desired effect is reached. Thus, the laser beam must track and follow a target if any great length of time is needed to achieve the desired effect.

Many parts of an aircraft or helicopter are highly resistant to an HEL weapon, but there are still enough thin-skin parts and sensitive areas to produce a devastating effect or destruction if hit precisely. On the other hand, it is obvious that at battlefield ranges even an extremely high energy laser weapon cannot penetrate the heavy armor on a tank or other armored vehicles and thus an HEL weapon is of no use for destroying resistant ground targets in the battlefield. However, sensors, optics, and related devices are still valid targets wherever they appear on the battlefield, even in a tank.

4.9 High Energy Laser (HEL) Safety Program

As high-energy lasers move from the safe confines of the laboratory into the outdoor domain, new problems arise in dealing with laser safety. The tri-Service laser bioeffects program at Brooks AFB will be examining the safety aspects of the new technologies and weapons systems to be employed in the future. Several new high-energy laser systems are now scheduled for deployment in the immediate future.

The Tactical High Energy Laser (THEL), will be a ground-mobile system which will use a chemical laser to destroy low-flying threats. Currently under development in a cooperative program with Israel, the THEL conducted test firing in FY1998, and continues several test phases at White Sands Missile Range today.

ABL on a refueling mission over California, December 2002

The Airborne Laser (ABL), with its megawatt-class laser systems, will engage tactical ballistic missiles during boost phase at altitudes over 40,000 ft. Its lasers will be test fired in FY 2003, with Engineering and Manufacturing Development scheduled to begin soon after that. The high-power Chemical Oxygen Iodine Laser will have nominal eye safe distances in the order of thousands of miles, and will produce reflection patterns off targets that also have the potential for causing eye damage at very large distances.

Combining these laser characteristics with the planned usage of these weapons systems, involving moving targets and possibly moving sources, results in a complex series of laser safety calculations to  allow safe testing and usage of high-energy lasers outdoors. The Air Force Research Laboratory, Optical Radiation Branch is developing new tools and techniques for calculating laser hazard areas which include computer modeling of the interaction of high energy lasers and moving targets, and the use of probabilistic methods to augment deterministic calculations.

One of the Missile Defense Agency's highest priority programs involves putting a weapons class laser aboard a modified Boeing 747-400 series freighter aircraft and using that laser to destroy ballistic missiles shortly after launch. The program is called the Airborne Laser, and its development could forever change the way that nations wage war.

4.9.1 Airborne Laser (YAL-1A)

Destroying ballistic missiles is a complicated process, one that is confounded even more by the revolutionary use of a directed energy device as a weapon rather than as a targeting or range-finding apparatus. To be successful, ABL must:

- Be housed aboard a stable platform that can stay aloft for hours on end above weather systems whose clouds could refract its laser beams and nullify its effectiveness;
- Be equipped with sensors able to locate a ballistic missile shortly after launch and hold the track long enough for other system elements to swing into operation;
- Be implemented with a sophisticated computer system capable of keeping track of dozens of missiles and prioritizing them so that the most threatening is targeted first;
- Have a highly developed optical system capable of measuring the amount of thermal disturbance between the aircraft and the target, then be capable of directing a beam of energy that self-compensates for the clear-air obstacles;
- Possess the ability to focus the killer beam on a rapidly rising target, which may be traveling at a speed of Mach 6 or more, then keep the shaft of energy in place long enough to burn a hole in the missile's metal skin;
- And lastly, be provided with a laser powerful enough to prove lethal at a distance of hundreds of kilometers.

Some of those requirements already have been tested:

- The first ABL aircraft – YAL-1A – made its virgin flight over western Kansas on July 18, 2002, staying aloft for one hour and 22 minutes before returning to the Boeing modifications facility in Wichita. Between then and the time it transitioned to its new temporary home at Edwards Air Force Base, California., in December, YAL-1A made an additional 13 flights logging more than 60 flight hours;
- As part of a Missile Defense Agency test over the Pacific Ocean in December 2002. ABL's infrared trackers successfully detected a Minuteman booster rocket as soon as it broke the clouds, holding a lock until the rocket's engines burned out 500 kilometers downrange;

First Flight

- Its battle management (computer) system was flight tested in late summer and early fall of 2002 to verify internal crew communications and the V/UHF radios, plus the data acquisition system and High Definition VHS;
- The six infrared search and track sensors were successfully flight tested;
- The first COIL module that will be installed on YAL-1A tested at 118 percent of anticipated power during a shakedown run at TRW's facility in San Juan Capistrano, Calif., in January 2002. Shortly afterwards, it was disassembled and shipped to Edwards Air Force Base.

In December 2002, YAL-1A was pulled into a hangar at Edwards' Birk Flight Test Facility where it will be grounded while the lasers and optical components can be tested and installed.

The goal of the Missile Defense Agency, which has overall management responsibility for the program, and the Airborne Laser System Program Office at Kirtland Air Force Base, N.M., is to have YAL-1A ready to shoot down a threat-representative ballistic missile by December 2004. Currently, the missile is scheduled to be launched from Vandenberg Air Force Base, Calif., with the shoot down to take place over the Pacific.

Construction and testing of YAL-1A (prototype attack laser, model 1A), the first aircraft in a proposed fleet of so-far undetermined size, are the results of an effort by MDA, the program office, the Air Force, and three major contractors – Boeing, Lockheed Martin, and Northrop Grumman Space Technologies (formerly TRW). In addition, the U.S. Air Force's Aeronautical Systems Center, headquartered at Wright-Patterson Air Force Base, Ohio, and has provided office personnel. The Air Combat Command, headquartered at Langley Air Force Base, Va., will assume control over the plane once it is declared operational and transferred back to the Air Force.

The ABL program office was formed in 1993. Three years later, in November 1996, the Air Force awarded a $1.1 billion contract to the Boeing Defense Group of Seattle, Wash., TRW Space and Electronics Group of Redondo Beach, Calif., and Lockheed Martin Missiles & Space of Sunnyvale, California

Boeing built the aircraft in Everett, Wash., and modified it in Wichita. The company also developed the hardware/software used in the battle management system and is managing integration of the main components. TRW built the megawatt-class COIL laser that produces the knockout punch to ballistic missiles, and Lockheed Martin is responsible for the optical system.

Another key organization is the Air Force Research Laboratory's Directed Energy Directorate, also at Kirtland Air Force Base, N.M., where the COIL was invented in 1977. For a quarter of a century, the Laboratory has been conducting research into a myriad of technologies needed to make a laser-carrying aircraft a reality. Besides the COIL, the Laboratory also developed the technologies that will increase the distance laser light can travel through the atmosphere to destroy attacking missiles.

The Aircraft – The Air Force bought a 747-400F straight off the Boeing Commercial Aircraft assembly line and flew it to Wichita, Kan., in January 2000. Boeing workers virtually rebuilt the aircraft, installing miles of wiring, grafting huge sheets of titanium to the plane's underbelly to protect the exterior from the heat of the laser exhaust and, most importantly, adding a 12,000-pound bulbous turret on the front of the aircraft to house the 1.5 meter telescope through which the laser beams will be fired. Company officials said it was the largest military modification to a commercial aircraft that Boeing had ever attempted.

Acquisition, Tracking & Pointing – In addition to a powerful laser, an airborne laser system also must be able to find and hit its targets. Numerous tests have been conducted at the White Sands Missile Range in southern New Mexico, both with lab-type instruments and with the actual aircraft, to demonstrate the system's ability to identify and follow a potential target.

The Lasers – Central to this system is the COIL. As a laser that generates its energy through chemical reaction, it has advantages over solid-state lasers, most notably in the amount of energy it can produce. COIL energy is produced by chemical reaction when oxygen and iodine molecules are mixed. A tremendous additional advantage is that the laser propagates at 1.315 microns in the infrared (invisible) spectrum. This wavelength travels easily through the atmosphere and has greater brightness – or destructive potential – on the target. There are three other important lasers aboard the aircraft: the Active Ranger System, which provides preliminary tracking data; the Track Illuminator Laser, which produces more refined data, and the Beacon Illuminator Laser, which measures the amount of atmospheric disturbance.

Systems Integration Laboratory (foreground)
Ground Pressure Recovery Assembly (background)

Correcting For Atmospheric Turbulence – The ability to find and track a boosting missile would be meaningless without a corresponding ability to lock onto and destroy the intended target. Since air, like water, is made up of many layers, scientists needed to find a way to compensate for these disturbances in the atmosphere in order to focus a high-energy beam on the target and hold the beam in place long enough for it to complete the destruction process. The system that will be installed on YAL-1A is the result of more than 15 years of research conducted by scientists at the Laboratory's Directed Energy Directorate and the Massachusetts Institute of Technology's Lincoln Laboratory. Working out of astronomical facilities at the Starfire Optical Range in the southeastern corner of Kirtland Air Force Base, researchers made revolutionary breakthroughs using lasers, computers and deformable optics.

The ABL Integrated Test Force – Actually a complex of buildings located at the historic Birk Flight Test Facility at Edwards Air Force Base, Calif. The gem of the ITF is the System Integration Laboratory (SIL), an 18,000 square-foot building housing a surplus 747-fuselage test stand that will serve as a laser template for the ABL aircraft. The six modules that compose the COIL component initially will be tested in the SIL. Once those tests have been completed, the modules will be disassembled, then reassembled on YAL-1A. Other resources in the ITF complex include a Ground Pressure Recovery Assembly (GPRA), which will enable simulation of ABL's anticipated cruising height, and a mixing area for Basic Hydrogen Peroxide, a vital ingredient to the  main laser's chemical reaction process.

History – Almost 20 years ago, the Air Force Research Laboratory and its predecessor units completed a project that showed the potential for an airborne laser. A KC-135A tanker airplane (a military version of the Boeing 707) was modified and equipped with a gas dynamic laser. This aircraft shot down a low-flying drone and five air-to-air missiles, proving the concept was possible. Later tests also were conducted at White Sands Missile Range aimed at finding out how effective a laser would be. For these tests, the nation's most powerful laser, the Mid-Infrared Advanced Chemical Laser, was used. In every case, scale models of typical targets were easily destroyed.

The System – Computer simulations indicate that an airborne laser would be very effective under battle conditions. Currently, the program will provide the United States with its only near-term boost-phase missile defense, that is, the ability to find and destroy a missile between the time it is launched and its booster rockets burn out.

The Laser Range Safety Tool (LRST) is being developed to permit range safety officers to properly assess hazards, and configure test scenarios such that these new weapons systems can be tested in a safe manner. For any given scenario, the tool assists in the evaluation of reflection patterns resulting 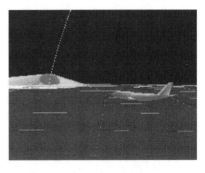 from targeting various types of moving targets, and predicts hazard zones and appropriate "keep out" areas. The tool is based on the ANSI Z136.1 standard for eye safety calculations along with new bio-effects data for the specific wavelengths associated with the new high-powered laser systems. Moreover, new risk assessment techniques using probabilities associated with the various aspects of exposure and injury will provide more realistic predictions for use by the range safety officers, as well as the operational users.

4.9.2 Tactical High Energy Laser for Air Defense

The U.S. Army Space and Strategic Defense Command are working on a new active defense weapon system concept to combat the threat to our forces from so-called "dumb munitions." The command's mobile Tactical High Energy Laser or THEL weapon system will provide an innovative solution for the acquisition and close-in engagement problems associated with these threats not offered by existing systems and give the air defense commander an option that he does not currently have. It will significantly enhance the force protection for combat forces and theater level assets for the Force XXI Army.

For the past several years, SSDC has been pursuing this concept that could provide new air and missile defense capability in force protection missions. Numerous Department of Defense high energy laser development programs over the last 20 years have proven and demonstrated the laser beam generation and beam pointing technologies for the THEL concept. Force XXI advancements in the area of real-time situational awareness now make it possible to capitalize on the attributes of a THEL in operational scenarios.

A THEL will be able to rapidly fire for close-in engagements where timelines are very short, and cost only a few thousand dollars per kill or less with a deep magazine to counter saturation attacks. Not only can THELs destroy, but they can also degrade, disrupt, or damage to enhance operational flexibility and effectiveness against a wide variety of air threats. This system can, therefore, operate as an effective new weapon node in the short- to medium-range air defense architecture.

The effectiveness of high-energy lasers against short-range rockets was tested and demonstrated in the "Nautilus" program, an outgrowth of Project Strong Safety, in collaboration with Israel. The program was conducted primarily at SSDC's High Energy Laser Systems Test Facility or HELSTF at White Sands Missile Range, N.M., and utilized a fraction of the power of the HELSTF Mid-Infrared Advanced Chemical Laser (MIRACL) to emulate the THEL weapon concept performance.

The MIRACL is a mega-watt class deuterium fluoride chemical laser that has been operational at HELSTF since the early 1980s. After a series of static and dynamic tests, the program successfully destroyed a short-range rocket in flight on Feb. 9, 1996. This success triggered the next development in the SSDC THEL effort.

In April 1996, then Prime Minister of Israel, Shimon Peres, met with President Clinton and Secretary of Defense William Perry. During the meeting, the U.S. made a commitment to assist Israel in the development of a THEL Advanced Concept Technology Demonstrator by the end of 1997, based on the success of the Nautilus program, to defeat the threat posed by Katyusha and other short-range rockets against the cities in northern Israel.

In July 1996, a contract was awarded by SSDC to TRW, Inc., of Redondo Beach, Calif., for the design, development, and fabrication of a THEL demonstrator, which will be a transportable, tactical sized deuterium fluoride chemical laser. Approximately 18 months will be required to design and build the system, followed by 12-18 months of testing.

If successful, the demonstrator may pave the way for future development of a THEL for use in U.S. peace keeping/contingency operations. The U.S. Army Air Defense Artillery School in Fort Bliss, Texas, already officially designated as the proponent for THEL by the Training and Doctrine Command, is planning to develop a mission need statement and operational concept that could lead to an operational requirement for a THEL system.

Evolving high-energy laser, beam control, and digital battlefield information technologies promise to combine into a highly effective force protection THEL weapon system for the Force XXI Army.

Prepared September 1996 by John J. Wachs, Weapons Directorate, MDSTC, SSDC High-Energy Lasers Weapons

4.10 Lasers for Air Defense

In its 1984 directed energy plan, SDIO planned to develop an acquisition, tracking, pointing, and fire control (ATPAWs) subsystem for directed energy weapons by fiscal year 1990 for $1,298 million. Through fiscal year 1993, SDIO allocated $1,634 million to this program, accomplishing some but not all of the program objectives. SDIO estimated that it will cost $180 million and take 3 years to resolve the majority of the remaining technical issues. For another $100 million, the ATP technology could be demonstrated in space.

All directed energy weapons need an ATP/FC system. In general terms, the system must quickly engage a large number of targets by placing a directed energy beam on the aim point of each target. These time and accuracy constraints dictate a rapid succession of handovers from one sensor to another. Each successive sensor in the system has a smaller field of view and greater accuracy.

The system locks on to the infrared signature of a missile (acquisition); calculates the flight path of the missile (tracking); calculates an aim point on the missile and directs the beam to the aim point (pointing); and assesses the results and selects the next target (fire control). Depending on the mission of the directed energy system, the ATP/ FC system must perform these functions when ballistic missiles are in their boost, post-boost, and/or midcourse phases of flight.

The basic goal of the program was to resolve the technical issues sufficiently to support a space test of a directed energy weapon by 1990. The overall technology performance objectives in the 1984 plan were as follows.

- Reduce the effect on the accuracy of pointing and tracking devices of vibrations caused by operation of the spacecraft and laser to less than 4 inches on the target.
- Develop the capability to rapidly retarget the laser beam from one target to another in less than 2 seconds.
- Develop the capability to track targets at ranges of 2,600 to 3,100 miles at an accuracy of about 4 inches.
- Develop fire control computer software to handle more than 100 targets at a rate of more than one target per second. The fire control functions are missile plume to missile hard body handover, tracking of multiple targets, target identification, aim point selection, and damage assessment.

The plan specified that $1,298 million would be required from focal years 1986 through 1990 to develop the system components and to fly space experiments to resolve integration and space operation issues. Experiments would permit the space test of a directed energy weapon in 1990.

SDIO met the plan's objectives for pointing and tracking technology and rapid retargeting technology for directed energy weapons. It did not meet the objectives for developing long-range fine tracking and fire control software. While not meeting all objectives, SD10 believes it has met the basic program goal of resolving technical issues sufficiently to support a space test of directed energy technology. Through fiscal year 1993, SDIO spent about $1,684 million developing ATP/FC technologies. This amount is about $286 million more than SD10 estimated was needed to accomplish the objectives. A majority of the funding was spent on a series of space- and ground-based experiments. All major space tracking experiments were canceled before completion due to a lack of funding. However, two space pointing experiments were completed.

At a cost of about $262 million, SDIO reported that it completed the Relay Mirror Experiment and the Low Power Atmospheric Compensation Experiment, which were focused on resolving issues related to the ground-based laser program. Each was placed in a separate orbit by one Delta booster in 1990. The Relay Mirror Experiment successfully demonstrated high-pointing accuracy, laser beam stability, and long-duration beam relays. The Low Power Atmospheric Compensation Experiment successfully demonstrated low-power technology to compensate for laser beam distortions, which occur when beams go through the atmosphere from ground to space.

SDIO had spent about $684 million from fiscal years 1985 through 1991 planning, designing, and fabricating hardware for four ATP/FC space experiments that were canceled before completion for the following reasons.

- Talon Gold was intended to demonstrate precision tracking and pointing in space for targeting satellites and boosters. After spending about $26 million on Talon Gold, SDIO canceled the experiment because the cost estimates for integration and launch had increased an additional $600 million.

- Pathfinder was started in September 1986 and was canceled in 1987 because it was too expensive. SD10 had spent about $40 million on this experiment, which was to address plume phenomenology using a sensor array on the space shuttle.
- The Starlab space experiment was intended to demonstrate precision tracking and would have used the space shuttle to accomplish the experiment. After spending about $603 million developing Starlab, SDIO canceled this experiment in part because the Challenger accident led to nearly a 3-year delay in the launch date, greatly increasing the overall cost. This coupled with changing priorities in the directed energy program led to changes in requirements and increased costs, which made the experiment too expensive to complete.
- Altair, which was canceled after SDIO had spent about $16 million in development costs, was intended to demonstrate the same types of technologies as Starlab and was planned to use some of the hardware developed for Starlab. An SDIO official estimated that it would have cost $330 million to complete Altair.

SDIO replaced the Altair space experiment with a nonspace ATP/FC experiment called High Altitude Balloon Experiment, This experiment was intended to achieve most of the same objectives as Altair but at a much lower estimated cost of $76 million. Balloons were used to carry AW/FC devices to an altitude of about 30 kilometers where these devices will be used to acquire and track missiles in the boost phase. SDIO'S program manager for ATP/FC expected this experiment to yield from 80 to 90 percent of the data that would have been obtained from a space experiment.

SDIO designed and constructed a Rapid Retargeting / Precision Pointing [R2P2] simulator that emulated the dynamics of a large spacecraft (e.g., motion and vibration). Using this facility, SDI0 developed and tested techniques for ensuring the stability, accuracy, and precision of a simulated directed energy weapon's pointing device under rapid retargeting situations. This project demonstrated, within the limits of a ground laboratory, that ATP/FC techniques should work in space at the levels established in the original program plan. SDIO will have spent about $42 million on this project from fiscal years 1986 through 1993.

Two other projects also demonstrated ATP/FC techniques. The Space Active Vibration Isolation project developed and tested ATP/FC techniques for negating the effects of spacecraft and weapon vibrations on the pointing device. This project produced hardware and technology that have improved the pointing stability of directed energy devices to below the program goal of less than 100 nanoradians, or about 4 inches from a distance of 1,000 kilometers. This project was followed by the Space Integrated Controls Experiment, which improved the pointing stability even further. SDIO spent about $37 million on these two projects from fiscal years 1986 through 1993.

As of 1993 SDIO estimated that it would cost $180 million and take three more years to resolve the vast majority of the ATP/FC technical issues and perform integrated ATP experiments against real targets from the High Altitude Balloon Experiment platform. This would substantially complete the objectives of the 1984 plan. An additional $100 million would be needed to demonstrate operation in space, assuming that it would be done as part of another directed energy space experiment such as Star LITE, the experiment planned for the chemical laser. The major technical issues to be resolved from 1993 through 1996 included long-range fine tracking, fire control, integrated ATP/FC, and additional concept development.

For long-range fine tracking, the Solid State baser Radar Source program produced two laser illuminators. They still need to be tested in realistic target environments to determine their effectiveness in changing conditions and against a wide variety of targets. In addition, their capabilities must also be developed to support aim point selection and maintenance and damage assessment.

Fire control decision software had been demonstrated in computer simulations, but its practicality and robustness had yet to be tested in an integrated field operation. Each of the individual fire control decision algorithms needs to be tested with several sets of scene conditions with real data. Functional integration with sensors and autonomous operation must also be demonstrated. SDIO plans to test the operation of the software on the High Altitude Balloon Experiment platform against boosting targets at the White Sands Missile Test Range.

4.10.1 Target Acquisition for Combat Operations

This section will be discussing Target Acquisition, Tracking and Combat operation by Direct Energy Weaponry Systems.

4.10.2 Overview

The goals of this sub-thrust can best be described in three major categories:

1. The measurement of atmospheric parameters on space and time scales required to support Air Force and Directed Energy Weapons System and its missions in Global Reach-Global Power,
2. The prediction of the future evolution of the atmosphere from a few hours to a few days, and,
3. The assessment of weather impact on Air Force Air Force and Directed Energy Weapons systems and operations.

4.10.3 Description

Theater Specification for Dominant Maneuvers sub-thrust conducts R&D programs to better understand the physical and dynamic processes of the lower atmosphere in order to design, develop, test, and transition remote sensing instrumentation, retrieval algorithms, and models in support of air and space war fighters.

Real-Time Measurements of Atmospheric Parameters from Satellites: The measurement goal emphasizes the application and interpretation of satellite sensor data, but also includes in-situ sensor development as part of the program. Measurement emphasis is on the three-dimensional determination of cloud cover at the highest spatial and temporal resolution to develop the models to support global surveillance and tactical warfare.

Atmospheric Optical Turbulence Measurements and Modeling: The technical objective is to specify and predict the atmospheric optical turbulence degradation to ground, air, and space based laser systems. Optical turbulence is highly variable from site to site, season to season, and day to day; however, as yet there are no good predictive models. In a program initiated in FY96, supported by the Airborne Laser (ABL) SPO, Phillips Lab is obtaining optical turbulence data in theaters of interest to the SPO

Tactical Remote Sensing: The technical objective is to provide from aircraft and satellite platforms remote sensing of battlefield gasses and emissions. The PL/GPOR lidar remote sensing program is set up to measure several atmospheric boundary layer parameters in high spatial resolution, including wind profiles, aerosol content and size distribution, as well as the detection of trace elements, both natural and man-made. Current assets include the following:

- 10.6 micron CO^2 Doppler range resolved wind profiler, dual tunable 9 to 11 micron CO^2 Doppler range resolved wind profiler and DIAL system to obtain range-resolved water vapor and trace gas profiles,
- 1.574 micron Portable, Environmental, Eye-safe Lidar (or Ladar) for range-resolved aerosol and cloud profiles in addition to cloud depolarization features.

New assets soon to be on hand include a coherent, tunable UV DIAL system for water vapor and ozone detection, a mechanical turbulence Lidar or Ladar for wind shear detection, and a refractive turbulence remote sensor to measure turbulence along a path.

The Theater Forecast for Precision Engagements FTA develops tailored weather products to support combat mission planning and execution worldwide.

Prediction of Clouds and Severe Weather: The prediction goal emphasizes the data fusion of satellite and indigenous data sources in the battlefield where data denial may be a factor. The resulting analysis fields will then be tested in theater-scale prediction models on time and space scales appropriate to tactical weapon delivery.

Virtual Weather: The goal of this program is to produce computer simulations of the atmosphere, with high physical fidelity, valid as a function of location, season, time of day and geometry. In order to address these requirements, simulation models must be developed that produce three-dimensional structure --the major shortfall of current capability. Initial efforts involve improving the physical reality of current cloud simulation models. Other projects include development of rain, fog, wind, humidity, lightning, and turbulence models. A strong emphasis is placed on physically correct visualization and the generation of radio-metrically correct atmospheric scenes.

Weather Impact Decision Aids (WIDA): The WIDA program is developing software technology for operationally predicting the impact of weather on the performance of airborne electro-optical navigation and weapon targeting systems. The program presently has four major ongoing and/or planned components: (1) Night Vision Goggle Operations Weather Software (NOWS), which will predict the impact of weather on night vision goggle detection range for AFSOC and ACC; (2) IR Target Scene Software (IRTSS), which is developing software that will determine the impact of weather on air-to-ground target scenes in the infrared, and produce an IR scene visualization for transition to the Air Force Mission Support System (AFMSS); (3) Weather Automated Mission Planning Software (WAMPS) a new start in FY97 to develop software to automatically incorporate weather impacts on airborne EO systems during theater mission planning in Theater Battle Management Core Systems (TBMCS); and (4) Target Acquisition Weather Software (TAWS), a new start in FY97, will provide a major upgrade to the current operational Electro-Optical

Tactical Decision Aid (EOTDA) used by Air Force Weather (AFW) support personnel to provide weapon lock-on and acquisition ranges for EO weapon systems used by ACC.

1. **User Impact:**
   None
2. **User Impact:**
   Concept/Technology
3. **Images:**
   None
4. **Related Initiatives:**
   - ➢ **Target Acquisition for Combat Operations** (See Section 5.1)
   - ➢ **Target Background Discrimination for Surveillance** (See Section 5.2)
5. **Related Requirements:**
   None
6. **Related Categories:**

Optical Surveillance Effects and Battle Space Operations

The importance of maintaining a reduced nuclear force and the emerging conventional ballistic force as a combat and cost effective weapon is recognized by Air Force Space Command (AFSPC) mission area plans and Space and Missile Systems Command (SMC) development plan has having the technology needs in Advanced Guidance technologies and Astrodynamics.

- • **The goals of Advanced Guidance are:**
   i. Global Positioning System (GPS) Range Standardization/ Safety Technology;
   ii. Development of new miniature systems to lower range costs 30% by replacing radar systems and enhance safety with greater accuracy and reliability by FY01;
   iii. GPS accuracy enhancements;
   iv. To increase cost effectiveness, missile navigation, testing accuracy with improved GPS/INS coupling by FY98;
   v. Development of Precision Fiber Optic Gyroscope (PFOG) with low loss integrated optics and fiber couplers and

Flexured Mass Accelerometer (FMA) with open loop, two back-to-back microwave resonant cavities by FY99.

vi. Decrease reliance on high cost, high precision inertial measurement systems with micromechanical updates on accelerometers and gyros by FY01;

vii. To fly the Missile Technology Demonstration III (MTD III) during FY01 to gain data on multiple penetrator warheads delivered on an ICBM;

viii. To develop anti-jam antennas;

ix. To integrate plasma physics with design; and

x. To develop and test materials for antenna windows.

- **The goals of Astrodynamics are to:**
  i. Improve differential correction (DC) accuracy 90%;

  ii. Improve propagation accuracy at the end of the prediction period by 90%;

  iii. Demo integrated performance of high accuracy lasers and astrodynamics algorithms to precisely locate and illuminate spacecraft;

  iv. Demo next generation initial orbit determination, DC and propagation for space surveillance;

  v. Show deficiencies in current operational DC and propagation which could be eliminated; and

  vi. Demonstrate capability to maintain independent high accuracy catalog of selected satellites (20-30 objects).

4.11 Target-Background Discrimination for Surveillance

4.11.1 Overview

Space-based surveillance, tracking, and interceptor systems must accurately and reliably discriminate target IR and optical signatures from the atmospheric and celestial IR and optical emissions against which the targets are viewed. When sensor specifications are optimized against realistic, accurate simulations of the atmospheric and celestial emissions in the sensor's field of view, then operational performance is significantly enhanced and system over-design is minimized, thereby making DoD space-based systems much more affordable. The Sub-thrust goals are to develop and demonstrate integrated background clutter mitigation technologies for SBIRS-High and -Low and next generation hyper-spectral Surveillance and Threat Warning systems, and to integrate clutter suppression technologies into hardware simulators to provide high-resolution spectral and spatial scene data of atmosphere, cloud, terrain, and celestial background clutter to support systems designs.

This sub-thrust:
1. Defines impact of optical and infrared backgrounds on Surveillance and Threat Warning, Theater and National Missile Defense, and Intelligence, Surveillance, and Reconnaissance systems.
2. Measures atmospheric and celestial infrared, ultraviolet, and visible backgrounds using satellite and rocket-borne sensors.
3. Models atmospheric and celestial optical and infrared backgrounds for the full range of operational conditions and system design trade space.
4. Provides real-world background scenes, global background statistics, and reliable background scene models to support systems engineering trade studies.
5. Measures and models in-flight infrared signatures of aircraft and missiles.
6. Distributes and provides on-line access to background phenomenology data.
7. Defines optical and infrared background requirements for surveillance systems and battle-space simulations.

4.11.2 Description

This sub-thrust defines impact of optical and infrared backgrounds on Surveillance and Threat Warning, Theater and National Missile Defense, and Intelligence, Surveillance, and Reconnaissance systems and measures atmospheric and celestial infrared, ultraviolet, and visible backgrounds using satellite and rocket-borne sensors. The two main project areas of this sub-thrust are backgrounds and targets phenomenology and background clutter mitigation.

The goals of the backgrounds and target Future Technical Architecture (FTA) are to: provide high-resolution spectral and spatial scene data of atmospheric, cloud, terrain, and celestial background clutter to support SBIRS designs; provide high-throughput data processing, analysis and distribution of back-ground phenomenology data for SBIRS, BMDO, and other DoD programs; measure in-flight infrared signatures of aircraft and missiles; and develop models capable of predicting the infrared characteristics of all aircraft, particularly in the design and development stages. A major task under this FTA is to construct infrared atmospheric and celestial background scenes from the superb data measured by the MSX satellite and atmospheric scenes from the highly successful MSTI-3 satellite mission. The combined data set will be used to up-grade models for design of the new SBIRS surveillance system.

The goals of the background clutter mitigation FTA are to: (1) characterize and predict atmosphere, cloud, and terrain infrared background clutter for full range of SBIRS operational conditions and system design trade space; and (2) assess impact of background clutter on SBIRS performance and mission capabilities. Spatial and temporal structure in atmospheric, cloud, and terrain backgrounds produce clutter against which infrared and optical sensor systems must detect and track theater ballistic missiles, cruise missiles, and aircraft threats as well as perform technical intelligence missions.

Under this program, tasks are being performed to:
(1) Provide background clutter codes to extrapolate measured background data to the full SBIRS design trade space and all SBIRS operational conditions;
(2) Provide background model uncertainty bounds;
(3) Assess and upgrade background clutter codes for SBIRS using MSX and MSTI-3 data;
(4) Develop dynamic, statistical background clutter models to support adaptive hyperspectral imaging; and
(5) Provide expert user interface for code applications.

1. **User Impact:**
   None
2. **User Impact:**
   Concept/Technology
3. **Images:**
   None
4. **Related Initiatives:**
   ➢ **Space-Based Infrared System – Low Earth Orbit (SBIRS-Low)**

   The Space-Based Infrared System (SBIRS) is in response to the U.S. military forces increasing need for accurate and timely warning of tactical missile attack. SBIRS will replace the current Defense Support Program (DSP) designed to meet U.S. infrared space-based surveillance and warning needs through the next two to three decades. SBIRS improves support to theater CINCs, U.S. deployed forces and allies by providing detailed information in the four mission areas of Missile Warning, Missile Defense, Technical Intelligence and Battle Space Characterization. SBIRS will provide significant performance enhancements over DSP by improving quality and timeliness of missile warning data. SBIRS should enhance information superiority and support the Joint Vision 2010 operational concepts of full-dimensional protection and precision engagement, by providing this data directly to theater commanders in a timely, survivable manner, thus enabling U.S. forces' immediate reaction to threat.

   The SBIRS space segment includes a high and low component. The high component comprises six satellites: four in Geosynchronous (GEO) earth orbit and two hosted payloads in Highly Elliptical Orbit (HEO). The low component includes approximately 24 Low Earth orbit (LEO) satellites. The SBIRS high component will meet a subset of the operational requirements, including all key threshold requirements. The SBIRS low component will provide a unique, precision, mid-course-tracking capability critical for effective ballistic-missile defense, as well as enhanced capability in support of other

SBIRS missions. SBIRS High, complemented by SBIRS Low satellites will meet all of its operational requirements.

The SBIRS ground segment includes a Continental U.S. (CONUS)-based Mission Control Station (MCS), a MCS backup (MCSB), a survivable MCS (SMCS), overseas relay ground stations, Multi-Mission Mobile Processors (M3P), and associated communication links. The SBIRS ground segment will be delivered incrementally. The first increment, scheduled to be operational in FY99, consolidates DSP and Attack and Launch Early Reporting to theater ground stations into a single CONUS ground station, and will operate with DSP satellite data. The second increment, scheduled for FY02, will provide the necessary ground segment functions required for the new high-altitude SBIRS satellites and the residual DSP satellites. Included in the second increment will be mobile terminals capable of fulfilling the Army Joint Tactical Ground Station in-theater and SBIRS strategic processing requirements. A third increment, which will be operational in FY03, will add the necessary ground segment functions for the first LEO satellite scheduled to be deployed in FY04.

Background Information:

SBIRS was initiated in 1995 as a replacement for the Follow-on Early Warning System acquisition, which was canceled due to cost and requirements problems. Since SBIRS satellites need to be completed before the last DSP satellite is launched, it was placed on an accelerated schedule and selected as a lead program for acquisition reform. Much of the traditional required documentation was reduced or consolidated into a Single Acquisition Management Plan, and emphasis was placed on direct involvement through Integrated Product Teams (IPTs) rather than traditional documentation reviews.

The SBIRS high component entered the EMD phase following a Milestone II DAB review in October 1996. This decision was supported by an OA conducted by AFOTEC and reviewed by DOT&E.

The first phase of IOT&E will be conducted in 1999 to verify performance of the Increment 1 ground station. Due to the critical role SBIRS plays in Integrated Tactical Warning and Attack Assessment (ITW/AA) of attack on the CONUS, DOT&E has become involved in this program early. DOT&E works closely with AFOTEC, the program office, and all users to ensure that the acquisition strategy fosters an operationally effective and suitable system while maintaining cost effectiveness. DOT&E has supported SBIRS acquisition reform through heavy involvement in IPTs, early involvement in combined developmental and operational tests, and consolidation of developmental and operational test plans into a single Integrated T&E Plan.

The SBIRS test program includes a combination of OAs, combined DT/OT testing, and dedicated IOT&E. These OT&E events will progress in a building-block manner beginning with analyses, modeling, and validated simulation and ending with Hardware-in-the-Loop (HWIL) test-beds and field tests. Modeling, simulation, and test-beds will be used to assess those areas in which field-testing cannot be conducted, such as actual missile attacks and operation in nuclear environments. SBIRS operational effectiveness and suitability will be assessed on the basis of IOT&Es of each of the three major increments, which will include fixed and mobile assets.

Test and Evaluation Activity:

In 1998, DOT&E approved an initial TEMP that defined the top-level test strategy and mapped it into the overall acquisition strategy. DOT&E also continued its oversight of the following areas: (each of which could impact schedule, cost and system performance)

- Progress towards Increment 1 IOT&E.

○ HWIL testbed definition and dynamic effects modeling for Increment 2.
○ Risk reduction efforts for Increment 3.
○ Testability of SBIRS/NMD requirements for Increment 3.

Progress towards Increment 1 IOT&E was assessed by an AFOTEC (OA) that addressed four areas: (1) major issues potentially affecting effectiveness and suitability; (2) programmatic voids; (3) testability of user requirements; and (4) ability of the program to support operational testing. DOT&E has specific program concerns about SBIRS Increment 1: (1) immature ground system software and delays in requirements performance verification; (2) delays in procuring high reliability communications links from the overseas ground stations to the Mission Control Station; and (3) adequate hardware for crew training. The Program Office is addressing many of these findings through specific risk reduction efforts to ensure readiness to enter IOT&E for the Increment 1 ground system in April 1999. There are still testability concerns involving the difficulty of testing SBIRS/NMD operational requirements within an acceptable confidence limit.

Test and Evaluation Assessment:

Year 2000 (Y2K) testing for SBIRS is well underway, and there are no anticipated problems with the system. Due to extensive use of commercial software and close cooperation between the contractor team and the Air Force, an adequate verification program is in place. Final Y2K testing will be complete prior to the start of IOT&E for the Increment 1 ground station in April 1999.

The major near-term challenge for the SBIRS program is to ensure a seamless transfer of operations from the current DSP ground stations to the new SBIRS Increment 1 MCS. This demanding task is complicated by the compressed timeline and issues associated with shared use facilities at the overseas relay ground stations. Additionally, there have been significant delays in validating software performance of the Increment 1 Ground System. Other near-term challenges for the SBIRS program include the adequacy of test-bed design and the scope of models and simulations needed to validate the stressing requirements for the SBIRS High satellites and MCS Increment 2; and the significant technical risks associated with accelerated deployment of the low component by FY04. The demanding SBIRS High requirements are a significant improvement over DSP's demonstrated performance, and require extensive testing to validate assure the system's performance. For HWIL test-beds, continued attention must be given to ensure that the testbeds are adequate to support OT&E, including the need to portray dynamic backgrounds that accurately portray the earth's background as seen from space.

DOT&E's assessment is that the SBIRS compressed schedule to achieve "On Line in '99" remains high risk, and delays in software integration and testing pose an increased risk in a "zero margin" schedule leading to Increment 1 IOT&E scheduled for April 1999. The primary challenge for Increment 1 is the verification of software performance and reliability. There have been significant delays in verifying software performance and reliability, as well as delays in hardware installation at the Remote Ground Stations. While this type of problem is not unusual, many systems interfacing with the SBIRS MCS are 1970s legacy reporting systems, whose interfaces may not be adequately documented. Delays in starting testing of these interfaces put an inordinate amount of pressure on first opportunity success. The "never fail" nature of ITW/AA systems requires extensive "on-line" testing to validate reliable Increment 1 operations and a period of parallel operations prior to declaration of IOC. Any significant delays to IOT&E would lead to "ripple effect" delays in the Increment 1 IOC date, and further delay the IOC dates for subsequent ground system increments. Also, there is concern that the SBIRS Increment 1 ground system includes voids in areas of fault detection and isolation, operator training, and manpower.

SBIRS Increment 2 (both space and ground elements) remain on schedule, but face continued challenges in the areas of simulation and test-bed development. For Increment 2, progress has been made in identifying real world, dynamic effects in the short and medium wavelengths detected by the greatly improved SBIRS High sensors. The operational impact of these effects must be quantified and the SBIRS High sensor design shown to be robust enough to handle these natural phenomenon. Resolution of these issues can be best accomplished by incorporation of adequate testing processes into the baseline sensor ground-testing program. Until this testing is completed, the capabilities of the SBIRS sensor and signal processing to operate in the space environment remain a major concern.

Continuing significant technical problems with the SBIRS Low PDRR satellites demonstrate the wisdom of an extensive PDRR test phase before entering EMD to start construction of operational SBIRS Low satellites. The current schedule of events is very compressed, and does not allow full evaluation of the PDRR satellites' performance. The current baseline SBIRS Low schedule requires successful completion of many difficult activities proceeding in parallel toward a successful FY04 first launch, thus violating recommendations outlined in the recently completed Welch Report on missile defense systems. Any additional delays in the PDRR competing contractors programs will require starting EMD prior to completion of PDRR to meet the congressional goal of an FY04 first launch. DOT&E is concerned that the baseline schedule, which includes the Flight Demonstrations System and the Low Altitude Demonstrations System, will be delayed, presenting very few opportunities to collect "real world" performance data on contractor designs to assess their ability to meet draft performance requirements. This period of evaluation of PDRR results is critical since "lessons learned" from PDRR test activities form the foundation for the government and contractor teams to perform Cost As an Independent Value satellite design trades. Any significant problems encountered during the PDRR phase (given the compressed schedule) may lead to premature launching of inadequately designed and tested satellites to maintain the FY04 initial deployment date.

To support Milestone II decisions, DOT&E has worked closely with AFOTEC, the program office, and the user community, to ensure that the acquisition strategy throughout the acquisition cycle fosters an operationally effective and suitable system, while maintaining cost effectiveness. This early involvement included active membership in IPTs, fostering combined developmental and operational tests, early validation of software maturity, and consolidation of developmental and operational test plans into a single Integrated T&E Plan.

5. **Related Requirements:**
   None

6. **Related Categories:**

   ➤ **Contributing Sensors**
   These sensors provide observation data on satellites to USSPACECOM on a contributing basis, but are not directly under the operational control of USSPACECOM. Both mechanical radars and electro-optical systems are included in this category.

   ➤ **Satellite Operations**
   The DoD procures, operates, and maintains a myriad of satellite systems to support national and tactical communications, missile warning, nuclear detonation detection, navigation, weather, and environmental monitoring. DoD's satellite operations include the Defense Satellite Communications System (DSCS), Milstar, Fleet SATCOM System (FLTSATCOM), UHF Follow-on (UFO) System, the Defense Support Program (DSP), the Nuclear Detonation Detection System (NUDET), the Global Positioning System (GPS, also referred to as POSNAVTIME or position, navigation

and time), and the Defense Meteorological Satellite Program (DMSP).systems are included in this category.

➢ **Space Based Warning System**
This category addresses space systems and sensors that have a surveillance and warning mission, which are operational, in development, or being studied.

➢ **DoD Space Surveillance Programs**
A constant and vigilant surveillance of potentially hostile military threats is critical in preserving the operational effectiveness of our armed forces around the world. Naval Space Command manages two distinct surveillance efforts in support of Fleet and Fleet Marine Forces: tracking satellites in orbit and monitoring over-the-horizon threats from sea and air forces.

Over one million satellite detections, or observations, are collected by this surveillance network each month. Data gathered is transmitted to a computer center at Naval Space Command headquarters in Dahlgren, where it is used to constantly update a data base of spacecraft orbital elements. This information is reported to Fleet and Fleet Marine Forces to alert them when particular satellites of interest are overhead. The command also maintains a catalog of all earth-orbiting satellites and supports USSPACECOM as part of the nation's worldwide Space Surveillance Network

CHAPTER FIVE: LASER DIRECTED ENERGY CONCEPTS

This chapter will discuss Directed Energy concepts for Strategic Defense. We will talk about defensive weapons as a countermeasure against any measure that is applied in term of a lethal weapon against friendly targets. Directed energy concepts can play unique roles in strategic defense because of their reaction time, speed of light engagement, and large geographic converge. This chapter discusses the main directed energy concepts, engagements in which they could have significant advantage and their expected performance in them. It covers both boost phase engagements and midcourse applications, and contrasts these results with those of earlier analyses.

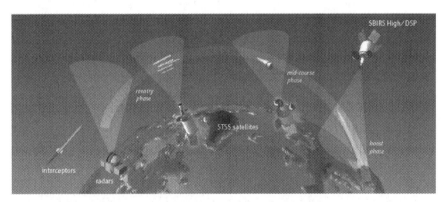

Figure 5-1: National Configurations of Space Tracking Surveillance System (STSS) and Spaced Based Infrared System (SBIRS)

5.1 Laser Beam and Material Interactions and its Lethality

Weapons are devices, which deliver sufficient energy to targets to damage them. Weapon design involves a dialog between weapon designers, and military planners. Designers create means of projecting energy, and planners have targets that they would like to destroy. Effective design requires knowledge of the targets and the circumstances of their engagement, and effective planning requires knowledge of the weapons and their characteristics. However, in new and emerging areas of weaponry, designers and planners often do not speak the same language. As a result, designers can operate in ignorance of operational realities, and planners can assume that anything involving new technology will meet all their needs.

Directed energy weapons are no different. However, while there are books and manuals that deal with the issues affecting the utility of nuclear missiles and rifles, there is no comparable source of information for directed energy weapons. I have tried to fill that void with this book as well as dealing with technical and theory of interaction of High Energy Laser in particular and avoid aspect of High Power Microwave in general as lethal weapons.

This book is way to explain High Energy Laser Power and how Directed Energy Weapons work, how the energy of high power laser as weapon is propagated to the target, and how the weapons/laser beam-target interaction creates effects (damage) in the target. The mathematics and physics of effects of high power laser radiation beam interacts with its targets and analyzing the damages within period of dual time.

This is a technical exposition, written at the undergraduate physics and engineering level that could serve either as a textbook or as a reference text for technical practitioners. The text touches upon Kinetic

Energy Weapons in addition to High Power Lasers and stays away from the other two aspect beam weapons namely Microwaves and Particle Beams. Numerous unclassified articles and literature both on High Power Microwaves and Particle Beams can be found on Internet that are published by expert in these **two fields** [xx, yy]. A directed-energy weapon is a type of weapon that emits energy in a particular direction by a means other than a projectile. It transfers energy to a target for a desired effect. Some of these weapons are real or practicable; some are science fiction. The energy is in various forms:

- Electromagnetic radiation (typically lasers or masers).
- Particles with mass (particle beam weapons).
- Fictional weapons often use some sort of radiation or energetic particle that does not exist in the real world; or where the physical nature of the energy and its means of transmission are not detailed and the visible effects would be impossible in the real world.

Some of these weapons are known as death rays or ray-guns and are usually portrayed as projecting energy at a person or object to kill or destroy.

Some lethal directed-energy weapons are under active research and development, but most examples appear in science fiction (or non-functional toys and film props).

5.2 Introduction to Effectiveness of Directed Energy Weapons

The effectiveness of a defensive weapons system is measured by its ability to deny the attacking system succession accomplishing its mission.

Lethality of a direct energy weapon (DEW) is, in simplest terms, its capability to destroy a target and incoming threat. It is appropriate to speak of lethality as the capability of directed energy weapons to prevent a target from accomplishing a particular mission. This requirement could be fulfilled in the form of "hard kill" (physical destruction of the warhead) or "soft kill" (mission impairment).

Further study of the "kill" phenomenon requires a distinction between immediate (within milliseconds) or delayed kill. The difference results in tracking assets wasted and the unnecessary dilution of defensive systems in a time critical situation[14].

To meet the kill requirements, weapons systems using three different energy sources have been proposed. Historically, chemical and nuclear explosives have been used. They, together, form the "Potential Energy" weapons (PEW) group. More recently, Kinetic Energy Weapons (KEW) and Directed Energy Weapons (DEW) have been proposed and engineering development has begun.

Thus, there may be several measures of lethality for a given target set. For an incoming missile threat, one may define lethality criteria to structure damage of the target in term of hard kill, and other criteria relating to destruction or indefinite interruption of the sensors or guiding system on which the missile depends to accomplish its function. Similarly, actual destruction of a booster or reentry vehicle sets certain lethality criteria; but methods of destroying accurate weapons delivery, such as destruction of guidance electronics, in term of soft kill, may also generate acceptable lethality criteria for system designers. However, in the latter case, verification of a kill becomes problematical.

The ability of laser beams (pulsed, Continuous wave (CW), and repetitively pulsed), at infrared, visible, ultraviolet, and x-ray wavelength to destroy various target is analyzed. First, the physics of the interaction of various laser beams as part of directed energy weapon with materials is examined. This information is used to assess the effect of a given incident power or energy flounce on the target and the ability of the target to perform its mission after such an attack. The arguments, then, are used to size weapons system to destroy enemy targets (lethality) and related safety factor and issues in regard to safety of friendly troops present in battlefield of such engagements.

The fundamental kill mechanism of CW or Quasi-CW repetitively pulsed laser beam is heating, with subsequent melting and/or evaporation of the wall of a liquid or solid booster rocket. Subsequently, ignition of booster fuel may take place, or mechanical failure of structures may occur before completion of burn-through. In a similar manner, the wall of the bus and components inside it may be damaged, so that the intended function of the missile is thwarted.

In addition to energy deposition, momentum is also transferred to the target by directed energy beams. Momentum transfer can damage targets through mechanical shearing or buckling. This damage mechanism has been demonstrated by pulsed laser beams for pulses less than or equal to 2 μs. Kill through repeated impulse damage has system-level advantages over thermal kill since the pointing requirements are far less sever. Momentum transfer may also be used as a discrimination tool for reentry vehicles and decoys in the mid-course such as technique employed in LIDAR (Laser Radar) Applications. The interaction of CW or Quasi-CW laser radiation with targets is discussed and lethality criteria for this type of beams are derived. Finally, summarizes the main conclusions, setting lower limits on power and energy that are imposed on a DEW of laser type system by the lethality requirements and as result the measurements that are need to take under consideration to address the issue of LRST to friendly troops in vicinity of target engagements field.

5.3 The Mathematics of Diffusion

The history of heat conduction and its mathematical theory principally starts with Fourier and was set forth by him in his *Theorie analytique de la Chaleur* with solutions of problems naturally arising from it. While Fourier treated a large number of cases, including most of those we shall see occasional consideration, his work was extended and applied to more complicated problem by his contemporaries Laplace and Poisson, and later by a number of others.

One of the most important applications that we can consider here is the Mathematical Diffusion Theory of Heat Conduction and principal of high-power laser beams and matter that both has industrial and military applications. This includes applications such as heating, melting, vaporization, and plasma production. These phenomena, which likewise can involve an interaction of a high-power laser beam, are indeed sometimes called laser effects. Some of these considerations will be out of scope of this book but its principle is presented here and further investigation in any particular application should be studied by reader. To introduce some general idea about how to go about these applications and laying out *The Mathematic of Diffusion* we start with the diffusion equation and the diffusion process.

5.3.1 The Diffusion Process and Basic Hypothesis of Mathematical Theory

Diffusion is the process by which matter is transported from one part of a system to another as a result of random molecular motions. Transfer of heat by conduction is also due to random molecular motions and there is an obvious analogy between the two processes [20]. This was recognized by Fick in 1855, which first put diffusion on a quantitative basis by adopting the mathematical equation of heat conduction derived some years earlier by Fourier in 1822. The mathematical theory of diffusion in isotropic substances is therefore based on the hypothesis that the rate of transfer of diffusing substances through unit area of a section is proportional to the concentration gradient measured normal to the section, i.e.

$$F = -D\frac{\partial C}{\partial X} \qquad \text{Eq. 5-1}$$

Where F is the rate of transfer per unit area of section, C the concentration of diffusing substances, x the space coordinate measured normal to the section, and D is called the diffusion coefficient. In some cases diffusion in dilute solutions, D can reasonably be taken as constant, while in others, e.g. diffusion in high polymers, it depends very markedly on concentration [20]. In case of heat transfer and solving problem involving the temperature field determination, one should obtain differential heat conduction. In this case the temperature increase along the normal to the isothermal surfaces is characterized by a temperature gradient ($grad\ T$). A temperature gradient is a vector along the normal to the isothermal surface in the direction of the increasing temperature, i.e.,

$$grad\ \boldsymbol{T} = n_0\ (\partial T / \partial n)$$

Eq. 5-2

Where n_0 denotes a unit vector, along the normal in the direction of the temperature change according to Figure 5-2 and $\partial T / \partial n$ is the temperature derivative along the normal (n) to the isothermal surface [21].

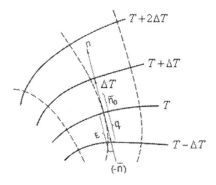

Figure 5-2: Isotherms of temperature filed [21].
(Letters with arrows corresponding to bold-face type in text)

The gradient is also denoted by ∇.

Gradient components along the Cartesian coordinates are identical to the appropriate partial derivatives, so that

$$grad\ \boldsymbol{T} = \vec{\nabla} \cdot \boldsymbol{T} = i\frac{\partial T}{\partial x} + j\frac{\partial T}{\partial y} + k\frac{\partial T}{\partial z}$$

Eq. 5-3

Where $\boldsymbol{i}$, $\boldsymbol{j}$ and $\boldsymbol{k}$ are mutual orthogonal vectors of a unit length along the coordinate axes. This relation is possible because any vector may be represented as a vectorial sum of three components along the coordinate axes.

The concept of a temperature-filed intensity may be introduced as follow;

$$\vec{E} = -grad\ T \qquad \text{Eq. 5-4}$$

The vector $\vec{E}$ is referred to as a vector of the temperature filed intensity.

The quantity of heat transferred per unit time per unit area of the isothermal surface is referred to as a heat flux; the appropriate vector is obtained by the relation

$$q = (-n_0)\frac{dQ}{dt}\frac{1}{S} \qquad \text{Eq. 5-5}$$

Where $\dfrac{dQ}{dt}$ quantity of heat is transferred per unit time, or the heat-flow rate, S is the isothermal surface area, and $(-n_0)$ is a unit vector along the normal to the surface area S in the direction of the decreasing temperature. In this case the vector q is therefore is designated as heat flux vector, the direction of which is opposite to that of the temperature gradient (both vectors follow the normal to the isothermal surface, but their directions are opposite to each other). The projection of the vector q on any arbitrary direction l is also the vector q_l, the scalar quantity of which is $q\cos(n,l)$.

The lines which coincide with the direction of vector q are referred to as heat-flow lines. These are perpendicular to the isothermal surfaces at the intersection points. A tangent to the heat-flow lines taken in the opposite direction yields the temperature gradient direction (See Figure 5-2).

The fundamental heat-conduction law may be formulated as follows: the heat flux is proportional to the temperature field intensity, or the heat flux is proportional to the temperature gradient, i.e.,

$$q = k\vec{E} = -grad\ T = -kn_0\ (\partial T / \partial n) \qquad \text{Eq. 5-6}$$

Where k the proportionality factor is called thermal conductivity. To reveal the physical significance of the thermal conductivity, we shall write the basic relation (Equation 5-6) for a steady one-dimensional temperature field for the situation where the temperature depends only on one coordinate which is normal to the isothermal surfaces. The scalar quantity of the heat flux vector is

$$q = -k\frac{dT}{dx} \quad \left(\frac{\partial T}{\partial x} = \frac{\partial T}{\partial y} = \frac{\partial T}{\partial z} = 0\right) \qquad \text{Eq. 5-7}$$

If the temperature gradient is a constant value ($\frac{\partial T}{\partial x} = \text{constant}$), which means the temperature variation with x follows the linear law, then it may be written as;

$$\frac{dT}{dx} = \frac{T_2 - T_1}{x_2 - x_1} = \text{constant} \qquad \text{Eq. 5-8}$$

Hence the heat flow rate $\frac{dQ}{dt}$ is also a constant value as;

$$\frac{dQ}{dt} = \frac{Q}{t} = \text{constant} \qquad \text{Eq. 5-9}$$

Where Q is the quantity of heat following in the time τ.

It follows from Equation 5-5 and 5-9 that;

$$\frac{Q}{St} = -k\frac{T_2 - T_1}{x_2 - x_1} = k\frac{T_2 - T_1}{x_1 - x_2} \qquad \text{Eq. 5-10}$$

Since $T_1 > T_2$ and $x_2 > x_1$.

Thus the thermal conductivity is equal to the heat flowing per unit time and per unit surface when the temperature difference per unit length of the normal is 1 degree. Thermal conductivity has dimensions of kcal/m.hr.°C or W/m.°C. Thermal conductivity is a physical property of a body characterizing its ability to transfer heat. The physical significance of the thermal conductivity and its dependence on basic properties of a body may be better understood when we consider the heat transfer mechanism in a body in a specific state [21].

The relation $k / (x_2 - x_1) = k / \Delta x$ (kcal/m².hr.°C or W/m².°C) is called thermal conductance of a certain portion of a body and the inverse value $\Delta x / k$ (m².hr.°C) or (m².°C/w) is the thermal resistance of this portion of a body and the magnitude of it varies for different materials over a wide range.

5.3.2 The Differential Equation of Diffusion Equation

The necessary condition for heat conduction is the existence of a temperature gradient. Experience shows that heat is transferred by conduction in the direction normal to the isothermal surface from a higher temperature level to a lower one.

To solve problems involving the temperature field determination, one should obtain a differential heat conduction equation. A differential of heat equation is a mathematical relationship between physical quantities characterizing the phenomenon considered, these quantities being functions of space and time. Such an equation characterizes the physical process at any point of a body at any moment. A differential heat equation provides a relation between temperature, time, and coordinates of an elementary volume. A differential equation will be derived by a simplified method. A one-dimensional temperature field is assumed (heat propagates in only one direction; say, in the direction of the x-axis). Under these conditions we assume that the thermal coefficients are to be independent of spatial coordinates and time. We single out an elementary rectangular parallelepiped of the volume $dxdydz$ from a uniform and isotropic infinite plate such as Figure 5-3 whose sides are parallel to the axes of coordinates and are of length dx, dy and dz.

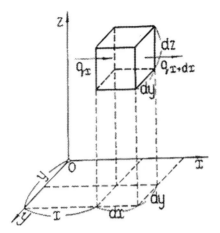

Figure 5-3: Heat Flux through elementary volume [21].

The fundamental differential equation of diffusion in an isotropic medium is derived from Equation 5-1 as follows.

The heat amount flowing in through the left side, $dydz$, into the parallelepiped per unit time is $q_x dydz$, and the heat amount flowing out through the opposite side per unit time is $q_{x+dx} dydz$.

Note: that from now on we represent temperature with capital T instead of small t or C to keep everything in perspective and not to make any mistake with time t and we shall also convert τ to t for time.

Therefore if $q_x > q_{x+dx}$, then the elementary parallelepiped will be heated. However the difference between these flows according to the law of energy conservation is equal to the heat accumulated in this elementary parallelepiped, i.e.

$$q_x dydz - q_{x+dx} dydz = c\rho \frac{\partial T}{\partial t} dxdydz \qquad \text{Eq. 5-11}$$

Note: that the heat accumulated is calculated from the elementary relation $\nabla Q = cM\nabla\Theta = c\rho V\nabla\Theta$, where $\nabla\Theta$ is a temperature increment in a body per unit time with the mass M and the volume V where c is representing specific heat and ρ is density of this mass (i.e. $M = \rho V$).

The quantity of q_{x+dx} is an unknown function of x. If it is expanded in Taylor's series (See Appendix A for Taylor's Series definition) and only the first two terms of the series are retained, it may be written as follow;

$$q_{x+dx} \approx q_x + \frac{\partial q_x}{\partial x} dx \qquad \text{Eq. 5-12}$$

Then substitution of Equation 5-12 into Equation 5-11 results

$$q_x dydz - (q_x + \frac{\partial q_x}{\partial x} dx) dydz = c\rho \frac{\partial T}{\partial t} dxdydz$$

$$q_x dydz - q_x dydz - \frac{\partial q_x}{\partial x} dxdydz = c\rho \frac{\partial T}{\partial t} dxdydz$$

$$-\frac{\partial q_x}{\partial x} dxdyd = c\rho \frac{\partial T}{\partial t} dxdydz$$

Using the heat conduction Equation 5-7 in form of $q_x = -k(\partial T / \partial x)$, we obtain

$$k\frac{\partial^2 T}{\partial x^2} c\rho \frac{\partial T}{\partial t}$$

or

$$\alpha \frac{\partial^2 T}{\partial x^2} = \frac{\partial T}{\partial t} \qquad \text{Eq. 5-13}$$

$\alpha = k / c\rho$ is the thermal diffusivity, a material-specific quantity depending on the *thermal conductivity*, k, the *mass density*, ρ, and the *specific heat capacity*, c and can noted as c_p from now on therefore α can be shown as $\alpha = k / c\rho$.

Equation 5-13 is a differential heat conduction equation for a one-dimensional heat flow. If heat propagates along the normal to the isothermal surfaces, then the vector $\mathbf{q}$ may be expanded in three components along the coordinate axes. The heat stored in the elementary volume of Figure 5-3 will be equal to the sum of;

$$-\left(\frac{\partial q_x}{\partial x} + \frac{\partial q_y}{\partial y} + \frac{\partial q_z}{\partial z}\right)dxdydz$$

Then the differential heat conduction equation can be written as follow;

$$\alpha\left(\frac{\partial^2 T}{\partial x^2} + \frac{\partial^2 T}{\partial y^2} + \frac{\partial^2 T}{\partial z^2}\right) = \alpha\nabla^2 T = \frac{\partial T}{\partial t} \qquad \text{Eq. 5-14}$$

where ∇^2 Laplacian operator in is Cartesian coordinates and is presented as follow

$$\nabla^2 = \frac{\partial^2}{\partial x^2} + \frac{\partial^2}{\partial y^2} + \frac{\partial^2}{\partial z^2} \qquad \text{Cartesian coordinates.}$$

$$\nabla^2 = \frac{1}{r}\frac{\partial}{\partial r}\left(r\frac{\partial}{\partial r}\right) + \frac{1}{r^2}\frac{\partial^2}{\partial \theta^2} + \frac{\partial^2}{\partial z^2} \qquad \text{Cylindrical coordinates.}$$

$$\nabla^2 = \frac{1}{r^2}\frac{\partial}{\partial r}\left(r^2\frac{\partial}{\partial r}\right) + \frac{1}{r^2\sin\theta}\frac{\partial}{\partial \theta}\left(\sin\theta\frac{\partial}{\partial \theta}\right) + \frac{1}{r^2\sin^2\theta}\frac{\partial^2}{\partial \phi^2} \quad \text{Spherical coordinates.}$$

For details of derivation of above relationship refer to Appendix B.

This operator can be expressed in Cylindrical and Spherical as well and are shown in above as results the Heat Conduction Equation can be expressed in those coordinates respectively;

Diffusion Equation in Cylindrical Coordinate

The Equation 5-14 can be expressed in cylindrical form by transformation of coordinates, or by considering elements of volume of different shape. Thus by putting

$$x = r\cos\theta$$
$$y = r\sin\theta$$

Or by considering an element of volume of a cylinder of sides dr, $rd\theta$ and dz we obtain the equation for diffusion in a cylinder as follow;

$$\frac{\partial T}{\partial t} = \frac{1}{r}\left\{\frac{\partial}{\partial r}\left(r\alpha\frac{\partial T}{\partial r}\right) + \frac{\partial}{\partial \theta}\left(\frac{\alpha}{r}\frac{\partial T}{\partial \theta}\right) + \frac{\partial}{\partial z}\left(r\alpha\frac{\partial T}{\partial z}\right)\right\} \qquad \text{Eq. 5-15}$$

in terms of the cylindrical coordinates r, θ and z.

Diffusion Equation in Spherical Coordinate

The corresponding equation for a sphere in terms of spherical polar coordinates r, θ and ϕ is obtained by writing

$$x = r\sin\theta\cos\phi$$
$$y = r\sin\theta\sin\phi$$
$$z = r\cos\theta$$

or by considering an element of volume of a sphere of sides dr, $rd\theta$ and $r\sin\theta d\phi$. It is

$$\frac{\partial T}{\partial t} = \frac{1}{r^2}\left\{\frac{\partial}{\partial r}\left(\alpha r^2 \frac{\partial T}{\partial r}\right) + \frac{1}{\sin\theta}\frac{\partial}{\partial \theta}\left(\alpha\sin\theta\frac{\partial T}{\partial \theta}\right) + \frac{\alpha}{\sin^2\theta}\frac{\partial^2 T}{\partial \phi^2}\right\} \qquad \text{Eq. 5-16}$$

If the thermal conductivity is independent of temperature then simplified forms of Equation 5-15 and 5-16 for pure radial diffusion, for example in a long cylinder where end effects are negligible or in a spherically symmetrical system can be expressed in terms of the nomenclature of vector analysis as follow;

$$\frac{\partial T}{\partial t} = div(\alpha\, grad T) = \alpha\nabla^2 T \qquad \text{Eq. 5-17}$$

For a one-dimensional symmetrical temperature filed, $\nabla^2 T$ is a function of one space coordinate.

5.3.3 Boundary and Initial Conditions

Before any solution can be presented for any governing diffusion equation, it is necessary to introduce additional physical information in the form of two conditions that are known as *Initial* and *Boundary* Conditions which the temperature satisfies in case of Conduction problems. These are partly the direct expression of the results of experiment and partly the mathematical statement of hypotheses founded upon these results [26]. We assume that in the interior of the solid T is a continuous function of x, y, z and t; and this holds also for the first differential coefficient with regard to t; and that this holds also for the first differential coefficients with regard to x, y, and z. At the boundary of the solid, and at the instant at which flow of heat is supposed to start, these assumptions are not made.

- *Initial Condition* (I. C.) is specification of the condition of the system at the start of the computation. The temperature throughout the body is supposed given arbitrary at the instant which we take as the origin of the time coordinate t . In a thermal and diffusion analysis problem for example, the temperature of the melt at the time of laser dwelling with target or some period of collapse time as an initial condition. Similar argument can readily provide good starting value for other independent variables such as the velocity or the concentration of various chemicals. If this arbitrary function is continuous, we require finding a solution of our problem which shall, as t tends to zero, tend to the given value. In other words, if the initial temperature is given by

$$T = f(x, y, z)$$

our solution of the equation

$$\frac{\partial T}{\partial t} = k\nabla^2 T$$

must be such that;

$$\lim_{t \to 0}(T) = f(x, y, z)$$

at all points of the solid. If the initial distribution is discontinuous at points or surfaces, these discontinuities must disappear after a short period of time, and in this case our solution must converge to the value given by the initial temperature at all points where this distribution is continuous [26].

- The surface *Boundary Conditions* (B. C.) usually arising in the mathematical theory of diffusion and heat transfer problem are described below. On the other hand defining the specification of boundary conditions is normally more difficult. In some cases especially in case of interaction of a high power laser weapon with its target very little is known about the actual thermal or dynamic of target condition at interface. However, there are basically three types of boundary conditions. The situation is simpler to analyze in the case of the thermal problem. The three types of boundary conditions for thermal problems are as follows.

1. At the outer boundary of the system the temperature is specified

$$T = T_s$$

2. The heat flux is zero (insulating boundary which means *no flux across the surface*)

$$k\nabla T = 0$$

3. The heat flux is specified as q, (heat exchange boundary, which means *prescribed flux across the surface*)

$$-k\nabla T = q_s$$

The book by Luikov (Analytical Heat Diffusion Theory) [21] offers different problems and associated solution for the above three types of boundary conditions and readers should refer to that reference extensively to understand how to solve heat diffusion equation under these boundary conditions. Luikov also offers different methods for calculating the heat flow in the process of heating and cooling, where a body receives or release a definite quantity of heat. His suggest method easily can be applied in case of Laser beam where the High Power Laser beam is used as part of Directed Energy Weapons.

5.3.4 Materials Response

The laser heating of a material is mainly determined by the material's *Absorptivity* (A) as function of laser wavelength. Accordingly the *Reflectivity* (R) of materials also is dominated by the laser wavelength and as result both of these properties are main driving factor and criteria for materials response to laser analysis. Absorptivity and reflectivity are part of optical properties of metals and in general condition of their surfaces and temperature, i.e. the laser heating rate. The heating rate of the metal of consideration is mainly determined by the its absorptivity for a given laser wavelength—a quantity which, in return, is determined by the optical properties of the metal itself and of the metal surface as well as the temperature range of the source, heating rate by the source, etc.

Given the above argument the Absorptivity (A) and Reflectivity (R) are main driving factor for the choice of the most appropriate laser system as a mean for a Directed Energy Weapons System. Surface hardening of the target of engagement also plays some part in this matter where the target lethality is under consideration. In case of dealing with incoming foe missile and destroying such threat in flight with a light beam such as laser, there are several possible approach. One is to damage the missile's target seeker and prevent the missile from acquiring the target, while another case is to cause the warhead or rocket fuel to detonate prematurely. It is also possible to damage the flight controls and force the missile into an uncontrollable flight preplanned and path. The most common method is structurally weakening the missile body so that the missile breaks up in flight. Throughout these destruction methods, the ways in which missile materials reacts to laser irradiation is threefold:

1. Light coupling to the material – The optical reflectivity of the material determines what fraction of the energy is absorbed and thus converted to thermal and mechanical energy.
2. Propagation of Thermal/Mechanical effects – This characteristic determines the efficiency in which the heat or shock transmits through the material.

3. Induced effects of the propagation of thermal/mechanical energy – The resulting process occurs when high energy is deposited on a material. For instance, melting, vaporization, shock loading, crack propagation and spalling.

5.3.4.1 Theory of Laser Interaction with Solids

Some of the first questions that should be asked when it comes to laser interaction with solids in particular if it is used as weapon to destroy a target are:

1. How much laser power is needed?
2. How long this power must be applied to dual target?
3. What side effects will be produced in addition to the heating process anticipated?

Off course, the last question in case of total target destruction is not important at this point.

Finally the last be not least is

4. Are these requirements compatible with specifications of available laser system? Whether is ABL (Air Born Laser) or GBL (Ground Based Laser) or the system is orbiting beyond the earth atmosphere.

Naturally, ABL and GBL system requires certain other analysis, considerations and effects such as Thermal Blooming, which causes the laser to defocus and disperse energy into the atmosphere. It can be more severe if there is fog, smoke, or dust in the air. As result of the thermal blooming and atmospheric attenuation of the laser beam, the beam diverges and loses its energy that is supposed to be delivered to the target.

In many instances, the answers to the first three questions can be obtained by performing a few simple calculations based on classical heat transfer theory. Usually the results of these calculations will suggest an answer to the forth question. The purpose of this discussion is finding some appropriate solution to the basic following heat equation under different Boundary and Initial condition which are obtained for laser heating of solids (target) under a variety of conditions that pertain to the particular use case and applications [27].

$$\nabla^2 T(x,y,z,t) - \frac{1}{\kappa} \frac{\partial T(x,y,z,t)}{\partial t} = -\frac{A(x,y,z,t)}{K} \qquad \text{Eq-5-18}$$

1. $A(x,y,z,t)$:   Heat rate supplied to target per unit time per unit volume.
2. κ: Thermal diffusitivity (units, cm²/sec).
3. K: Thermal conductivity (units, W/cm °C)
4. $T(x,y,z,t)$:   Temperature (°C)

which are obtained for laser heating of solids under a variety boundary, initial and laser/target conditions that pertain to practical applications? Solution to Equation D-18 can only be obtained in simple analytic form when one is prepared to make a variety of assumptions concerning the spatial and temporal dependence of the impressed laser heat source and the geometry of the ·sample that is being irradiated. As the description of these boundary conditions becomes more and more rigorous in terms of the actual spatial and temporal dependence of the heat source and the geometry of the work piece, analytical solutions can no longer be obtained and the resulting expression for $T(x,y,z,t)$ can only be expressed numerically. Solutions to problems of this sort are of little use except in specialized studies and will not be discussed here. We will show that in many cases even quite crude approximations to the actual source and sample boundary calculations are capable of yielding predictions of $T(x,y,z,t)$ that correspond quite closely to actual temperature-time profiles in the solid. Where possible, these predictions have been generalized (i.e., expressed in reduced variable form), so that they may be applied to any material when thermal constants of that material are known [27].

One of the most important effects of high power energy laser irradiation is the conversion of the optical energy in the beam into thermal energy into material of target of interest. This is a classical heat transfer problem based on diffusion equation of 5-18 and we will summarize this thermal response using the Initial and Boundary Condition defined in above. The solution to conduction of heat transfer equation 5-18 in a three-dimensional solid is given in general by the solution to the following Cartesian form of Heat Transfer equation 5-19.

$$\rho C \frac{\partial T}{\partial t} = \frac{\partial}{\partial x}\left(K\frac{\partial T}{\partial x}\right) + \frac{\partial}{\partial y}\left(K\frac{\partial T}{\partial y}\right) + \frac{\partial}{\partial z}\left(K\frac{\partial T}{\partial z}\right) + A(x,y,z,t) \qquad \text{Eq. 5-19a}$$

or

$$\nabla^2 T - \frac{1}{\kappa}\frac{\partial T}{\partial t} = -\frac{A(x,y,z,t)}{K} \qquad \text{Eq. 5-19b1p1.5}$$

Where the thermal conductivity K, the density ρ, and the specific heat C are dependent both on temperature and position, and heat is supplied by laser beam to target surface materials at the rate of $A(x,y,z,t)$ per unit time per unit volume [27,28]. These thermal parameters and the temperature dependency on them make the Equation 5-19 to be none-linear one and in return solutions under different initial and boundary conditions become very difficult to obtain although numerical solutions are possible in a limited number of cases when the temperature dependence of $\kappa = (K/\rho C)$ [Thermal Diffusitivity], K [Thermal Conductivity], ρ [Material Density of Target Surface], and C [Heat Capacity or Specific Heat] is known. With simple assumption of that thermal properties of most materials dot change greatly with temperature $T(x,y,z,t)$ they can often be assumed independent of temperature and can be assigned an average value for the temperature range of interest [27].

In order to support any experimental result of heat transfer data with theoretical calculations we must have information on thermal parameters of the materials under consideration. See below;

- K: Thermal conductivity (units, W/cm °C),
- κ: Thermal diffusitivity (units, cm²/sec),
- C_p: (or C) the heat capacity or specific heat at constant pressure(units, J/gm °C) or ρC (units, J/cm² °C)

The average values of these parameters over the temperature range from 0^0 to T^0 C can be designated as K_{avg} and κ_{avg} where mathematically can be written as follows [27]

$$K_{avg} = (1/T) \int_0^T K(T)dT \qquad \text{Eq. 5-20}$$

$$\kappa_{avg} = (1/T) \int_0^T \kappa(T)dT \qquad \text{Eq. 5-21}$$

These integrals may be evaluated numerically when K and κ are not simple function of T. In case of thermal properties varying with the temperature but independent of position, then Equation 5-19a turns into following form;

$$\rho C \frac{\partial T}{\partial t} = K\nabla^2 T + \frac{\partial K}{\partial T}\left\{ \left(\frac{\partial T}{\partial x}\right)^2 + \left(\frac{\partial T}{\partial y}\right)^2 + \left(\frac{\partial T}{\partial z}\right)^2 \right\} + A(x,y,z,t) \qquad \text{Eq. 5-22a}$$

Equation 5-22a clearly is a none-linear case and under this condition may be reduced to a simpler form by introducing a new variable as follow [26];

$$\Theta = \left(\frac{1}{K_0}\right) \int_0^T KdT \qquad \text{Eq. 5-22b}$$

Where K_0 is the value of K at $T = 0\,^0C$. These, and the lower limit of integration, are merely introduced to give θ the dimensions of temperature and a definite value [26]. Note that Θ is essentially a potential whose gradient is proportional to the flux then from Equation 5-22b [26] follows that;

$$\frac{\partial \Theta}{\partial t} \quad \frac{\partial}{K\,\partial t}, \quad \frac{\partial \Theta}{\partial x} = \frac{K}{K_0}\frac{\partial T}{\partial x}, \quad \frac{\partial \Theta}{\partial y} = \frac{K}{K_0}\frac{\partial T}{\partial y}, \quad \frac{\partial \Theta}{\partial z} = \frac{K}{K_0}\frac{\partial T}{\partial z}$$

This results in Equation 5-19a to be reduced to the following equation;

$$\nabla^2 \Theta - \frac{1}{\kappa}\frac{\partial \Theta}{\partial t} = -\frac{A}{K_0} \qquad \text{Eq. 5-22c}$$

Where, in Equation 5-22c, A and $\kappa = K/\rho c$ are expressed as function of the new variable Θ, therefore in terms of this new variable the heat conduction Equation 5-19b is preserved with the condition that diffusitivity κ now is function of Θ [26]. In most cases the variation of κ with temperature is not important as K,

Bahman Zohuri

so that, to a reasonable approximation it can be considered to be a constant. For example, if a metal surface is being near absolute zero, both K and c are approximately proportional to the absolute temperature. In such cases, if A is independent of T, Equation 5-22c becomes of type Equation 5-19b and solutions for the case of constant conductivity may take over immediately by replacing T by Θ, provided that the boundary conditions prescribed only T or $K\frac{\partial T}{\partial n}$, if they are of the form $(\frac{\partial T}{\partial n}) + hT = 0$ where h is a constant, this remark does not hold [26]. Note that $\partial/\partial n$ represents differentiation along the outward-drawn normal to the surface.

In steady-state cases the situation is very important as well since Equation 5-22c turns to Poisson's Equation if A is constant and reduces to Laplace's equation if A is equal to 0. Then in these cases finding solution to heat conduction problem is straight forward.

Another useful form may be obtained by introducing W, the heat content per unit mass of the material (measured from some arbitrary zero of temperature). In this case Equation 5-19a reduces to the following equation;

$$\rho C \frac{\partial W}{\partial t} = \frac{\partial}{\partial x}\left(K\frac{\partial T}{\partial x}\right) + \frac{\partial}{\partial y}\left(K\frac{\partial T}{\partial y}\right) + \frac{\partial}{\partial z}\left(K\frac{\partial T}{\partial z}\right) + A(x,y,z,t) \qquad \text{Eq. 5-23}$$

Or, in term of Θ defined by Equation 5-22b, we have

$$\frac{\rho}{K_0}\frac{\partial W}{\partial t} = \nabla^2\Theta + \frac{A}{K_0} \qquad \text{Eq. 5-24}$$

where W is related to Θ in a known manner. The introduction of W has advantages in problems involving latent heat. We will further discuss the case of thermal properties varying with temperature and solving Equation 5-22c for different boundary condition imposed by the problem in hand, utilizing *Boltzmann's Transformation* with constant diffusivity for the infinite composite solid scenario [26].

If the target or materials on surface of target is irradiated with a laser beam, the temperature in the vicinity of the focal spot on target will usually rise rapidly to within an order of magnitude

More commonly, the approximation is made that Equation 5-19b can be used with averaged values of the thermal constants over the temperature range of interest. Then Equation-19b becomes

$$\nabla^2 T - \frac{1}{\kappa_{avg}} \frac{\partial T}{\partial t} = -\frac{A(x,y,z,t)}{K_{avg}} \qquad \text{Eq. 5-25}$$

In this case, solutions are possible for a number of cases in which thermal properties vary discontinuously (i.e. composite solids) or in those cases where a simple analytic expression is available for the spatial variation of K [27]. All these condition are valued so long as we assume the solid is taken to be homogeneous and isotropic, then Equation 5-19a reduces to Equation 5-19b where again we have assumed that $\kappa = K / \rho C$ is the thermal diffusivity and holds. In the steady state situation where $(\partial T / \partial t) = 0$ Equation 5-19b reduces to

$$\nabla^2 T = -\frac{A(x,y,z)}{K} \qquad \text{Eq. 5-26}$$

Note that in dynamic laser heating process where laser beam weapon interacting with moving target, it may not be appropriate to use Equation 5-20 and 5-21 since these equations give equal weight to all temperatures in the range $0 \to T$ to determine a weighting factor for each $K(T)$ and $\kappa(T)$.

Both Equation 5-19b and 5-23 can be solved in a large number of cases using different methods such as separation of variables or utilizing Fourier or Laplace transformation based on initial and boundary condition of the case in hand. Furthermore if no heat is applied to the surface of the material, the $A = 0$ and Equation 5-19b and 5-25 both reduce to

$$\nabla^2 T = \frac{1}{\kappa} \frac{\partial T}{\partial t} \qquad \text{(Transient-State case)} \qquad \text{Eq. 5-27}$$

$$\nabla^2 T = 0 \qquad \text{(Steady-State case)} \qquad \text{Eq. 5-28}$$

With appropriate boundary and initial condition applied in most cases whether heat source is present or absent usually heat transfer problem (Heat Conduction) can be solved either by Equation 5-24 or Equation 5-26 by applying such boundary considering as heat flux transfer cross the surface of the target or solid. In summary we can reduce the full conduction heat Equation 5-18 that is, conduction with heat source or generation to very special cases. When the thermal conductivity K is constant, the first term of Equation 5-18 becomes Laplacian of temperature T. The Laplacian's of temperature in the three principle coordinate system are listed in Table 5-2 while the general heat conduction equation with variable thermal conductivity, in three principal coordinate systems are listed in Table 5-1. The three special forms of the conduction Equation 5-18 with constant thermal conductivity K is listed below.

1. **Laplace's Equation.**
   This is for constant K, steady state heat transfer so that the term $(\partial T / \partial t) = 0$, and no heat generating or $A = 0$, which is basically presented by Equation 5-24 in above.

   $$\nabla^2 T = 0 \qquad \text{Eq. 5-29}$$

   where $\nabla^2 T$ is Laplacian of the temperature T.

2. **Poisson's Equation.**
   This is for constant K and steady state heat transfer so that the term $(\partial T / \partial t) = 0$ with heat source being present therefore $A \neq 0$.

   $$\nabla^2 T + \frac{A(x, y, z)}{K} = 0$$

   or

   $$\nabla^2 T + \frac{A}{K} = 0 \qquad \text{Eq. 5-30}$$

3. **Fourier's Equation.**
   This is for constant K and no heat generation or $A = 0$. Which is basically representation of Equation 5-27 or transient state with no heat source?

   $$\nabla^2 T = \frac{1}{\kappa} \frac{\partial T}{\partial t} \qquad \text{Eq. 5-31}$$

The parameter κ is the thermal diffusivity, $\kappa = K / \rho C$.

Coordinate System	$\nabla \cdot (K\nabla T) + A = \rho C \dfrac{\partial T}{\partial t}$
Rectangular	$\dfrac{\partial}{\partial x}\left(K\dfrac{\partial T}{\partial x}\right) + \dfrac{\partial}{\partial y}\left(K\dfrac{\partial T}{\partial y}\right) + \dfrac{\partial}{\partial z}\left(K\dfrac{\partial T}{\partial z}\right) + A = \rho C\dfrac{\partial T}{\partial t}$
Cylindrical	$\dfrac{1}{r}\dfrac{\partial}{\partial r}\left(Kr\dfrac{\partial T}{\partial r}\right) + \dfrac{1}{r^2}\dfrac{\partial}{\partial \phi}\left(K\dfrac{\partial T}{\partial \phi}\right) + \dfrac{\partial}{\partial z}\left(K\dfrac{\partial T}{\partial z}\right) + A = \rho C\dfrac{\partial T}{\partial t}$
Spherical	$\dfrac{1}{r^2}\dfrac{\partial}{\partial r}\left(Kr^2\dfrac{\partial T}{\partial r}\right) + \dfrac{1}{r^2\sin\theta}\dfrac{\partial}{\partial\theta}\left(K\sin\theta\dfrac{\partial T}{\partial\theta}\right) + \dfrac{1}{r^2\sin^2\theta}\dfrac{\partial}{\partial\phi}\left(K\dfrac{\partial T}{\partial\phi}\right) + A = \rho C\dfrac{\partial T}{\partial t}$

Table 5-1: Heat Conduction equation with variable thermal conductivity in the three principal coordinate systems.

Coordinate System	$\nabla^2 T$
Rectangular	$\dfrac{\partial^2 T}{\partial x^2} + \dfrac{\partial^2 T}{\partial y^2} + \dfrac{\partial^2 T}{\partial z^2}$
Cylindrical	$\dfrac{\partial^2 T}{\partial r^2} + \dfrac{1}{r}\dfrac{\partial T}{\partial r} + \dfrac{1}{r^2}\dfrac{\partial^2 T}{\partial\phi^2} + \dfrac{\partial^2 T}{\partial z^2}$
Spherical	$\dfrac{1}{r^2}\dfrac{\partial}{\partial r}\left(r^2\dfrac{\partial T}{\partial r}\right) + \dfrac{1}{r^2\sin\theta}\dfrac{\partial}{\partial\theta}\left(\sin\theta\dfrac{\partial T}{\partial\theta}\right) + \dfrac{1}{r^2\sin^2\theta}\dfrac{\partial^2 T}{\partial\phi^2}$

Table 5-2: The Laplace of temperature in the three principle coordinate

In summary to find the solutions to various heat conduction problems, we need boundary conditions in space and time since both temperature T and heat generation term A are function of x, y, z and time t. In general, there are seven constants of integration. There is the first-order derivation with respect to the time variable and second-order derivatives with respect to each variable. The number of conditions for each independent variable is equal to the order of the highest derivative of that variable in the equation. Hence, one initial condition is required for all time dependent problem; two boundary conditions are needed for each coordinate.

The spatial boundary conditions may be classified into three principal classes as we mentioned in Section 5.2.3 in above and they can be summarized as follows [29]

1. The First kind or **Dirichlet** boundary conditions.
2. The Second kind or **Neumann** boundary conditions.
3. The Third kind or **Robin** boundary conditions.

Each of these boundary conditions is described again as follows [29];

1. First kind or (**Dirichlet**) Boundary Conditions.
   Here, the temperatures are known at the boundaries.

   $$T(\vec{x},t)\big|_{surface} = T_s \qquad \text{Eq. 5-32}$$

   An example of the first kind of boundary conditions for one-dimensional heat conduction is

   $$T(x,t)\big|_{x=0} = T_0 \qquad \text{and} \qquad T(x,t)\big|_{x=L} = T_L$$

   An example of the first kind of boundary conditions for two-dimensional heat conduction is

   $$T(x,y,t)\big|_{x=0} = T_0(y) \qquad \text{and} \qquad T(x,y,t)\big|_{x=L} = T_L(y)$$

   where T_0 and T_L are prescribed functions of y. If these functions are zero, these boundary conditions are called first kind homogeneous boundary conditions

2. Second Kind (**Neumann**) Boundary Conditions.
   Here, the heat fluxes are known at the boundaries.

   $$q_s = -K\frac{\partial T}{\partial x}\bigg|_{surface} \quad \text{is known} \qquad \text{Eq. 5-33}$$

   An example of the second kind of boundary conditions for one-dimensional heat conduction is

   $$\frac{\partial T}{\partial x}\bigg|_{x=0} = \frac{-q_1(y)}{K} = f_1(y) \text{ where } f_1 \text{ is a prescribed function of } y.$$

   If this function is zero, the boundary condition is called the second kind homogeneous boundary condition.

3. Third Kind (**Robin or Mixed**) Boundary Conditions.
    Here, the convection heat transfer coefficients are known at
    the boundaries

$$q = h\Delta T = -K \frac{\partial T}{\partial \eta} \quad \text{is known} \qquad \text{Eq. 5-34}$$

An example of the third kind of boundary conditions for one-dimensional heat conduction is

$$h_1(T_\infty - T_{x=0}) = -K \frac{\partial T}{\partial x}\bigg|_{x=0} \quad \text{or} \quad \left[-K \frac{\partial T}{\partial x}\bigg|_{x=0} + h_1 T_{x=0} \right] = h_1 T_\infty = f_1$$

where f_1 is a prescribed function of y.

Other boundary conditions include nonlinear type boundary conditions. When there is radiation, phase change or transient heat transfer at the boundary conditions are nonlinear in nature.

Example 5-1: For a steady-state heat conduction problem with heat generation in a rectangular medium, write the governing equation and the mathematical representation of the boundary conditions. For $x = 0$, there is convection with heat transfer coefficient h_1. For $x = a$, the boundary is insulated. For $y = 0$, there is constant heat flux q. For $y = b$, there is convection with heat transfer coefficient h_2.

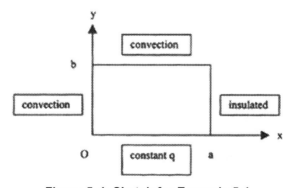

Figure 5-4: Sketch for Example 5-1

Solution: The governing energy conservation (heat conduction) equation is given by;

$$\frac{\partial^2 T}{\partial x^2} + \frac{\partial^2 T}{\partial y^2} + \frac{A}{K} = 0 \quad \text{for} \quad 0 \leq x \leq a \text{ and } 0 \leq y \leq b$$

The boundary conditions are

$$-K\frac{\partial T}{\partial x} + h_1 T = h_1 T_\infty \quad \text{at} \quad x = 0 \quad (1)$$

$$\frac{\partial T}{\partial x} = 0 \quad \text{at} \quad x = a \quad (2)$$

$$-K\frac{\partial T}{\partial y} = q \quad \text{at} \quad y = 0 \quad (3)$$

$$-K\frac{\partial T}{\partial x} + h_2 T = h_2 T_\infty \quad \text{at} \quad y = b \quad (4)$$

5.3.4.2 Laser Radiation, Effects on Solid Target

The fundamentals of which are given in this book and particular Chapter 5 and 6 is a systematic and in-depth study of the physical and chemical mechanism governing the interaction of laser radiation with solid targets, among them metals in different gaseous environment, and for a wide range of beam parameters.

The laser-solid interaction is crucial, particularly the amount of laser energy that is absorbed.

It is shown that the dependence of the reflection coefficient of absorbing media (metals) on the polarization of light may give rise to anisotropy of the absorption of powerful laser radiation in these media. This anisotropy is demonstrated by bending of the laser damage channel. When the polarization of light is linear, such bending occurs in a plane perpendicular to the plane of polarization and the direction of bending is governed by an asymmetry of the distribution of the intensity in a cross section of the beam in this plane. The effect is weaker when the polarization is circular. The position of the bending plane is then governed by the nature of the asymmetry of the distribution of the intensity over the beam cross section.

The experiments have shown that the emission is essentially due to rapid heating of the surface spot which the laser beam strikes, and temperatures as high as 9000 °K have been reached in some samples by using lasers with an output of 1 Joule [34]. Laser-induced electron and ion emission from metals has recently been observed by several authors [35-37].

By focusing extremely high power energy laser beam radiation to its target production of light fluxes at the coupling interface with target takes place.

The highest radiation power (see Table 5-3 below) has been produced using solid-state neodymium-doped glass lasers (wavelength $\lambda = 1.06$ microns [μ]) and gas lasers ($\lambda = 10.6$ μ). The specific features of laser radiation have led to the discovery of a number of new physical phenomena, the range of which is expanding rapidly as the power of lasers is increased.

Laser Type	Pulse duration (sec)	Pulse energy (J)	Power (W)	Maximum radiation flux density (W/cm²)
CO^2	Continuous	—	10^3	up to 10^7
Nd + glass	10^{-3}	10^4	10^7	up to 10^7-10^{11}
CO^2	6×10^{-8}	3×10^2	5×10^{19}	10^{13}
Nd + glass	10^{-9}	3×10^2	3×10^{11}	10^{16}
Nd + glass	$(0.3) \times 10^{-11}$	10–20	10^{12}-1013	10^{15}-10^{16}

Table 5-3: Characteristics of certain types of lasers

Effect of high power laser radiation on absorbing solid target can be explained for different applications are as follows;

Developed vaporization of metals. When laser radiation (for example, pulses of a neodymium laser lasting several microseconds) with a radiation flux density of 10^6-10^8 watts per sq cm (W/cm²) acts on metals, the metal in the zone of irradiation disintegrates, and a characteristic crater appears on the surface of the target. The bright luminosity of a plasma flare, which is a moving vapor heated and ionized by the laser radiation, is observed near the target. The reaction pressure of the vapor ejected from the surface of the metal imparts a recoil impulse Q to the target (Figure 5-5).

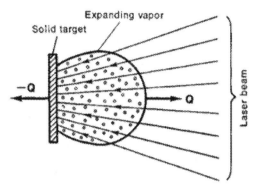

Figure 5-5: Motion of vapor near the surface of a metal and transfer of momentum to a target from incident laser radiation: (Q) momentum vector of vaporized substance, (-Q) momentum imparted to solid target

Vaporization takes place from the surface of a thin layer of liquid metal heated to a temperature of several thousand degrees. The temperature of the layer is determined by the equality of the absorbed energy and the losses to the cooling associated with vaporization. The role of thermal conduction in cooling the layer in the process is insignificant. In contrast to ordinary vaporization, this process is called developed vaporization.

The pressure in the layer is determined by the recoil force of the vapor and, when a gas-dynamic flow of vapor forms from the target, is one-half of the saturated vapor pressure at the surface temperature. Thus, the liquid layer is superheated, and its state is meta-stable. This makes it possible to study the conditions of maximum superheating of metals, under which rapid volumetric boiling-up of the liquid takes place. Upon heating to a temperature close to the critical temperature, an abrupt drop in electrical conductivity may take place in the liquid layer of the metal, and it may acquire the properties of a dielectric. In the process an abrupt drop in the light reflection coefficient is observed.

Irradiation of solid targets. As in the previous case, plasma is formed in the vapor flux from the vaporizing target upon irradiation of virtually all solid targets with millisecond pulses of laser radiation having a radiation flux density of the order of 10^7-10^9W/cm^2. The plasma temperature is 10^4-10^5 °K. This method may be used to produce a large quantity of dense, chemically pure low-temperature plasma to fill magnetic traps and for various industrial purposes. The vaporization of solid targets by laser radiation is used extensively in engineering.

When nanosecond laser pulses with a radiation flux density of 10^{12}-10^{14} W/cm^2 are focused on a solid target, the absorbing layer of the substance is heated so intensely that it immediately becomes plasma. In this case it is no longer possible to speak of vaporization of the target or of a phase interface. The energy of the laser radiation is used to heat the plasma and advance the disintegration and ionization front into the target. The plasma temperature is so high that multiply charged ions, in particular Ca^{16+}, are formed in it. Until recently, the formation of ions of such high multiplicity of ionization was observed only in the radiation of the solar corona. The formation of ions with a nearly stripped electron shell is also interesting from the standpoint of the possibility of conducting nuclear reactions know as ICF (Inertial Controlled Fusion) using heavy nuclei in accelerators of multiply charged ions.

Laser spark (optical breakdown of a gas). When a laser beam with a radiation flux density of the order of 10^{11} W/cm^2 is focused in the air at atmospheric pressure, a bright burst of light is observed at the focal point of the lens, and a loud sound is heard. This phenomenon is called the laser spark. The duration of the burst exceeds the duration of the laser pulse (30 nanoseconds) by a factor of 10 or more. The formation of the laser spark may be represented as consisting of two stages: (1) the formation at the focal point of the lens of primary (seed) plasma, which ensures strong absorption of the laser radiation, and (2) the spread of the plasma along the beam in the area of the focal point. The mechanism of formation of seed plasma is analogous to the high-frequency breakdown of gases; hence the term "optical breakdown of a gas." For picoseconds pulses of laser radiation ($I \sim 10^{13}$-10^{14} W/cm^2)

the formation of seed plasma is also due to multi-photon ionization. The heating of the seed plasma by laser radiation and its spread along the beam (against the beam) are caused by several processes, one of which is the propagation of a strong shock wave from the seed plasma. The shock wave heats and ionizes the gas beyond the shock front, leading in turn to the absorption of the laser radiation—that is, to maintenance of the shock wave itself and of the plasma along the beam (light detonation). In other directions the shock wave attenuates quickly.

Since the lifetime of the plasma formed by laser radiation greatly exceeds the duration of the laser pulse, at great distances from the focal point the laser spark may be considered as a point explosion (the nearly instantaneous release of energy at a point). This explains, in particular, the high intensity of the sound. The laser spark has been studied for a number of gases at different pressures, under different conditions of focusing, and for various wavelengths of laser radiation, with pulses lasting 10^{-6}-10^{-11} sec.

A laser spark may also be observed at much lower intensities if absorbing seed plasma is generated in advance at the focal point of the lens. For example, in air at atmospheric pressure a laser spark is developed from electric-discharge seed plasma at a laser radiation intensity of approximately $10^7 W/cm^2$; the laser radiation "captures" the electric-discharge plasma, and during the laser pulse the luminosity spreads over the caustic surface of the lens. When the laser radiation is of relatively low intensity, the spread of the plasma is due to thermal conduction, as a result of which the rate of spread of the plasma is subsonic. This process is analogous to slow combustion, hence the expression "laser spark in the slow combustion mode."

Steady-state maintenance of a laser spark has been accomplished in various gases by means of a continuous CO^2 laser with a power of several hundred watts. The seed plasma was developed by a pulse CO^2 laser.

Thermonuclear fusion. Controlled thermonuclear fusion may be produced using laser radiation. For this purpose it is necessary to form extremely dense and hot plasma with a temperature of approximately 10^8 °K (in the case of fusion of deuterium nuclei). For the energy liberation resulting from the thermonuclear reaction to exceed the energy added to the plasma during heating, the condition $n\tau \approx 10^{14}$ cm^{-3} sec must be fulfilled, where n is the density of the plasma and τ is its lifetime or confinement time. For short laser pulses this condition is satisfied at very high plasma densities. Here the pressure in the plasma is so great that it is virtually impossible to contain it magnetically. The plasma that appears near the focal point disperses at a speed of the order of 10^8 cm/sec. Therefore, τ is the time in which the dense plasmoid is unable to change its volume significantly (the inertial confinement time of the plasma). For thermonuclear fusion to occur, the length of the laser pulse t_l obviously must not exceed τ. The minimum energy e of the laser pulse for a plasma density of n = 5 × 10^{22} cm^{-3} (the density of liquid hydrogen), a confinement time of τ = 2 × 10^{-9} sec, and a plasmoid with linear dimensions of 0.4 cm should be 6 × 10^5 joules (J). Effective absorption of light by the plasma under conditions of inertial confinement and satisfaction of the condition $n\tau \approx 10^{14}$ occur only for certain wavelengths λ and that is $\lambda_{cr} > \lambda > \left(\lambda_{cr} / \sqrt{40}\right)$, where $\lambda_{cr} \sim 1/\sqrt{n}$ is the critical wavelength for plasma with density n. When n = 5 × 10^{22} cm^{-3}, λ lies in the ultraviolet region of the spectrum, for which powerful lasers do not yet exist. At the same time, when λ = 1 μ (a neodymium laser), even for n = 10^{21} cm^{-3}, corresponding to λ_{cr}, a value of e = 10^9 J for the minimum energy, which is difficult to realize, is obtained. The difficulty of feeding the energy of laser radiation in the visible and infrared bands into dense plasma is fundamental. Various ideas exist for surmounting this difficulty; one such idea that is of interest is the production of a super dense hot plasma as a result of adiabatic compression of a spherical deuterium target by the reaction pressure of plasma ejected from the surface of the target under the action of laser radiation.

High-temperature heating of plasma by laser radiation was accomplished in the first time by optical breakdown of the air. In 1966–67, X-radiation from the plasma of a laser spark with a temperature of the order of (1-3) × 10^6 °K was recorded for a laser radiation flux density of the order of 10^{12}-10^{13} W/cm^2. In 1971 plasma with a temperature of 10^7 °K (measured on the basis of X-radiation) was produced by irradiating a solid spherical hydrogen-containing target with laser radiation having a flux density of up to 10^{16} W/cm². A yield of 10^6 neutrons per pulse was observed in the process. These results, as well as the existing possibilities for increasing the energy and output of lasers, create the prospect of producing a controlled thermonuclear reaction using laser radiation [38-40].

Chemistry of resonance-excited molecules. A selective effect on the chemical bonds of molecules, making possible selective intervention in the chemical reactions of synthesis and dissociation and in the processes of catalysis, is possible under the action of monochromatic laser radiation. Many chemical reactions reduce to the scission of some chemical bonds in molecules and the formation of others. Interatomic bonds are responsible for the vibrational spectrum of a molecule. The frequencies of the spectral lines depend on the binding energy and mass of the atoms. A certain bond may be "built up" under the action of monochromatic laser radiation of the resonance frequency. Such a bond may easily be broken and replaced by another. Therefore, vibrationally excited molecules prove to be chemically more active (Figure 5-6).

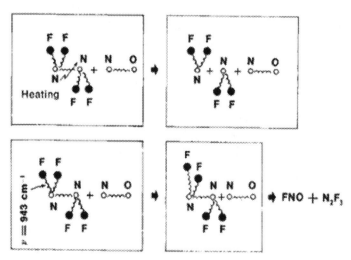

Figure 5-6: Diagram of the reaction between tetrafluorohydrazine (N_2F_4) and nitric oxide (NO) upon heating (top) and upon resonance excitation of the N - F bond by laser radiation (bottom). The wavy lines represent chemical bonds.

Molecules with differing isotopic compositions may be separated by means of laser radiation. This possibility is associated with the dependence of the vibrational frequency of the atoms comprising a molecule on the mass of the atoms. The monochromaticity and high power of laser radiation make possible selective pumping of molecules of a specific isotopic composition to the pre-dissociation level and the production of chemical compounds of mono-isotopic composition or the isotope itself in the dissociation products. Since the number of dissociated molecules of a given isotopic composition is equal to the number of quanta absorbed, the effectiveness of this method may be high in comparison with other methods of isotope separation.

The effects mentioned above do not exhaust the physical phenomena caused by the action of laser radiation on matter. Transparent dielectrics are destroyed under the action of laser radiation. When certain ferromagnetic films are irradiated, local changes in their magnetic state are observed. This effect may be used in developing high-speed switching devices and computer memory units. When laser radiation is focused within a liquid, the light-hydraulic effect, which makes possible production of high pulse pressures in a liquid, occurs. Finally, for radiation flux densities of approximately 10^{18}-10^{19} W/cm^2, the acceleration of electrons to relativistic energies is possible. A number of new effects, such as the production of electron-positron pairs, are associated with this.

5.3.4.3 Absorption of Laser Radiation by Metals

The laser heating of materials is mainly determined by thermal parameters of the materials under consideration and particularly absorptivity of given metals at the respective laser wavelength. The metal absorptivity or alternatively, the reflectivity of the metal at given laser wavelength plays a major roles in laser interaction with metal target. In this section we are trying to identify the key quantities of absorptivity/reflectivity as well as thermal conductivities to the optical properties of metals, the general condition of their surfaces and temperature, i.e. laser heating rate through heat conduction equation under different boundary and initial conditions. We shall discuss the physical processes that occur during the interaction of high-power laser radiation with materials. Understanding of concept of these processes is important to have the knowledge and limitation s of laser-based material processing. We pay attention and put emphasizes on metallic targets, but much of what we will discuss is applicable to other types of absorbing materials.

When laser duals with a target surface, part of it are absorbed and part is reflected. The energy that is absorbed beings to heat the surface. There are several regimes of parameters that should be considered, depending on the time scale, duration of engagement and on the irradiance. The heating rate of metal sample or target surface is mainly determined by the target material absorptivity for a given wavelength—a quantity which, in turn, is determined by the optical properties of the metal itself and of the target surface, as well as by the temperature range, heating rate, etc at the time of engagement. That is why the metal absorptivity, A, or alternatively the metal reflectivity, R, stand as main criteria guiding the choice of the most appropriate laser system for destroying the metallic parts of the target or damages it enough that the incoming target is no longer a threat [41]. For example, losses due to thermal conduction are small if the pulse duration is very short, but they can be important for longer pulses. Under some conditions, there can be important effects due to absorption of energy in the plasma formed by vaporized material above the target surfaces. We note that losses due to thermal re-radiation from the target surfaces are usually insignificant [42].

The heating effects due to absorption of high-power beam can take place very rapidly. The surface temperature quickly rises to its melting point. Laser-induced melting is of interest because of target destruction during engagement. One often desires maximum melting under conditions where surface vaporization does not occur. Melting without vaporization is produced only within a fairly narrow range of laser parameters [42]. If the laser irradiance is too high, the surface begins to vaporize before a significant depth of molten material is produced. In case of industrial application of laser welding, this means that there is a maximum irradiance suitable for this purpose, but in our case where we are interested in target destruction any damage to target as incoming threat falls as part of target lethality requirement that is mentioned in section 5.2.4. Alternatively, for a given total energy in the laser pulse, it is often desirable to stretch the pulse length.

Melting of a material by laser radiation depends on heat flow in the material, where in turn depends on the thermal conductivity K. But on the other hand the rate of thermal conductivity is not the only factor where the rate of change of temperature is depending on. The rate of change of temperature also depends on the specific heat c of the material at constant pressure. In fact Equation 5-19b shows that, the heating rate is inversely proportional to the specific heat per unit volume, which is equal to ρc, where ρ is the material density. The important factor for heat flow is $K / \rho c$. This factor has the dimension of cm^2/sec, which is per Equation 5-19b is characters tic of diffusion coefficient which is known as *"Thermal Diffusivity"* [42].

The factor $K / \rho c$ is involved in all unsteady-state heat flow processes, such as pulsed laser heating. The significant of this material property is that it determines how fast a material will accept and conduct thermal energy. Thus the higher thermal conductivity allows larger penetration of the fusion front with no thermal shock or cracking, on the other hand lower thermal conductivity on the target material surface makes it harder for the laser to duel with it and limits the penetration of laser into material. Although low values of thermal diffusivity mean that the heat does not penetrate well into the material. But high value of thermal diffusivity can also allows rapid removal of heat from the surface and this may cause reduction of melting amount. To compensate for these effects, one should vary the laser parameters for optimum effects for different materials. Table 5-4 lists the thermal diffusivity of several metals and alloys.

Metal	Thermal diffusivity (cm²/sec)	Thermal time constants (msec)			
		0.01 cm thick	0.02 cm thick	0.05 cm thick	0.1 cm thick
Silver	1.70	0.015	0.059	0.368	1.47
Aluminum alloys					
Commercially pure	0.850	0.029	0.118	0.74	2.94
2024 alloy	0.706	0.035	0.142	0.89	3.54
A13 Casting alloy	0.474	0.053	0.211	1.32	5.27
Copper alloys					
Electrolytic (99.95%)	1.14	0.022	0.088	0.55	2.19
Cartridge brass	0.378	0.066	0.265	1.65	6.61
Phosphor bronze	0.213	0.117	0.470	2.93	11.74
Iron alloys					
Commercially pure	0.202	0.124	0.495	3.09	12.38
303 stainless steel	0.056	0.446	1.786	11.16	44.64
Carbon steel	0.119	0.210	0.840	5.25	21.01
(1.22 C, 0.35 Mn)					
Nickel alloys					
Commercially pure	0.220	0.114	0.454	2.84	11.36
Monel	0.055	0.455	1.818	11.36	45.46
Inconel	0.039	0.641	2.564	16.03	64.10

Table 5-4: Thermal Diffusivity and Thermal Time Constant [42].

The depth of penetration of heat in time t is given approximately by the Equation 5-35 below;

$$D = (4kt)^{1/2} = \left(\frac{4Kt}{\rho c} \right)^{1/2} \qquad \text{Eq. 5-35}$$

where D is the depth of penetration of the heat and $k = K / \rho c$ is the thermal diffusivity. Typically for a metal with thermal diffusivity 0.25 cm²/sec, heat can penetrate only about 3 x 10⁻⁴ com during a pulse of 90 nsec duration (typical of a Q-switched laser). During a pulse of 100 μsec duration (typical of a normal pulse laser) heat can penetrate about 0.01 cm into the same metal [42].

The amount of light absorbed by metallic surface is proportional to $1 - R$ where is the reflectivity. Quantitatively, the absorption A is the ration of the intensity absorbed by the metallic surface, I_a, to incident intensity, I, at a certain moment in the process of laser heating. Accordingly, the reflectivity, $R = 1 - A$, is the ratio between the reflected (specularly and/or diffused) intensity, I_r, and the incident intensity, I [41]. The absorptivity of metals shows a general trend to increase when the incident radiation wavelength decreases from the infrared to the ultraviolet spectral range [6 and 27]. At the CO^2 laser wavelength of 10.6 μm, where R is close to unity, $1 - R$ becomes small as result A is small. This means that only small fraction of the light incident on the surface is absorbed and is available for heating the engagement surface of the target. The difference in the value of R becomes important at long wavelengths. For copper or silver for example at 10.6 μm, $1 - R$ is about 0.02, whereas for steel it is about 0.05. Steel then absorbs about 2.5 times as much of the incident light as silver or copper. In practice, this means that steel surfaces are easier to engage with a CO^2 laser than are metals such as aluminum or copper [42].

The wavelength variation is also important. At shorter wavelengths, the factor $1 - R$ is much higher than at long infrared wavelengths. For example, the factor $1 - R$ for steel is about 0.35 at 1.06 μm, about 7 times as great as its value at 10.6 μm, This means that, at least initially, 7 times as much light is absorbed from a Nd:YAG laser than from a CO^2 laser for equal irradiance from the two lasers. In some cases it will be easier to carry out target destruction with a shorter wavelength laser because of the increased coupling of light into the metal surface of target [42]. In general the shorter the wavelength the better coupling with the surface of the target.

Figure 5-7 shows some data on the reflectivity of a stainless steel surface struck by a 200-nsec-duration pulse from a CO^2 TEA laser, which delivered an irradiance of 1.5 x 108 W/cm² to the target.

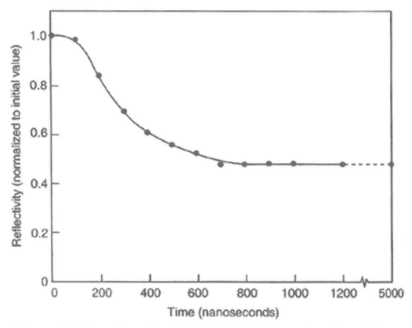

Figure 5-7: Specular reflectivity at 10.6 μm as a function of time for a stainless steel surface struck by a CO^2 TEA laser pulse delivering 1.5 x 108 W/cm² in a pulse of 200 nsec long [42].

Note that one of the important factor for a battle management of some sort on ABL, SBL or GBL platforms can possibly to collect some information from its laser finder such as LADAR (Laser Detection and Ranging) and target acquisition system the correct information using indirect determination of absorptivity A based upon measuring the reflectivity R. This method generally encounters its own several difficulties. First, we can note that the signal reflected by target surface actually consists of a specular component as well as scattered (diffused) component—so that the value of total reflection coefficient R is $R = R_R + R_D$, where R_R and R_D are the coefficients of specular reflection and scattering, respectively.

A FASOR used at the Starfire Optical Range for LIDAR and laser guide star experiments is tuned to the sodium D2a line and used to excite sodium atoms in the upper atmosphere

LIDAR (Light Detection And Ranging) is an optical remote sensing technology that measures properties of scattered light to find range and/or other information of a distant target. The prevalent method to determine distance to an object or surface is to use laser pulses. Like the similar radar technology, which uses radio waves, the range to an object is determined by measuring the time delay between transmission of a pulse and detection of the reflected signal. LIDAR technology has application in Geomantic, archaeology, geography, geology, geomorphology, seismology, forestry, remote sensing and atmospheric physics.[1] Applications of LIDAR include ALSM (Airborne Laser Swath Mapping), laser altimetry or LIDAR Contour Mapping. The acronym LADAR (Laser Detection and Ranging) is often used in military contexts. The term "laser radar" is also in use even though LIDAR does not employ microwaves or radio waves, which is definitional to radar.

The ability of lasers to produce intense pulses of light energy leads to heating, melting, and vaporization of the target. The feature of laser that allows it to be used in Directed Energy Weapons is, of course, its ability to deliver very high values of irradiance to a target surface. Irradiance can be defined as the incident laser power per unit area at the surface; it has units of W/cm^2. Only an electron beam can compare with a laser in this respect [42].

When laser radiation strikes a target surface, part of it is absorbed and part is reflected. The energy that is absorbed begins to heat the surface. There are several regimes of parameters that should be considered, depending on the time scale and on the irradiance. For example, losses due to thermal conduction are small if the pulse duration is very short, but they can be important for longer pulses. Under some conditions, there can be important effects due to absorption of energy in the plasma formed by vaporized material above the target surface. We note that losses due to thermal reradiation from the target surface are usually insignificant [42].

Since our interest on laser concentrates on its application as Directed Energy Weapons, therefore type of destruction effects on incoming threat, weather it is melt or vaporization due to heat conduction from chosen laser, is not important. So long as the threat or the incoming target gets destroyed or cannot deliver its assigned mission to its own pre-selected targets then, we have achieved our mission of creating a DEW system.

In other application of laser with matter such as welding or cutting industries, the interest is melting before we reach vaporization and plasma gets introduced. The heating effects due to absorption of high-power beams can occur very rapidly. The surface quickly rises to its melting temperature. Laser-induced melting is of interest because of welding applications. One often desires maximum melting under conditions where surface vaporization does not occur. Melting without vaporization is produced only within a fairly narrow range of laser parameters. If the laser irradiance is too high, the surface begins to vaporize before a significant depth of molten material is produced. This means that there is a maximum irradiance suitable for welding applications. Alternatively, for a given total energy in the laser pulse, it is often desirable to stretch the pulse length as we have described in above and presented in Equation 5-35..

Effective melting and welding with lasers depends on propagation of a fusion front through the sample during the time of the interaction, at the same time avoiding vaporization of the surface. Figure 5-8 shows the time dependence of the penetration of the molten front into a massive nickel sample for an absorbed irradiance of 10^5 W/cm^2. About 4 msec after the start of the pulse, the surface begins to vaporize. We note that the depth of penetration without surface vaporization is limited. To obtain greater depth, one can tailor the laser parameters to some extent. Generally, one lowers the irradiance and increases the pulse duration. The control is rather sensitive. One must make careful adjustments to achieve a balance between optimum penetration depth and avoidance of surface vaporization. (The results shown in Figures 5-8 and 5-9 are calculated using an analog computer routine developed by M. I. Cohen [43])

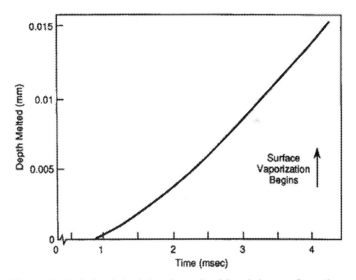

Figure 5-8: Calculated depth melted in nick as a function of time for an absorbed laser irradiation of 10^5 W/cm^2

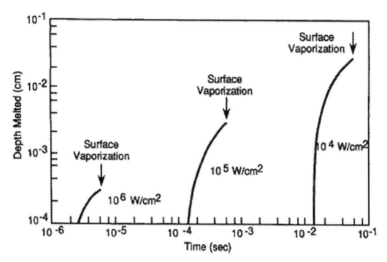

Figure 5-9: Calculated depth melted in stainless steel for several different values of laser irradiance. The time at which surface vaporization begins is indicated for each curve [42].

One is interested primarily in welding under conditions where surface vaporization does not occur. Melting without vaporization is produced only within a narrow range of laser parameters. If the laser irradiance is too high, the surface begins to vaporize before the fusion front penetrates deep into the material. This means that there is a maximum irradiance suitable for welding applications.

Alternatively, for a given total energy in the laser pulse, it is often desirable to stretch the pulse length to allow time for penetration of the fusion front through the work piece. Figure 5-9 shows depth of melting in stainless steel as a function of time. Good fusion can be achieved over a range of pulse lengths if the laser energy is carefully controlled. For pulses shorter than 1 msec, surface vaporization is difficult to avoid [42].

One might think that one should use lasers with very high peak power in order to increase material removal. Paradoxically, it is not the highest laser powers that are optimal for material removal. The very high powers from a Q-switched laser vaporize a small amount of material and heat it to a high temperature. Early in the laser pulse, some material is vaporized from the surface. The vaporized material is slightly thermally ionized and absorbs some of the incident light. This heats the vapor more, producing more ionization and more absorption in a feedback process. Our earlier assumption that the laser light does not interact with the vaporized material is no longer valid if the irradiance becomes very high. Rather, the vaporized material does interact and absorb the incoming laser beam, so that the surface is shielded from the laser light [42]. Under some condition, most of the material may be removed as liquid. Figure 5-10 shows data on the fraction of the material ejected as liquid by a Nd:glass laser pulse with 30 kW power. Early in the pulse, most of the material was removed as vapor, but after a few hundred microseconds, about 90 percent of the material removal occurred as liquid droplets.

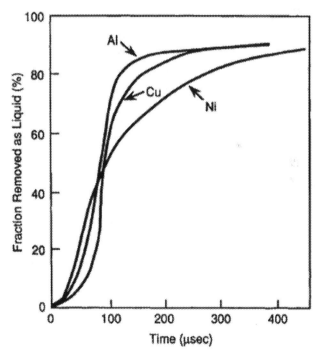

Figure 5-10: Fractional of material removed in liquid form. Results are shown as a function of time for several metals struck by a Nd:glass laser pulse. (From M. K. Chun and K. Rose, J. Applied. Phys. 41, 614 (1970).)

Thus, new physical processes become important as the irradiance becomes very high. This is shown schematically in Figure 5-11, which shows depth vaporized as a function of time. The laser pulse shape is also shown for comparison. This is a typical pulse shape for Q-switched lasers. Early in the pulse, the surface starts to vaporize. Then the vaporized material, heated and ionized by the laser, forms a hot, opaque, ionized plasma, which absorbs essentially all of the incoming laser light. The flat portion of the curve represents the period when the surface is shielded by the plasma, so that vaporization ceases. Finally, late in the pulse, the plasma has expanded and become transparent again. Light can again reach the surface, and some additional material is vaporized. Because of these effects, the amounts of material that can be removed by short-duration, high-power pulses, as from a Q switched laser, are limited. Such lasers are not well suited for hole drilling or for cutting.

The shielding of the target by a hot opaque plasma leads to a phenomenon called a Laser Supported Absorption (LSA) wave. The LSA wave is plasma that is generated above the target surface and propagates backward along the beam path toward the laser. It is accompanied by a loud noise and a bright flash of light. Thus, the LSA wave makes an impressive demonstration, but while present it effectively shields the target surface and reduces the material removal. It can also drive a shock wave into the target.

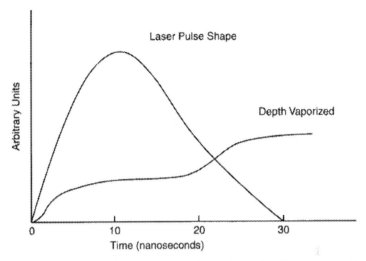

Laser Pulse Shape

Depth Vaporized

Arbitrary Units

0   10   20   30

Time (nanoseconds)

Figure 5-11: Schematic representation of the depth vaporized in a metallic target as a function of time by a 30-nsec-duration laser pulse with the indicated temporal profile. The effect of shielding of the target surface by blowoff material produced in the laser pulse is apparent [6]

We now try to explain one of the important of physical phenomena that occur during the interaction of high-power laser radiation with target surface, and we can summarize that again like we did in Section 5.2.4.2 in above. The physical phenomena are depicted in Figure 5-12 below. If the top left portion of the figure indicates absorption of the incident laser light according to the exponential absorption law

$$I(x) = I_0 e^{-\alpha x} \qquad \text{Eq. 5-36}$$

where $I(x)$ is the laser light intensity at depth x and I_0 is the incident laser light intensity, and α is the absorption coefficient. Based on this figure, fraction of light that is reflected was neglected [42]. For metals, the absorption coefficient is of the order of 10^5 cm^{-1}. Thus, the energy is deposited in a layer about 10^{-5} cm thick. The light energy is transformed into heat energy essentially instantaneously, in a time less than 10^{-13} Seconds [42]. Thus the laser energy may be regarded as an instantaneous surface source of heat.

The heat energy then penetrates into the target by thermal conduction. When the surface reaches the melting temperature, a liquid interface propagates into the material, as indicated in the top portion of Figure 5-10. With continued irradiation the material begins to vaporize, as indicated in the bottom left portion of Figure 5-12, and a hole begins to be drilled [42]. If the irradiance is high enough, absorption in the blow off materials leads to hot opaque plasma. The plasma can grow back toward the laser as Laser Supported Absorption (LSA) wave. The LAS is defined in above. The plasma absorbs the light and shields the surface, as shown in the bottom right portion of Figure 5-12. The ranges of laser irradiance for which individual processes dominate the interaction are given in Table 5-5. Values are stated for two wavelength regions: the visible and near infrared region (around 0.5-1 μm) and the far infrared region near 10 μm. The values in the table are approximate and will vary according to the exact parameters of the laser irradiation, such as pulse duration, target properties, and the like. At relatively low irradiance, melting is the main effect. At somewhat larger irradiance, vaporization becomes the most important effect. This is conventional vaporization, with minimal interaction between the incident light and the vaporized material [42].

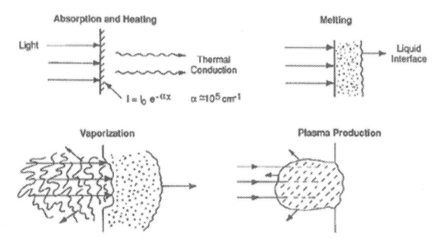

Figure 5-12: Physical phenomena occurring when a high-power laser beam strikes an absorbing surface [42].

At still higher irradiance, LSA waves are kindled and dominate the physical processes, whereas vaporization is diminished. The threshold for kindling the LSA waves are those appropriate to one specific case, namely, a titanium target with laser pulse duration in the microsecond regime. The threshold will vary as the circumstances change. But the numbers in Table 5-5 will serve to identify an order of magnitude at which certain types of interaction occur. The LSA wave dominates at a lower value of irradiance for far infrared lasers than for visible and near infrared lasers.

Process	Range for visible and near infrared laser (W/cm^2)	Range for far infrared laser (W/cm^2)
Melting	$\sim 10^5$	$\sim 10^5$
Vaporization	$10^6 - 1.5 \times 10^8$	$10^6 - 2.5 \times 10^7$
Laser-supported absorption (LSA) wave	$> 1.5 \times 10^8$	$> 2.5 \times 10^7$
Plasma-collective effects	$\geq 10^{13}$	$> 10^{13}$

Table 5-5: Approximate Ranges of Laser Irradiance at which Various Processes Dominate the Laser-Surface Interaction [42]

We summarize these phenomena in Figure 5-13, which identifies various regimes of interaction and their potential applications. The figure defines these regimes in terms of irradiance and the duration of the interaction. The ordinate represents the pulse duration for a pulsed laser (or the time that the beam dwells on a spot for a continuous laser). Below the line marked "No Melting," the surface is not heated to the melting point. In this region, one may have heat treating applications. In the region marked "Welding," one obtains a reasonable depth of molten material, and welding applications are possible. Above the line marked "Surface Vaporization," the surface begins to vaporize and welding applications are less desirable. To the left of the welding region, the penetration of the fusion front is small because of the short interaction time. To the right of the welding region, the heat spreads over a broad area, and the desirable feature of localized heating is lost. Thus, welding operations usually require careful control to remain within this process window. Similarly, the figure identifies regimes useful for cutting, hole drilling, and material removal for small amounts of material, such as vaporization of thin films, that is, trimming. Above the line marked "Plasma Production," the LSA wave develops. The only potential application identified in this region has been shock hardening [42].

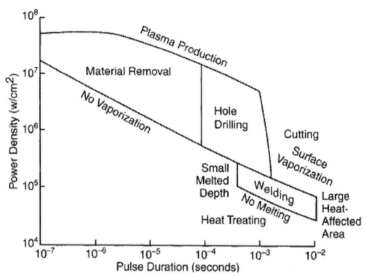

Figure 5-13: Regimes of laser irradiance and interaction time for material processing application [42]

The regions identified in Figure 5-13 are not exact; they will vary with target material, laser wavelength, and so forth. Still, they define regimes of laser parameters where certain applications are most likely to be productive. The engineer desiring to apply a laser in a specific material processing application must identify the process parameters suitable for that particular application [42].

5.3.4.4 Reflectivity at normal incident

Consider an electromagnetic wave in vacuum, with field components of the form[15]

$$E_y(incident) = E_y(inc) = B_z(incident) = Ae^{i(kx-\omega t)}$$

Let the wave be incident upon a medium of dielectric constant å and permeability $\mu = 1$ that fills the half-space $x > 0$. Show that the reflectivity coefficient $r(\omega)$ as defined by $E(\text{refl}) = r(\omega)B(\text{inc})$ is given by

$$r(\omega) = \frac{n + ik - 1}{n + ik + 1}$$

where $n + ik \equiv \varepsilon^{1/2}$, with n and k real. Further we show that the reflectance is

$$R(\omega) = \frac{(n-1)^2 + k^2}{(n+1)^2 + k^2}$$

The reflected wave in vacuum may be written as

$$-E_y(\text{reflected}) = -E_y(\text{refl}) = B_z(\text{reflected}) = A'e^{-i(kx+\omega t)}$$

where the sign of E_y has been reversed relative to B_z in order that the direction of energy flux (Poynting vector) be reversed in the reflected wave from that in the incident wave. For the transmitted wave in the dielectric medium we find

$$E_y(\text{transmitted}) = E_y(\text{trans}) = ck\frac{B_z(\text{transmitted})}{\varepsilon\omega} = \varepsilon^{-1/2}B_z(\text{transmitted})A''e^{-(kx-\omega t)}$$

by use of the Maxwell equation $\text{curl}\,H = \varepsilon\dfrac{\partial E}{\partial t}$ and the dispersion relation $\varepsilon\omega^2 = c^2 k^2$ for electromagnetic waves.

The boundary conditions at the interface at $x = 0$ are that E_y should be continuous: $E_y(\text{inc}) + E_y(\text{refl}) = E_y(\text{trans})$ or $A + A' = A''$. Also B_z should be continues, so that $A + A' = \varepsilon^{1/2}A''$. We solve for the ratio A/A' to obtain $A + A' = \varepsilon^{1/2}(A - A')$, whence

$$\frac{A}{A'} = \frac{1 - \varepsilon^{1/2}}{1 + \varepsilon^{1/2}}$$

and

$$r \equiv \frac{E(\text{refl})}{E(\text{inc})} = -\frac{A}{A'} = \frac{\varepsilon^{1/2} - 1}{\varepsilon^{1/2} + 1} = \frac{n + (ik - 1)}{n + (ik + 1)}$$

The power reflectance is

$$R(\omega) = r^*r = \left(\frac{n-(ik-1)}{n-(ik+1)}\right)\left(\frac{n+(ik-1)}{n+(ik+1)}\right) = \frac{(n-1)^2+k^2}{(n+1)^2+k^2}$$

Some of the most interesting phenomena associated with lasers involve the effects produced when a high-energy power laser beam is absorbed at an opaque surface.

The most spectacular effects involve a change of phase of the absorbing material; for example, the luminous cloud of vaporized material blasted from a metallic surface and often accompanied by a shower of sparks[16].

For an opaque solid, the fraction of incident radiation absorbed is

$$\varepsilon = 1 - R_0$$

where ε is the emissivity and R_0 is the reflectivity at normal incidence. R_0 and ε can be calculated from measurements of optical constants or the complex refractive index. For a complex refractive index,

$$m = n - ik$$

then based on above derivation the reflectivity at normal incidence is

$$R_0 = \frac{(n-1)^2+k^2}{(n+1)^2+k^2}$$

The emissivity is then

$$\varepsilon = \frac{4n}{(n+1)^2+k^2}$$

In General, n and k for metallic materials are functions of wavelength and temperature. The variation of n and k with wavelength and corresponding changes in ε for Ti at 300 K are shown in figure 5.14.

It is apparent that both n and k are relatively slowly varying functions of λ over the range 0.4< λ <1.0 μm and ε is large in this range.. At longer wavelengths, n and k both increase rapidly with λ and ε decreases to a small fraction of its value at shorter wavelength. In the infrared $\varepsilon \propto \lambda^{1/2}$ at constant temperature. Since $\propto$ $^{1/2}$, where r is the electrical resistivity, while r increases with temperature, $\varepsilon(\lambda)$ increases with temperature in the infrared [27]. The temperature dependence of $\varepsilon(\lambda)$ for $\lambda \le 1 \mu m$ is more complex; however, the net change in ε is smaller than observed in the infrared. In visible region of the spectrum ε often decreases slightly with increasing temperature [33].

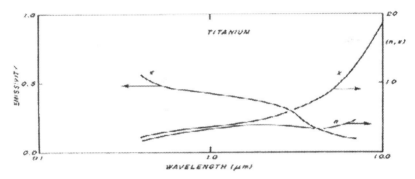

Figure 5-14: Wavelength dependence of ε, n, and k for Ti at 300 ^{0}K [33]

Emissivities for metals at wavelengths characteristic of Ar⁺, ruby, Nd-YAG, and CO^2 lasers are summarized in Table 5-6. The temperature dependence of ε for some metals at 1000 nm and 10.6 μm is shown in Figure 5-15 and 5-16, respectively. Data on ε (1000 nm) vs. were obtained from the observations of Barn [44]. That for ε (10.6 μm) was calculated from the temperature-dependent emissivity from the expression given by Duley [27].

$$\varepsilon_{10.6\,\mu m}(T) = 11.2[R_{20\,^0C}(1+\gamma T)]^{1/2} - 62.9[R_{20\,^0C}(1+\gamma T)] + 174[R_{20\,^0C}(1+\gamma T)]^{1/2} \qquad \text{Eq. 5-37}$$

where $R_{20\,^0C}$ is the resistivity at 20 ^{0}C and γ is the coefficient of resistivity change with temperature T ^{0}C.

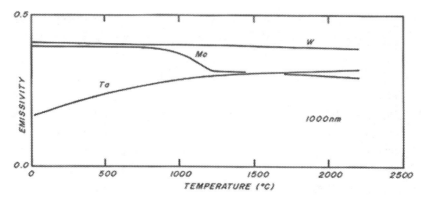

Figure 5-15: Temperature dependent of emissivity for several metals at a wavelength of 1000 nm [33]

Note: The Equation 5-37 is valid for the metals heated in vacuum without a surface oxide layer. The presence of surface films will greatly increase $\varepsilon_{10\,\mu m}(T)$ [27].

Metal	Emissivity[a]			
	Ar^+ (500 nm)	Ruby (700 nm)	Nd–YAG (1000 nm)	CO_2 (10 μm)
Aluminum	0.09	0.11	0.08	0.019
Copper	0.56	0.17	0.10	0.015
Gold	0.58	0.07	—	0.017
Iridium	0.36	0.30	0.22	—
Iron	0.68	0.64	—	0.035
Lead	0.38	0.35	0.16	0.045
Molybdenum	0.48	0.48	0.40	0.027
Nickel	0.40	0.32	0.26	0.03
Niobium	0.58	0.50	0.32	0.036
Platinum	0.21	0.15	0.11	0.036
Rhenium	0.47	0.44	0.28	—
Silver	0.05	0.04	0.04	0.014
Tantalum	0.65	0.50	0.18	0.044
Tin	0.20	0.18	0.19	0.034
Titanium	0.48	0.45	0.42	0.08
Tungsten	0.55	0.50	0.41	0.026
Zinc	—	—	0.16	0.027

[a]At 20°C.

Table 5-6: Values of Emissivity for various metals at laser wavelengths [33]

Inspection of the data in Table 5-6 and Figure 5-15 and 5-16 shows that the absorption of laser light by metal surfaces at 20 °C is almost and order of magnitude larger at visible wavelengths than at infrared wavelengths [33].

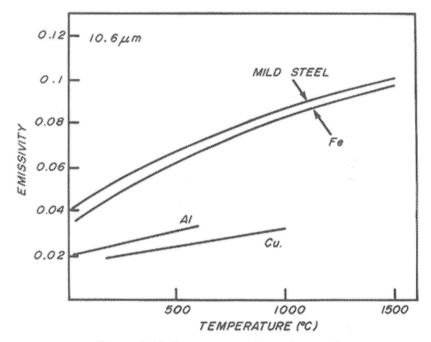

Figure 5-16: Temperature dependence of emissivity at 10.6 μm for several metals [33]

As we said in above note the validation of these analyses takes place in absence any surfaces film. In most practical applications of laser heating this assumption will not be valid because of oxide formation or presence of surface contamination and possible other films (i.e. paints). When this is the case, values of ε in the infrared can be increased at visible wavelength. Thus, under practical conditions the difference between $\varepsilon_{10.6\ \mu m}$ and $\varepsilon_{visible}$ is unlikely to be as large as suggested by Duley [33] and data provided in Table 5-6. Duley et al. (1979) [45] have investigated the effect of oxidation on $\varepsilon_{10.6\ \mu m}$ for several metals heated in air. This follows work by Wieting and De Rosa (1979) [46] and Wieting and Schriempf (1976) [47] on the absorptance of stainless steel and Ti-6A1-4V alloy at high temperatures in vacuum.

Data obtained by Wieting and de Rosa on the absorptivity, ε, of type 304 stainless steel at 10.6 μm and presented by Duley [33] in his book are shown in different figures and we suggest the reader to refer to his book.

The further study of interaction of high power laser beam with materials and producing plasma at the target surface (See Figure 5-12) will introduce to the research done by Sturmer and Von Allmen [48]. The time evolution of target shielding via plasma formation has been followed in details by them in 1978. They identify three separate absorption regimes when a high-intensity pulse of long duration is incident on a metallic target in air or other atmosphere. These are:

1. Strong reflection from target.
2. Absorption by plasma and target shielding.
3. Dissipation of plasma and enhanced coupling to target.

As we discussed in pervious section to some degree, during Step 1, which occurs during the initial stages of laser heating, the target has high reflectivity and ε is small. Material evaporated from the focus may seed the gas in front of the target initiating plasma breakdown and lead to the formation of a Laser Supported Detonation (LSD) wave. This wave absorbs practically all the incident laser radiation (Step 2) and shields the target. It dissipates by moving away from the target toward focusing lens. This results in a reduction of plasma density followed by a decrease in opacity. The surface is then exposed to the last part of the laser pulse (Step 3) which couples efficiently to the damaged target. Subsequent LSD wave ignition is suppressed by the low gas density left in front of the target following dissipation of the initial LSD wave.

While ε may be important in the initial stages of the heating of metallic targets with laser radiation, it is unimportant in many practical laser heating applications. The importance of ε is diminished when material removal has proceeded to the point where a cavity or keyhole has formed in the workpiece (target surface). In this case, the cavity acts as a blackbody absorber with ε effectively equal to unity. It has been shown [Shewell (1977)] [49] that control over the fitting of parts to be joined can also be effective in increasing ε. Under conditions in which laser radiation is absorbed in a keyhole, Steen and Eboo (1979) [50] have shown that plasma absorption occurs within the keyhole yielding $\varepsilon = 1$.

The data contained in Table 5-6 can be used to obtain an estimate of the relative merit of Ar+, ruby, Nd-YAG, and CO^2 sources for laser heating. Heat transfer calculations show that the limiting temperature at the center of a Gaussian focal spot on a bulk target is

$$T = \frac{\varepsilon I_0 d\pi^{1/2}}{K} \qquad \text{Eq. 5-38}$$

where I_0 is the peak laser intensity (W cm^{-2}), d the Gaussian beam radius, and K the thermal conductivity. With optimum focusing $d \propto \lambda$, where λ is the laser wavelength. Since $I_0 \propto P / \lambda^2$, where P is the laser power, one has

$$P \propto \frac{KT\lambda}{\varepsilon} \qquad \text{Eq. 5-39}$$

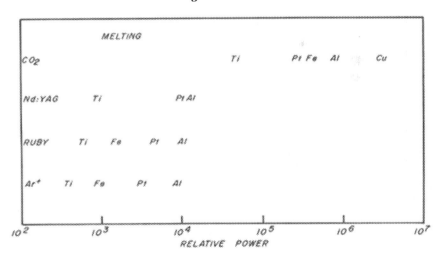

Figure 5-17: Relative power to produce surface melting with various laser sources [33].

If we assume that useful thermal effects are produced only when $T = T_m$ or T_b, where T_m is the melting temperature while T_b is the boiling temperature, then this expression can be used to obtain an estimate of the relative difficulty of machining with different laser sources. A comparison of this sort is shown in Figures 5-17 and 5-18 for the production of melting and boiling, respectively [33].

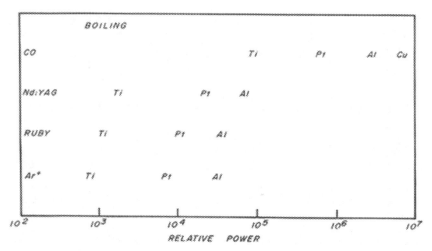

Figure 5-18: Relative power to produce surface melting with various laser sources [33].

The correlations shown in these two figures are, of course, highly approximate because they assume room temperature values for ε and K can be used to high temperatures [33]. The uncertainly in these estimates can be reduced somewhat by taking $\varepsilon = 1$. A comparison calculated on this basis is shown in Figure 5-19. If we compare powers required to melt or boil Ti from this figure we see that $P(CO^2)/P(Ar+)\sim20:1$. Taking $\varepsilon < 1$ as shown in Figure 5-14, the corresponding ratio is ~120. Thus, while higher powers are required to initiate surface damage with infrared lasers than with visible lasers, when damage has occurred (i.e., $\varepsilon \sim 1$), much of the effect of the increased spot size of infrared lasers has disappeared [33].

At anything other than normal incidence the reflection of laser radiation depends on polarization. This also well explained in Appendix F of this book. The geometry at some general angle of incidence ϕ is shown in Figure 5-20. The reflectivity for the two polarization direction s and p, R_s and R_p, will in general be different. This means that the reflection coefficient for polarized laser light will be dependent on the orientation of the polarization vector relative to the metal surface. An example of the angular dependence of R_s and R_p for Cu at 10.6 µm is shown in Figure 5-21. It can be seen that R_s is high for all angles. However, R_p becomes very small at close to grazing incidence. Thus ε for incident light polarized perpendicular to the metal surface is larger under these conditions and enhanced coupling occurs. This has some important consequences in laser probing target where the efficiency of material removal depends on the relation between polarization direction and the direction of translation of the metal substrate. This also can be demonstrated in the following section also known as *Fresnel Absorption*.

5.3.4.5 Fresnel Absorption

Energy absorption by the work piece from the laser can involve a direct process [51, 52, 53, 54] with the laser light incident on a surface as well as other indirect processes. There exists a simple electromagnetic model for absorption at a metal surface that is widely used, especially in the context of keyhole modeling at the wavelength of a CO^2 laser. At that wavelength the assumptions of a simple model of electromagnetic interaction involving resistive dissipation are justifiable as a useful approximation, although at shorter wavelengths it becomes progressively more suspect. The model does not make allowance for surface impurities and must therefore be used with an understanding of its limitations.

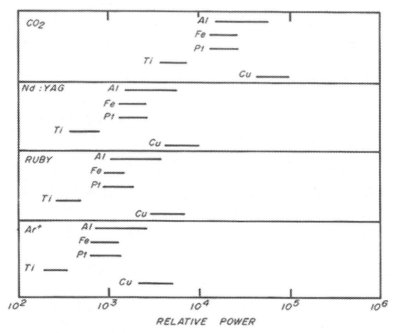

Figure 5-19: Relative power to reach temperatures between T_m and T_b assuming $\varepsilon = 1$ [33]

This direct absorption process is usually referred to as *Fresnel Absorption*. A formula for the reflection coefficient $\Re$ that is frequently quoted [55], and which applies to circularly polarized light, is

$$\Re = \frac{1}{2}\left(\frac{1+(1-\varepsilon\cos\phi)^2}{1+(1+\varepsilon\cos\phi)^2} + \frac{\cos^2\phi+(\varepsilon-\cos\phi)^2}{\cos^2\phi+(\varepsilon+\cos\phi)^2}\right) \qquad \text{Eq. 5-40}$$

where ϕ is the angle of reflection that the light makes to the normal and ε is a material-dependent quantity defined by

$$\varepsilon^2 = \frac{2\varepsilon_2}{\varepsilon_1 + \sqrt{\varepsilon_1^2 + (\sigma_{st}/\omega\varepsilon_0)^2}} \qquad \text{Eq. 5-41}$$

where ε_0 is the permittivity of a vacuum, ε_1 and ε_2 are the real parts of the dielectric constants for the metal and the air or vapor through which the beam is being transmitted, and σ_{st} is the electrical conductance per unit depth of the work-piece. The value of ε_0 is 8.854x10^{12} F m^{-1}, and typical values for the other terms are approximately unity for ε_1 and ε_2, and 5.0x10^5 Ω^{-1}m^{-1} for σ_{st}. For a CO^2 laser a wavelength of 10.6μm gives a value for ω of 1.78x10^{14} s^{-1}, and so ε has a value of about 0.08. Figure 5-22 shows the graph of $\Re$ as a function of ϕ.

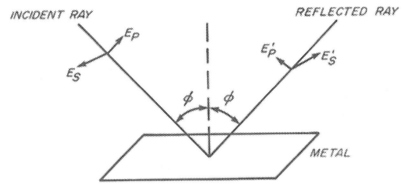

Figure 5-20: Incident and reflected waves at a metal surface [33]

It will be seen that there is a strong dependence on the angle of incidence with a marked minimum close to $\phi = \frac{1}{2}\pi$, indicating that absorption is strongest at near-grazing incidence. For normal incidence, however, as much as 85% of the incident power can be reflected. This figure can be very greatly modified by surface impurities or other additives introduced as part of the process.

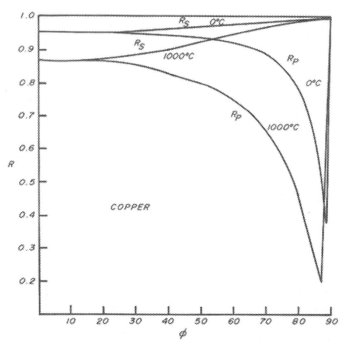

**Figure 5-21: Angular dependence of reflectivity for s and p
polarizations with 10.6-µm radiation incident on Cu at 20 and 1000 ºC** [33]

Absorption of light by insulating materials is a strong function of
wavelength. In the infrared, absorption arises from vibrational modes
of the crystal lattice or organic solids by intermolecular vibration.
Absorption coefficients $\alpha \sim 10^2 - 10^4$ cm^{-1} is typical within these
bands. In the visible band, absorption may occur due to impurities (e.g.
transition metal ions, crystal defect centers, etc.) Absorption can also
occur due to discrete electronic transitions in molecular crystal (e.g.,
many organic solids) [33]. Absorption coefficients are typically $10^3 - 10^6$
cm^{-1} within absorption bands. Figure 5-23 shows absorptions, α, for
several refractory materials in the visible and ultraviolet α can be
related to the transmission of a sheet of thickness t via;

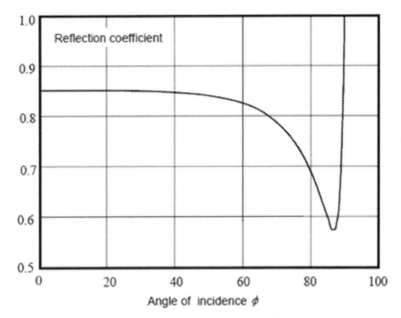

**Figure 5-22: The reflection coefficient $\Re$ as a function
of the angle of the incident beam to the normal** [56]

$$\frac{I}{I_0} \times 100 = \text{Transmission in percent} = 100e^{-\alpha t}$$

or

$$\frac{I}{I_0} = e^{-\alpha t}$$

Eq. 5-42

where I_0 is the incident intensity and I is the transmitted intensity. A useful measure of the thickness required for significant of incident radiation is given by

$$L = \alpha^{-1}$$

where L is the attenuation length. A strong absorber has $\alpha = 10^6$ cm^{-1} and L cm while a relatively weak absorber has $\alpha = 10^1$ cm^{-1} and $L = 10^{-1}$ cm.

The relation between α and refractive index is given by Equation 5-43 where k is imaginary term in the complex refractive index

$$\alpha = \frac{4\pi k}{\lambda}$$

Eq. 5-43

while λ is the wavelength of the incident light. In the visible region, nominally transparent materials will typically have $\alpha \sim 10^{-5}$ or $\alpha \sim 10$ cm-1. The absorption due to $k = 0.1$ is shown in Figure 5-23.

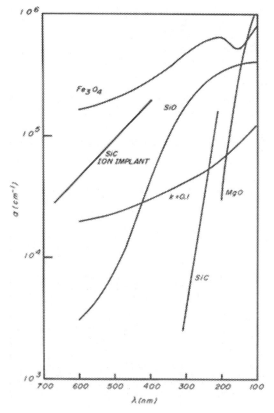

Figure 5-23: Absorption coefficient α for several insulators at wavelengths between 100 and 700 nm [33]

Note that: In Figure 5-23 the curve at $k = 0.1$ corresponds to the absorption that would be produced by a material with an imaginary refractive index equal to this value.

As we have mentioned the optical properties of materials at UV wavelengths (i.e. typical CO_2 at λ=10.6μm) using the knowledge of electromagnetic radiation (See Appendix F) with condensed matter can be characterized in terms of a complex frequency-dependent dielectric constant $\varepsilon(w)$ [97].

$$\varepsilon(w) = \varepsilon_1(w) + i\varepsilon_2(w) \qquad \text{Eq. 5-44}$$

where $\varepsilon_1(w)$ and $\varepsilon_2(w)$ are related to the complex refractive, m, as follows:

$$\varepsilon_1(w) = n^2 - k^2 \qquad \text{Eq. 5-45}$$

$$\varepsilon_2(w) = 2nk \qquad \text{Eq. 5-46}$$

with

$$m = n - ik \qquad \text{Eq. 5-47}$$

Where n and k are both frequency-dependent. Under an ideal vacuum circumstances $n = 1$ and k is zero accordingly. The presence of matter causes both n and k to deviate from these values. With condensed matter, the density is many times larger than that of a gas. And deviations of n and k from vacuum values are correspondingly larger. It is not unusual to have $n, k \gg 1$ over a wide wavelength range in most solids.

Physically, the dependence of n on wavelength leads to dispersive effects in optical systems whereas the absorption at a particular wavelength n is directly related to k. It can be shown that the real and imaginary terms either in the dielectric constant or in the refractive index are related through the Kramers-Kronig integrals [101]. For the dielectric constant $\varepsilon(w)$ these are [97];

$$\varepsilon_1(w) = 1 + \frac{2}{\pi} P \int_0^{\infty} \frac{w^1 \varepsilon_2(w^1)}{(w^1)^2 - w^2} dw^1 \qquad \text{Eq. 5-48}$$

$$\varepsilon_2(w) = \frac{-2w}{\pi} P \int_0^{\infty} \frac{[\varepsilon_1(w')-1]}{(w')^2 - w^2} dw' \qquad \text{Eq. 5-49}$$

where p is the principal part of the integral. These relations show that knowledge of either ε_1 or ε_2 over the frequency range $0 < w < \infty$ provides information on the value of the other at a specific frequency w. These relationships are often used to verify the consistency of experimental data for ε_1 and ε_2.

The absorption of light propagation through a medium characterized by refractive indices and is given by Beer-Lambert law [102].

$$I(x) = I_0 e^{-\alpha x} \qquad \text{Eq. 5-50}$$

where I_0 is the intensity at $x = 0$ and is the intensity after a distance $I(x)$. The attenuation coefficient

$$\delta^{-1} = \alpha = \frac{4\pi k}{\lambda} \qquad \text{Eq. 5-51}$$

is found to be directly proportional to the imaginary term in the refractive index. At UV wavelength, a transparent material would have $\alpha \leq 1$ cm^{-1} whereas strong absorbers such as semiconductors or metals would have a $\alpha = (2-3) \times 10^6$ cm^{-1}. The characteristic penetration depth (i.e. Skin Depth $\delta = \alpha^{-1}$) for radiation under these conditions is then α^{-1}. Note that Equation 5-50 is valid only under conditions in which I_0 is much less than the intensity at which non-linear effects may become significant. This can be shown in following analysis and more details can be found in Schriempf report [28] as well. For the examples given the penetration depth would be about 300-500 nm (metal) and ≥ 1 cm (transparent media). These values show that surface effects will dominate in interaction of UV radiation with metals and many semiconductors. Surface roughness and composition are also important in determining the coupling of laser radiation to solids [98-100].

5.3.4.6 Optical Reflectivity

To consider the coupling of the laser energy to a material, we need first to know the optical reflectivity R and the transmissivity T for light incident on a surface which divides two semi-infinite media. The transmissivity plus the reflectivity equals unity at a *single surface*:

$$R + T = 1 \qquad \text{Eq. 5-52}$$

(See Appendix F for proof). In most practical situations we are dealing with more than one surface; typically, we have a slab of material with light impinging on one surface. Some light is reflected, and the rest is either absorbed or passes completely through the slab. In such a situation we shall describe the net result of all the reflection, after multiple passes inside the slab and appropriate absorption has been accounted for, in terms of the reflectance R, the absorptance A, and the transmittance T:

$$R+A+T=1 \qquad \text{Eq. 5-53}$$

What we really are interested in from the point of view of material response is A, the absorptance of the material. In most materials of interest from the practical aim of using lasers to melt, weld, etc., T is zero, and

$$R+A=1 \qquad \text{Eq. 5-54}$$

Schriempf [28] arguers how to consider the relationship between R and R.

To understand reflectivity, we must use some general results from the theory of electromagnetic waves. Let us summarize these briefly at this point. The electric field of the electromagnetic wave, from the following Equation 5-55 which, is

$$E = \text{Re}[E_0 e^{-2\pi kz/\lambda} e^{i\omega(t-nz/c)}] \qquad \text{Eq. 5-55}$$

This equation is well defined in Appendix F of the book (Volume 2). The relationships we need are those among the index of refraction

n, the extinction coefficient k, and the material properties. These relationships can be derived by substituting Equation 5-55 in the wave equation

$$\frac{\partial^2 E}{\partial z^2} = \mu\varepsilon\frac{\partial^2 E}{\partial t^2} + \mu\sigma\frac{\partial E}{\partial t} \qquad \text{Eq. 5-56a}$$

Where

E :   is the electric field of the radiation.
Re :   stands for the real part of the complex quantity in brackets.
E_0 :   is the maximum amplitude.
k :   is the extension coefficient; in vacuum, $k = 0$.
z :   is the direction in which the wave is propagating.
λ :   is the wavelength.
t :   is time
n :   is the index of refraction: in a vacuum, $n = 1$.
c :   is the velocity of light in vacuum.
σ :   electric conductivity or conductivity.
μ :   magnetic permeability.
ε :   dielectric function.
ω :   is angular frequency

This results in the following expression known as Equation 5-56b

$$\left(\frac{2\pi k}{\lambda} + \frac{i\omega n}{c}\right)^2 = \mu\varepsilon(-\omega^2) + i\omega\mu\sigma \qquad \text{Eq. 5-56b}$$

Note that Schriempf [28] is using rationalized MKS units throughout. The material properties enter through μ, ε, and σ, which are the magnetic permeability, the dielectric function, and the electric conductivity of the medium. Using the usual equations between the field vectors as follows (See Appendix F and Equation F-42 as well);

$$\begin{cases} \vec{D} = \varepsilon\vec{E} \\ \vec{B} = \mu\vec{H} \\ \vec{J} = \sigma\vec{E} \end{cases} \qquad \text{Eq. 5-57}$$

Plugging the following assumption in Equation 5-57 we get and the results final result into Equation 5-56b along with some algebra work we obtain Equation 5-59;

$$\begin{cases} \varepsilon = K_e \varepsilon_0 \\ \mu = K_m \mu_0 \end{cases} \quad \text{Eq. 5-58}$$

$$(k + in)^2 = -K_e K_m \varepsilon_0 \mu_0 c^2 + iK_m \mu_0 \sigma \frac{c^2}{\omega} \quad \text{Eq. 59}$$

Where

ε_0 : electric permittivity of vacuum.

μ_0 : magnetic permeability vacuum.

K_e : dielectric constant of metal.

K_m : magnetic permeability of metal.

Finally, if we introduce $c^2 = (\varepsilon_0 \mu_0)^{-1}$ and some more algebra we have;

$$n - ik = \sqrt{K_m} \sqrt{K_e - i \frac{\sigma}{\varepsilon_0 \omega}} \quad \text{Eq. 5-60}$$

This equation relates the material parameters K_m, K_e, and σ, which in general may be complex, to *index of refraction* n and *extinction coefficient* k. To describe the propagation of the light wave thus requires a knowledge of K_e, K_m, and a. Before we describe these, let us look at two more general properties of our propagating electromagnetic wave.

The first of these is absorption. If the medium is absorbing, the intensity will fall off to $1/e$ of its initial value in a distance δ, obtained by setting E^2 of Equation 5-55 equal to $(1/e)E_{max}^2$, or

$$\begin{cases} \dfrac{4\pi k \delta}{\lambda} = 1 \\ \\ \delta = \dfrac{\lambda}{4\pi k} \end{cases} \quad \text{Eq. 5-61}$$

From this equation we can see why k is called the *extinction coefficient*, for it determines *skin depth* δ. Equation 5-61 is fairly general in that once k is known, δ can be calculated, providing that knowledge of the material of interest or target material properties is required to calculate k. Some information is discussed in Chapter 6 how to measure of these issues experimentally and more can be found in report by Joseph S. Accetta and David N. Loomis [95].

Schriempf [28] is deriving the second general property which we present here and is expression for reflectivity, in terms of n and k again.

To do this, consider light impinging normally onto an ideal solid surface, as shown in Figure 5-24. Here we have illustrated the incident E_i, reflected E_r, and transmitted E_t electric waves at a vacuum-material interface. For the present, we limit our discussion to the case of normal incidence. We now consider the boundary condition. We have for the electric field

$$E_i + E_r = E_t \qquad \text{Eq. 5-62}$$

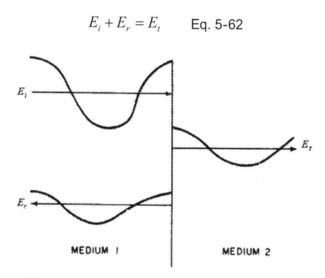

Figure 5-24: Normal incident, transmitted, and reflected electric vectors at an interface

For the magnetic field $\vec{B}$, we write

$$B_i - B_r = B_t \qquad \text{Eq. 5-63}$$

The minus sign is before B_r because $\vec{E} \times \vec{B}$ is positive in the direction of propagation of the wave. Now, the relationship between $\vec{B}$ and $\vec{E}$, or, since $\vec{B} = \mu\vec{H}$, between $\vec{H}$ and $\vec{E}$, is required in order to proceed further. This follows directly from Maxwell's equations (See Appendix F):

$$\nabla \times \vec{E} = -\mu\frac{\partial\vec{H}}{\partial t} \qquad \text{Eq. 5-64}$$

$$\nabla \times \vec{H} = \sigma\vec{E} + \varepsilon\frac{\partial\vec{E}}{\partial t} \qquad \text{Eq. 5-65}$$

It is convenient to rewrite Equation 5-55 and introduce $\omega\lambda = 2\pi c$, to have $\vec{E}$, explicitly in terms of ω instead of both ω and λ. Recall that $\vec{E}$ is a vector, and take it as being along the x-direction. Thus

$$E_x = E_0 e^{i\omega t} e^{-\frac{i\omega}{c}z(n-ik)} \qquad \text{Eq. 5-66}$$

Here we have dropped the "Re" notation, and shall simply note that we always mean the real part when we write the wave in exponential form. We shall use unit vectors $\hat{x}$ and $\hat{y}$.

Now the curl expressions (See Appendix B on Vector Analysis) reduces to

$$\nabla \times E \quad \hat{y}\frac{\partial}{\partial}$$

Which with Equation 5-64, tells us that $\vec{H}$ has a y component

$$\nabla \times \vec{E} = \hat{y}\frac{\partial E_x}{\partial z} \qquad \text{Eq. 5-67}$$

Thus Equations 5-64 and 5-65 becomes

$$\frac{\partial E_x}{\partial z} = -\mu \frac{\partial H_y}{\partial t} \qquad \text{Eq. 5-68}$$

$$-\frac{\partial H_y}{\partial z} = \sigma E_x + \varepsilon \frac{\partial E_x}{\partial t} \qquad \text{Eq. 5-69}$$

and of course, $E_y = E_z = H_x = H_z = 0$. Putting the expression for E_x from Equation 5-66 into Equation 5-68 to find that;

$$H_y = \frac{n - ik}{\mu c} E_0 e^{-\frac{i\omega}{c} z(n - ik)} e^{i\omega t}$$

This is the desired relationship:

$$H_y = \left(\frac{n - ik}{\mu c} \right) E_x \qquad \text{Eq. 5-70}$$

At this point we note in passing that Equation 5-69 or 5-56b could be used to yield the relationship of n and k to μ, ε, and σ. If the reader is unfamiliar with these relationships, it is instructive to carry out the algebra. Returning to our consideration of the reflected electric and magnetic fields, we rewrite Equation 5-62 and 5-63 with the help of the relationship between $\vec{H}$ and $\vec{E}$, from Equation 5-70;

$$E_i + E_r = E_t$$

and

$$\mu_1 H_i - \mu_1 H_r = \mu_2 H_t$$

becomes

$$E_i - E_r = \left(\frac{n_2 - ik_2}{n_2 - ik_1} \right) E_t$$

Solve for E_r / E_i by eliminating E_t;

$$\frac{E_r}{E_i} = \frac{n_1 - n_2 - i(k_1 - k_2)}{n_1 + n_2 - i(k_1 + k_2)}$$

Finally, the reflectivity R at the surface is;

$$R = \left|\frac{E_r}{E_i}\right|^2 = \frac{(n_1 - n_2)^2 + (k_1 - k_2)^2}{(n_1 + n_2)^2 + (k_1 + k_2)^2} \qquad \text{Eq. 5-71}$$

Take medium 1 as a vacuum and drop the subscript 2. This gives, since in a vacuum $n_1 = 1$ and $k_1 = 0$.

$$R = \frac{(n_1 - 1)^2 + k^2}{(n_1 + 1)^2 + k^2} \qquad \text{Eq. 5-72}$$

Equation 5-72 is the second relationship we will find useful in discussing the coupling of optical relationship with metals. Note that it is derived for the special case of normal incidence and is applicable to a vacuum material interface.

5.4 Effects Caused by Absorption of Laser Radiation at Surface

Effects produced by a high power laser beam focusing and is absorbed by an opaque target surface is raising very interesting phenomena. The most spectacular effects involve a change of phase of the absorbing material such as the luminous cloud of vaporized material blasted from metallic surface and often accompanied by a shower of sparks. The irradiance in the focal spot can lead to rapid local heating, intense evaporation, and degradation of the material. The most attractive feature of laser excitation is its capability to probe insulator within focal spot and depositing heat energy into it. The most common mechanism of laser desorption is a thermally activated process induced by surface heating of the sample or surface of target at focal point. In this regime the amount of material transport across the surface is negligible (Figure 5-25a). Laser heating of the solid surface and induced plume leads to the generation of different chemical species. Protonation and alkalination reactions are often the source of the most characteristic species in the ion cloud [103]. Increasing the energy deposition into sample, the surface temperature reaches a point where material transfer across the surface becomes significant (Figure 5-25b).

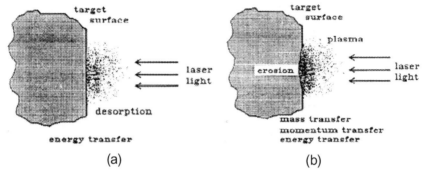

(a)   (b)

Figure 5-25: Different regimes of laser-target interaction under vacuum. In laser desorption (a) material transport across the surface is negligible. Laser volatilization (b) is characterized by considerable transport of mass, momentum, and energy and occasional plasma formation [104]

The initial process in the conversion of high power laser radiation to heat during irradiation involves the excitation of electrons to states of high energy. This is basically is simple conversion of optical energy of the beam into thermal energy in the material. This is the base of many laser applications including its weaponry application as directed energy weapons. We shall summarize here this thermal response through its basic classical heat flow problem and solving heat diffusion equation under different conditions.

Before we go further into this matter, we have to understand basic optical energy from atomic physics point of view and to understand how the principle of laser works. More correctly described a laser is a device for producing light that is almost totally coherent. It works in principle like this: An atom emits a photon of light when it decays from an excited energy state to a lower state; the difference in energy between the two states ΔE determines frequency v according to

$$\Delta E = hv \qquad \text{Eq. 5-73}$$

where h is Planck's constant. This is illustrated in Figure 5-26. This is the case for any light source, whether laser, flame, incandescent body, etc. In the conventional light source, atoms emit photons in a random, sporadic manner and spontaneously decay to lower states when excited by heat or electric current. In a laser, on the other hand, the photons are emitted in phase and the electromagnetic radiation thus produced is, more or less, simply a propagating sinusoidal radiation field that can be described on a macroscopic level by Equation 5-55 and further on by Maxwell's set of equations as described in above sections.

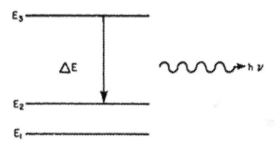

Figure 5-26: Energy levels

For this process to occur, vacant states have to be available to accept excited electrons. When the photon energy hv is small, as for example when 10.6 μm laser radiation is absorbed, only electrons within a narrow range hv near the Fermi energy, ε_F, can participate in absorption. At 0 K, the highest energy reached upon absorption is $\varepsilon_F + hv$.

At higher temperature, electrons occupy a range of states given by the Fermi-Dirac distribution. This reduces to a Boltzmann function for electron energies ε such that $\varepsilon - \varepsilon_F \gg kT$, where T is the metal temperature. Absorption of photons then populates those states with energy $\varepsilon_F + hv$. Since is usually several electron-volts, whereas

$hv = 0.117$ eV for CO^2 laser photons, absorption of IR laser radiation then acts to distribute electrons among states close to those on the Fermi surface.

Fermi Energy

The Fermi energy is a concept in quantum mechanics usually referring to the energy of the highest occupied quantum state in a system of fermions at absolute zero temperature.

The Fermi energy ε_F of a system of non-interacting fermions is the increase in the ground state energy when exactly one particle is added to the system. It can also be interpreted as the maximum energy of individual fermions in this ground state.

Fermi Energy for Metal

As we defined above, the Fermi energy is the maximum energy occupied an electron at 0 K. By the Pauli exclusion principle, we know that electrons will fill all available energy levels, and the top of that "Fermi Sea" of electrons is called the Fermi energy or Fermi level. The conduction electron population for a metal is calculated by multiplying the density electron state $\rho(\varepsilon)$ times the Fermi-Dirac function $f_{FD}(\varepsilon)$. The number of conduction electrons permit volume per unit energy is.

$$\frac{dn}{d\varepsilon} = \rho(\varepsilon)f_{FD}(\varepsilon) = \underbrace{\frac{8\sqrt{2}\pi m^{3/2}}{h^3}\sqrt{\varepsilon}}_{\substack{\text{Electron Density of} \\ \text{state}}} \underbrace{\frac{1}{e^{(\varepsilon-\varepsilon_F)/kT}+1}}_{\substack{\text{Fermi-Dirac} \\ \text{distribution function}}}$$

The total population of conduction electrons per unit volume can be obtained by integrating this expression

$$n = \int_0^\infty \rho(\varepsilon)f_{FD}(\varepsilon)d\varepsilon = \frac{8\sqrt{2}\pi m^{3/2}}{h^3}\int_0^\infty \frac{\sqrt{\varepsilon}}{e^{(\varepsilon-\varepsilon_F)/kT}+1}d\varepsilon$$

At 0 K the top of the electron energy distribution is defined as ε_F so the integral becomes

$$\varepsilon_F = \left(\frac{(hc)^2}{8mc^2}\right)\left(\frac{3}{\pi}\right)^{2/3} n^{2/3}$$

For example if we consider element of Au having Fermi Energy 5.53 eV, then the free electron density is $n \cong 0.5906466 \times 10^{29}$ electron/m³.

This situation is different at excimer laser wavelength, since hv is then comparable to or larger than the work function, φ, of many metals. When $hv > \varphi$, electrons may be directly excited from states near the Fermi surface to continuum states associated with the ejection of an electron from the metal. These electrons will originate from levels within the skin depth δ. Those electrons that are not ejected will dissipate their excess energy as heat within the skin depth. Photoelectrons, as they leave the surface with kinetic energy about $hv + kT - \varphi$, will *cool* the surface [97].

Figure 5-27 shows a plot of photoelectron current density versus laser intensity for 248 nm KrF laser radiation incidents on several metals.

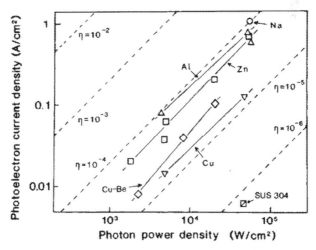

Figure 5-27: Quantum efficiencies for photoelectron emission from various metal subjected to 248 nm KrF laser radiation [105]

Transfer of energy from the electron gas to the metal to produce local heating and macroscopic thermal effects results from scattering of electrons by photons and defects.

In order to study pulsed-laser heating and evaporation of solids, we constructed a one-dimensional model consisting of two parts: the first dealt with the heating and melting of the target and predicted the temperature, density, and flow velocity of the particles emerging on the liquid-vapor interface, whereas the second followed the expansion of the plume expelled from the surface. In the following sections we present the framework of the calculations.

The distribution of this heat in response to a radiative source with defined spatial and temporal properties can then be calculated using the heat equation as follows;

$$\nabla^2 T(\vec{r},t) - \frac{1}{\kappa}\frac{\partial T(\vec{r},t)}{\partial t} = -\frac{A(\vec{r},t)}{K} \qquad \text{Eq. 5-74}$$

Where

κ : is thermal diffusivity (cm^{-2} s^{-1}) in MKS units.
K : is the thermal conductivity (Wcm^{-1} $^{\circ}$C^{-1}) in MKS units.

In the above equation $A(\vec{r},t)$ is the position-dependent rate of heat production per unit time per unit volume (Wcm^{-3}). Equation 5-74 assumes that K and κ are independent of temperature and do not vary across the metal surface of target.

As we discussed in Section 5.2.4.5 and Equation 5-51, the deposition of heat under laser irradiation of opaque surface occurs over a depth (i.e. Skin Depth $\delta = \alpha^{-1}$) defined by the single-photon absorption coefficient α cm^{-1}. In metals, at optical frequencies this dimension is typically about 10^{-6} cm. Since α^{-1} is usually much smaller than the lateral spatial extent of focused eximer beam the heat conduction equation (Eq. 5-74) can be linearized. Then in one-dimensional space we can reduce it to the following form;

$$\frac{\partial^2 T(z,t)}{\partial z^2} - \frac{1}{\kappa}\frac{\partial T(z,t)}{\partial t} = -\frac{A(z,t)}{K} \qquad \text{Eq. 5-75}$$

where z is a coordinate extending from the sample surface into the material. Because $A(z,t)$ is a volume heat source, it must be evaluated over some incremental length Δz local at z. Assuming a homogeneous absorbing medium at target surface, we can write;

$$A(z,t) = (1-R)I_0(t)\alpha e^{-\alpha z} \qquad \text{Eq. 5-76}$$

where R is the surface reflectivity and $I_0(t)$ is the time-dependent laser intensity incident at the surface. Then

$$\int_0^\infty A(z,t)dz = (1-R)I_0(t) \qquad \text{Eq. 5-77}$$

Substitution of Equation 5-77 into Equation 5-75 results in the following equation;

$$\frac{\partial^2 T(z,t)}{\partial z^2} - \frac{1}{\kappa}\frac{\partial T(z,t)}{\partial t} = -\frac{1-R}{K}I_0(t)\alpha e^{-\alpha z} \qquad \text{Eq. 5-78}$$

Equation 5-78 then describes the solution for the temperature profile produced inside a semi-infinite half space exposed to a uniform surface heat irradiation by laser beam source of $(1-R)I_0(t)$ distributed as $e^{-\alpha z} = \exp(-\alpha z)$ with depth know as skin depth defined in pervious sections of this chapter.

The solution for the heat transfer Equation 5-78 can be expressed in analytical form only when the system possesses certain symmetrical boundary conditions. When this is not the case, the heat transfer equation can be solved numerically. Detailed analysis of almost any practical laser heating problem requires that a numerical approach be adopted in particular for DEW application. However, as considerable physical insight into laser heating mechanisms can often be obtained from approximate solutions expressed in analytical form, available analytical solutions are summarized in this section.

These solutions, together with relevant boundary conditions, are shown presented by Duly [16]. While this does not represent a complete set of possible solutions, the examples shown have been chosen to be representative of boundary conditions most often encountered in laser drilling. Further examples and discussion can be found elsewhere [Carslaw and Jaeger [26], Ready [6], and Duley [27]]. One form of these solutions is demonstrated in Section 5.4.1 below.

5.4.1 Heating without Phase Change

In time of the duration of a laser pulse or irradiation, the electrons which absorb the photon will make many collisions, both among themselves and with lattice phonons. The energy absorbed by an electron will be distributed and passed on to the lattice. We can therefore regard the optical energy as being instantaneously turned into heat at the point at which the light was absorbed. The distribution occurs so rapidly on the time scale of Q-switched and normal laser pulses that we can regard a local equilibrium as established rapidly during the pulse. Therefore, the concept of temperature will be valid and we are allowed to apply the usual equations for heat flow such as Equation 5-78.

In case that absorption coefficient α is relatively small and we are interested in the temperature at depth z of the order skin depth $\delta = 1/\alpha$ the solution is give by Equation 5-79 below. Assumption is that the temporal pulse shape is flat; (i.e., $A(t) = A_0 = \text{constant}$ for $t \geq 0$) and A_0 being *Incident Intensity or beam Flux* with dimension (W/cm^2 or Jules/cm^2.sec). Under these conditions, in a material of thermal conductivity K and thermal diffusivity κ, the solution to the heat flow Equation 5-78 (The solution for this equation can be found using the Laplace Transform Method presented in Appendix E of this book) is given by.

$$T(z,t) = (2A_0 / K)(\kappa t)^{1/2} ierfc[z / 2(\kappa t)^{1/2}] - (A_0 / \alpha K)e^{-\alpha z}$$
$$+ (A_0 / 2\alpha K)\exp(\alpha^2 \kappa t - \alpha z)erfc[\alpha(\kappa t)^2 - z / 2(\kappa t)^{1/2}]$$
$$+ (A_0 / 2\alpha K)\exp(\alpha^2 \kappa t + \alpha z)erfc[\alpha(\kappa t)^2 + z / 2(\kappa t)^{1/2}]$$

Eq. 5-79

In this equation, *erfc* and *ierfc* denote the complimentary error function and its integral that are well define in Appendix E as well.

In case that the optical absorption coefficient of the absorbing material will be larger for a typical metals where α is of the order of 10^5 to 10^6 cm^{-1} then, the solution is proved in the following form;

$$T(z,t) = [2A_0(\kappa t)^{1/2} / K]ierfc[z / 2(\kappa t)^{1/2}]$$

Eq. 5-80

For the case that large absorption coefficient is under consideration and varying temporal pulse shape with an infinite uniform spatial is extended, we may obtain the solution by applying Duhamel's theorem to Equation 5-78 and present it as follow;

$$T(z,t) = \int_0^\infty \int_0^\infty \frac{A(\tau)}{A_0} \frac{\partial}{\partial t} \frac{\partial T'(z',t-\tau)}{\partial z'} dz' d\tau$$

Eq. 5-81

Where T' is the solution of the heat flow equation for the case of a square pulse of absorbed flux density A_0.

Typical results for a calculated temperature rise as function of depth, with time as a parameter, in a copper sample initially at 0 °C, are shown in Figure 5-28 for the indicated laser pulse shape.

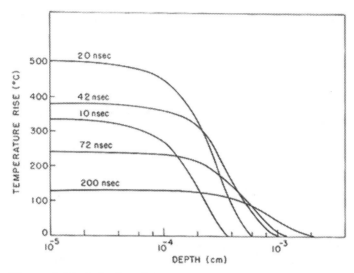

Figure 5-28: Calculated temperature rise as a function of depth, with time as a parameter, caused by absorption of a Q-switched laser pulse in copper [33]

Further temperature profiles for a laser pulse with a typical shape discussion can be found in Ready [6].

5.4.2 Heating with Phase Change

When the surface temperature reaches the melting temperature of T_m a melt region is formed adjacent to the surface. In the absence of perturbations this molten will propagate into the substrate at a speed υ_m that is give as following equation [16];

$$\upsilon_m = \frac{\varepsilon I_0}{\lambda_m + \rho C T_m} \exp\left(-\frac{\upsilon \Delta}{\kappa}\right) \qquad \text{Eq. 5-82}$$

The geometry of this equation is depicted in Figure 5-29 below and λ_m is the latent heat of fusion with MKS dimension of (J km³), C the heat capacity holding the dimension of (J g⁻¹ °C⁻¹), Δ the melt thickness, and υ_m is in cm s⁻¹.

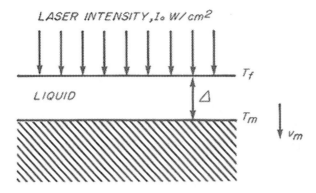

Figure 5-29: Geometry of melt region on the surface of semi-infinite region heated uniformly over its surface

W. W. Duley [16] is an excellent discussion about dealing with this aspect of laser irradiation target and heating with change of phase. If the liquid melt is not removed while the melting wave propagates into the solid, the temperature of the melt rises in response to the continuation of absorption at the melt-vapor interface. If the incident radiation is of sufficient intensity then the temperature may rise to the boiling point, T_v, or higher. This is accompanied by the onset of a vaporization wave with a speed when $T = T_v$.

$$\upsilon_v = \frac{\varepsilon I_0}{\lambda_v + \rho C T_v} \qquad \text{Eq. 5-83}$$

where λ_v is the latent heat of vaporization and all quantities have the same units as in the case for υ_m. As I_0 increases, υ_v increases accordingly until it approaches the speed of sound υ_s in the material, When $\upsilon \to \upsilon_s$, then the equation for υ is written as follows;

$$\upsilon = \upsilon_s \exp\left(\frac{-\lambda Z}{\rho N_A k_B T_v}\right) \qquad \text{Eq. 5-84}$$

Where
Z : is the atomic number of material.
N_A : is the Avogadro number.

k_B : is the Boltzmann constant.

Since υ is not dependent on I_0 in this regime, the speed of the vaporization rate saturates at high flux levels [16]. For most metals this saturation occurs when $\upsilon \sim 10^5 - 10^6$ cm$\cdot$s^{-1} and $I_0 \geq 10^8$ W$\cdot$cm^{-2} . Note that vaporization rates of this magnitude can be sustained only for short period of time i.e. pulsed laser beam excitation [16]. Further discussion can be found in Carslaw and Jaeger [26], Ready [6], and Duley [27]

5.4.3 Melt through of a Metal Plate

Increasing the energy deposition into the sample target, it causes that the surface temperature to reach a point where material transfer across the surface becomes significant (see Figure 25b). Experimental observations by various researches show that target erosion appears in the form of craters. In theoretical terms it means that the energy balance equation has to be supplemented by the balance equations for mass and momentum phenomena. The flow, the heating, and the expansion of evaporated target material are governed by the equation of hydrodynamic. Solving the couple partial differential equations of the conservation law provides insight into the factors determining crater depth, cloud extension, ion yield, relative sensitivity factors, and ion kinetic energy distributions. Calculated and measured values of these quantities show promising correlations for different lasers kind and different types of materials [106-108].

Depth of melting can be determined as a function of laser parameters (energy density and pulse duration in case of pulsed laser and engagement or dual time for continues laser beam).

Mathematical analysis and calculation are done by different researchers and few that are recommended for further study is by Carslaw, H. S. and J. C. Jaeger [26], A. V. Luikov [21] and M. N. Ozisik [109].

Problem of heat conduction involving melting or solidification are complicated because the interface between the solid and liquid phase moves as latent heat is absorbed or librated at the surface and under these type of regime all the boundary conditions associated with such heat flow problem more or less should be treated as *Lagrangian* rather than *Eulerian* types.

In fluid dynamics and finite-deformation plasticity the **Lagrangian** specification of the flow field is a way of looking at fluid motion where the observer follows an individual fluid parcel as it moves through space and time. Plotting the position of an individual parcel through time gives the path-line of the parcel. This can be visualized as sitting in a boat and drifting down a river.

The **Eulerian** specification of the flow field is a way of looking at fluid motion that focuses on specific locations in the space through which the fluid flows as time passes. This can be visualized by sitting on the bank of a river and watching the water pass the fixed location.

The Lagrangian and Eulerian specifications of the flow field are sometimes loosely denoted as the Lagrangian and Eulerian frame of reference. However, in general both the Lagrangian and Eulerian specification of the flow field can be applied in any observer's frame of reference, and in any coordinate system used within the chosen frame of reference.

In such condition the location of the moving interface is not known a priori, and the thermal properties of solid and liquid are different. Ozisik [109] is handing solution of heat transfer flow equation at the Moving Interface including problems involving Ablation. He also analyses cases that for a Semi-Infinite Region with *Variable Surface Heat Flux* as well as *Constant Surface Temperature* at x=0. His approaches also deal with problems involving temperature-dependent thermal properties of target surface materials as well as time dependency.

5.4.3 Vaporization of a Target

Vaporization is very easy to produce with lasers. Vaporization by a high power laser beam is a striking phenomenon. There is a shower of sparks characteristic of molten material expelled along with the vaporization. Induced plasma due to vaporization has its own implication on laser beam being absorbed by the surface of target. This situation is to some degree has been discussed in Section 5.2.4.3 under title of Absorption of Laser Radiation by Metals

In case utilizing laser as DEW (Directed Energy Weapons) vaporization of target is not much of concern. By the time the time this phase is met we are way beyond target assigned mission in order to have any impact. Hopefully incoming threat has lost all its momentum and path during melting phase. But for those readers that are interested in studying this aspect of laser irradiation target, lots of literature and references are provide by different researchers including few that have been mentioned during course of this chapter and we recommend them to those type of readers.

CHAPTER SIX: HIGH ENERGY LASER BEAM WEAPONS

In this section we talk about Beam Weapons and their applications as Directed Energy Weapons. With the origin of laser technology dated back to a prediction made in 1916 by Albert Einstein where he suggested that an atom or molecule could be stimulated to emit light of a particular wavelength when light of that wavelength reached it, a phenomenon called stimulated emission. It had already been recognized that atoms and molecules emit and absorb light spontaneously, without outside intervention. In 1928 R. Ladenburg showed that Einstein's prediction was right. At the time stimulated emission seemed to be a very rare occurrence that was inevitably overwhelmed by spontaneous emission. It would be many years before physicist learned how to create the right conditions to make practical use of stimulated emission in lasers, the physics of which we know today. 1970s saw a series of breakthroughs that rekindled military interest in high-energy laser weaponry. These developments were centered in two areas, carbon dioxide and chemical lasers, the technology of which are known today. The CO^2 laser's potential for high-power output was recognized soon after it was first demonstrated by Patel although technology of gas dynamic laser was invented in 1967. Similar work was reported at about same time by a Russian group which may have stimulated from American research works [57].

6.1 Introduction

Are laser and beam weapons purely defensive weapons that will protect us as if they were a colossal umbrella?. Or are they dangerous and destabilizing new elements in an accelerated arms race?. With the administration considering plans to spend billions of government and as result tax payers' dollars on the research and development of laser and particle beam weapons, the time has arrived to consider seriously their implication.

The effectiveness of a defensive weapons system is measured by its ability to deny the attacking system succession accomplishing its mission. It takes much more than a powerful beam to make an effective weapon system. The beam must be aimed and focused through a generally uncooperative atmosphere or over long distances. It must concentrate high power on a small area long enough to do fatal damage, a requirement that typically means the beam must follow the target along its path. Most of the targets envisioned for beam weapons are fast enough that automatic tracking and identification are needed. In the case of systems for defense against nuclear attack, there should be a way to verify "kill" from far away.

There are several ways to look at the problems in destroying targets with beam weapons, and the job is complicated by the very complexities involved. The problems are best defined for laser weapons, and for that reason in this section, we concentrated primarily on lasers as directed energy weapons than other beam weapons such as particle beams or electromagnetic weapons which involve quite different physics and they have their own sections and are presented from their own sources. In laser beam weapons there are several tasks involved and some of might have common ground in respect to the other beam weapons and they are as follows [58]:

1. Identify the target (which generally will not be sitting stationary by itself on a target range) and a vulnerable spot on it.
2. Track the target both until the weapon is ready to fire and while it is firing.
3. Point the weapon in the direction of vulnerable spot on the target
4. Focus the beam so it has the desired intensity (generally the highest possible) at the target. In case Laser beam as normal of incident as possible.
5. Compensate for atmospheric effects (i.e. Thermal Blooming) that otherwise would tend to make the beam wander off target or disperse the beam's energy.
6. Maintain focus of the beam on target during the attack.

7. Make sure that as much as possible of the energy in the beam is deposited on the target, not deflected away from it. Verify that the target has been disabled.

These are all a good wishing goals for a good DEW system, many of which are hard to achieve with the technology of lasers that we are aware of it today. In order for DEW system to achieve such goals military folks along with system developer's lump summing them under *target acquisition and fire control.* A process that process that provides detailed information about targets and locates them with sufficient accuracy to permit continued monitoring or target designation and engagement. This will includes target acquisition for both direct and indirect fire weapons as well as for information operations that can be part of *Artificial Intelligence* (AI) system of DEW platform where the system is hosted and it is coupled with firing control of weapon as part of its Command, Control, Communication and Intelligence (C^3I) overall system.

AI is nothing more than the science and engineering of making intelligent machines, especially intelligent computer programs. It is related to the similar task of using computers to understand human intelligence, but AI does not have to confine itself to methods that are biologically observable. Early target discrimination is very important task for an AI system coupled with DEW platform to shoot the right target since the total cost of ownership and operating cost for such DEW system in today's dollar is not cheap and shot from firing system of DEW should not be wasted on wrong target during its engagement. In this case, Surveillance and Target Acquisition is an important role assigned to AI units and/or DEW equipment. It involves watching an area to see what changes (surveillance) and then the acquisition of targets based on that information. So in an all beam control involves steering the beam and focusing it onto a target, in the process compensating for atmospheric distortions (i.e. Thermal Blooming) in case GBL (*Ground Based Laser*), ABL (*Airborne Based Laser*) where the beam goes through some layer of atmosphere. Off course any DEW in form of SBL (*Space Based Laser*) does not fall into this category unless it is engaging in initial phase of target boosting from its ground lunching platform.

The emerging body of *Reconnaissance, Surveillance,* and *Targeting Acquisition* (RSTA) resources brings a powerful contribution to battle-space domination. Diverse RSTA operations occur simultaneously within the battle space--keyed to support a range of users from decision makers to "shooters". In addition to collecting information that develops situational awareness, RSTA assets contribute too many battle space activities: Intelligence Preparation of the Battle space, Indications and Warning, situation development, force protection, Battle Damage Assessment, targeting and collection queuing. Given this multi-dimensional capability, it is no longer desirable to relegate RSTA assets solely to the realm of intelligence collection management. The command and control of finite, high value RSTA resources is ultimately the Commander's responsibility.

Surveillance and Target Acquisition is a military role assigned to units and/or their equipment. It involves watching an area to see what changes (surveillance) and then the acquisition of targets based on that information.

Fire control in conjunction with a RSTA system is the aiming and firing of the weapon, a task which includes identifying and tracking targets and providing information which the beam-control system can uses to point the beam (AI) and triggering shots from the weapon, spotting vulnerable points on the target, and making sure that target is crippled or destroyed.

Beam control is unique to directed-energy weapons, but fire control is a well-established military technology that is used in many kinds of weapon systems. Interestingly, the fire-control systems used with many modern missiles and "smart" bombs incorporate low-power lasers to mark potential targets with a laser spot that can be detected by a sensor in the bomb or missile. Low-power lasers can also measure the distance to a target to aid artillery fire-control system in pointing weapons. But although fire-control equipment is used widely in conventional weapons and battlefield of today, directed energy weapons would demand more than current equipment and existing technology that can deliver. Indeed, many observers believe that beam and fire control are much more difficult problems than building a big laser. The difficulties arise because of the very demanding missions envisioned for beam weapons [58].

One of deriving factor for designing a good fire control system for DEW is the mission requirements assigned to such weapon system. The different missions proposed for target engagement of beam weapons imposes distinct requirements for each of these missions and as result on beam and its fire control system as well as RSTA couple with DEW platform. In general the mission can be roughly divided into two categories that are known by early definition of Strategic Defense Intuitive (SDI) threats. The two groups are;

1. **Endoatmospheric** threats and target engagement within the atmosphere.
2. Exoatmospheric threats and target engagement within the outer space, where there is no air to deal with such as thermal blooming and beam divergence effects or encountering particles in the air.

Although some proposed systems fall into a hazy intermediate category because they require sending a laser beam up from the ground into space or look down and shoot down from space in boost phase of incoming threat such as continental ballistic missile.

Directed Energy Weapons intended for use in the atmosphere typically have tactical missions on or above the battlefield. That means that they must be able to function over ranges measured in miles or kilometers. For all practical purposes a beam traveling at or near the speed of light can reach such a target instantaneously. However, the atmosphere can bend, distort, or break up the beam, and sophisticated compensation techniques are needed to concentrate the beam energy onto the right point of the target. Many missions, such as defense of a battleship against an onslaught of cruise missiles, would probably require extremely fast response to engage and zap many targets before they could reach the designated target of their mission (i.e. ships). Speed might not be as critical in some other missions, such as destroying comparatively slow-moving helicopters, but in most cases the system would have to pinpoint enemy targets in a field that included friendly forces. Typical targets would require concentration of enough power at a critical point to physically disable them, but in some cases much lower powers would be sufficient to blind a sensor and thereby disable the target without any damage to friendly force [i.e. *Bidirectional Reflection Distribution Function* (BRDF)] effects, See Chapter Two on Laser Safety) [58].

Ground- and air-based anti-satellite (ASAT) weapons present rather different design constraints. Their range would be hundreds or perhaps thousands of kilometers or miles, depending on the orbit of the target satellite. Moderate powers reaching the satellite should be sufficient if the goal was to blind sensors or disable vulnerable sensing systems or electronics, probably the most effective way to kill current satellites. Seen from the ground, satellites would be slow-moving targets. Some compensation for atmospheric effects (i.e. Thermal Blooming) might be needed, but the task would be easier than if high powers had to be delivered to a small point on the target.

Considering that if we divide the target acquisition and engagement into three stages as follows;

1. Initial course or boost phase (endoatomospheric scenario).
2. Mid course phase for incoming ballistic missile (exoatmospheric scenario).
3. Final course (endoatomospheric scenario).

Then defending the country against a nuclear attack requires a different system and would have very different set of requirements. In an all-out attack hundreds of targets would simultaneously appear thousands of kilometers or miles away, and the weapon system would have to go after them as rapidly as possible at that distance. Except for X-ray lasers, any weapon system would have to destroy a series of many targets in succession. The degree of devastation caused by a nuclear bomb would make it important to kill as many targets as possible (ideally all of them) and to know which ones were not disabled so other weapons could shoot at them. If the lasers were in space, there would be no need to worry about atmospheric effects at all. If the lasers were on the ground, transmitting their beams to "battle mirrors" in space, compensation for atmospheric effects could be performed both by the optics on the laser and by the large mirrors in space, which together would form the beam-control system.

Additional differences come from the nature of the weapon itself. It takes different techniques to direct beams of visible light, X-rays, charged particles, uncharged particles, and microwaves. Fire-control techniques for such weapons would be more closely related to each other, although there would be some notable differences. Our focus in this chapter is based on the high energy laser weapon system. The different ways in which other types of beam would be controlled will be covered in Chapter Seven and Eight of this book, which describes the principal directed energy alternative to lasers in more details.

6.2 Directed Energy Weapons Engagements

Target engagements with Directed Energy Weapons (DEW) are very likely to be considerably different from conventional engagements with kinetic weapons. They will demand a much more detailed knowledge of the specific target engaged, and it will be harder to perform damage assessment during and after the engagement.

First, the target knowledge required for a DEW engagement will most likely be significantly different and much more detailed than that required for a kinetic engagement. The variation in effectiveness of DEWs against multiple target sets is likely to be quite large. It is not likely that weapon developers can produce devices that will be as universally effective as typical kinetic weapons. It will be important for DEWs to be employed against specific components in most targets, and those components will need to be identified prior to the engagements.

Second, our ability to perform damage assessment after a DEW engagement is likely to be significantly different than currently used methods. Physical damage may not be easily observable. Anomalous behavior may be the only clue to a directed energy weapon's effectiveness on a specific target. A simple example would be that of an air-to-air engagement. With a kinetic weapon, an attack on an aircraft will be recognized as successful if the aircraft bursts into flames, or it dives uncontrollably toward the earth. Both observations will indicate a successful kill. With a DEW system, the attack may never produce a physical change in the target that is observable, only the uncontrolled behavior of diving toward the earth would indicate a successful kill. Attacks on ballistic missiles in the boost phase may well produce easily observed explosions as well as anomalous behavior as a result of irradiation.

The details of how these two factors are handled will vary with the type of DEW, whether it is a laser device, a high power microwave device, or a particle beam device.

Consider first the laser weapon. Any laser system is likely to be fairly expensive, though it may have a low cost per target engagement. Therefore it will be desirable for the laser system to be able to engage targets outside of their kinetic kill range. It should be fairly easy for a laser to do this and it is one of the advantages of this type of DEW that it will have a long range of effectiveness by conventional standards.

Consider the following table for the potential spot sizes generated by laser weapons operating at 1.0 and 10.0 microns with diffraction limited beams.

Range	Spot Size radius at 1.0 m	Spot Size radius at 10.0 m
100 m	0.1 mm	1.0 mm
1 km	1.0 mm	10.0 mm
10 km	1.0 cm	10.0 cm
100 km	10.0 cm	100.0 cm
1000 km	1.0 m	10.0 m
10000 km	10.0 m	100.0 m

Of course optics will never be perfect and the atmosphere (Thermal Blooming Effects, etc in case of laser beam weapons) will perturb the beam significantly, but it would appear that engagements out to 1 to 10 km are possible.

At these ranges a typical radar return is probably not adequate to locate a target accurately enough to commit to firing. Therefore a tracking laser of some sort will be required to accurately locate the target and aim the high power laser. The tracking laser will also be required to image the target as the spot sizes at these ranges are small enough that a specific aim point on a target can be selected to maximize the beams effect. For this to be accomplished, a reasonably detailed knowledge of the target geometry must be available. Boresighting the tracking laser and the high power laser will require great precision. For actual laser weapon systems the acquisition, pointing and tracking challenges are at least as great as the beam generation challenges.

To get a feel for the issues involved, it is probably useful to discuss the actual successful target engagements accomplished by the Airborne Laser Laboratory (ALL) in 1983 [1]. The ALL used a 10.6 micron laser to engage two targets, an AIM-9B Sidewinder missile and a BQM-34A Aerobe drone in separate test series. The AIM-9B test series addressed the aircraft self-defense scenario against an air-to-air missile. The BQM-34A test series addressed the fleet defense scenario against a cruise missile.

The first two AIM-9B engagements started at approximately 3 kilometers range and had beam on times of 4.8 seconds and 3.8 seconds. The beam spot sizes were estimated to be less than 10 cm in radius. In both engagements the tracking laser acquired the missile and aimed the high power laser so as to hit the missile. The returned glint off the body of the missile allowed the beam to be walked forward to the nose section containing the tracker head of the missile guidance system. The beam then dwelled on the tracker head resulting in burn through of the nose dome. The actual burn through took less than a second. When the tracker head failed, the missile veered off course and crashed into the ground. The entire engagement was observed on the tracking screen in the ALL fire control center. The engagement was computer controlled as the response times and tracking maneuvers exceeded any human capability. Kill confirmation occurred when the missile veered off course. However, the AIM-9B was instrumented in such a fashion that burn through of the nose dome and failure of its tracking mechanism were transmitted to an instrumentation aircraft following the ALL to confirm the effects of the laser irradiation. Still there were no visible indications of missile kill comparable to a kinetic kill and subsequent explosion of the missile.

So for the third engagement, a small spotting charge was rigged to a break-wire in the nose of the missile. It would explode if the wire burned through due to laser irradiation. This time the scanning, movement of the beam to the nose of the missile, and burn through of the dome took 2.4 seconds and the missile exploded with a puff of white smoke. This provided an additional confirmation of missile kill suitable for publication in the press but of no consequence for system validation. The fourth and fifth engagements required 3.6 seconds and 3.1 seconds respectively to observe the AIM-9B's fatal veering off course and crash.

The engagements were successful because the computer on the ALL had enough information on the return from the AIM-9B's to know the most likely strongest glint return from the Sidewinders body and the offset from this point to the nose dome of the missile. The engagements could also be terminated with a reasonable beam on time because the veering off course was a clear indication that the missiles guidance system had failed. All tracking was accomplished by computer and no visible laser beam was ever observed. The engagements were significantly different than conventional engagements, but just as successful in terms of destroying the target as kinetic kills would have been.

For the engagements of the BQM-34A, an aim point just forward of the wing root was chosen to install a stainless steel tank to simulate a fuel tank on a cruise missile. The glint from the nose of the drone was used as the reference point for tracking and the aim point was offset from that reference. On the first ALL engagement, the laser hit the tank and dwelled long enough to detonate some fuel within the tank but the explosion was not strong enough to destroy the drone. The drone ran out of fuel and crashed into the ocean. In the second ALL engagement the beam control allowed the beam to shift off the fuel tank and drift down to the wing root. This drone was recovered from the ocean and had obvious damage to the wing root. But the damage was not enough to cause the drone to veer out of control and destroy itself. (One could draw an analogy to the vehicle being hit by small arms fire and not being destroyed.) On the third ALL engagement, the aim point was shifted from the fuel tank to the area of the fuselage containing the flight control system, slightly behind the wing. At a range of 1.8 kilometers, the ALL placed the beam on the surface above the flight control box. Almost immediately the flight control signals being telemetered to the tracking aircraft were disrupted. The drone rocked rapidly back and forth, and then it took a hard 90-degree roll to the right and dove into the water. Once again kill confirmation was obtained by anomalous behavior of the target.

Based on these two sets of kills by an engineered high power laser system, future systems will require;

1. Detailed target knowledge, if the target is larger than a few tens of centimeters,
2. Computer controlled tracking utilizing multiple lasers and recognition of laser return signals from a spatially diverse target,
3. Kill confirmation by anomalous target behavior.

These requirements appear achievable, but they are somewhat different than kinetic system requirements.

Not all laser engagements are anticipated to occur against aircraft or missile targets. Engagement of ballistic targets is not likely to give indications that would be useful for kill confirmation. If a kill cannot be easily confirmed, then it becomes difficult to determine when to terminate dwell time on the target. Engagement of fixed targets on the ground suffers from a similar lack of kill confirmation mechanism.

High Power Microwave (HPM) Weapons or Electromagnetic Pulse Weapons suffer from the same difficulties to some extent. Aiming an HPM weapon is much easier than a laser because the radiation is far less collimated and in many cases may almost be isotropic. This however presents a major limitation to employment, as the device must get much closer to its target before emitting. It also presents problems of "suicide" or "fratricide" to the weapons delivery system or systems.

When it comes to target knowledge for an HPM system, there are classically two types of effects or couplings into the target. In Front Door coupling, the attacking system uses an antenna that is tuned for a specific frequency or range of frequencies to overpower the receiver of the target. This is usually a solvable problem and the power on target can be estimated. However, Front Door coupling is only useful against systems having a receiving antenna that is accessible and necessary for its continued operation. This applies primarily to communication systems.

In Back Door coupling, the attacking system attempts to couple into the target through some method that is out of band and/or does not come in through an antenna. This is a much more difficult problem and pretty much not capable of being solved by analysis. Simply put, an attacker must have available samples of systems that will be attacked and be able to test for the effects desired prior to carrying out an attack. There are many ways that an electromagnetic signal can couple into a circuit inside a porous body, but accurate analysis is extremely difficult to perform from first principles. Shielding against inadvertent entry of electromagnetic signals can be accomplished and systems can be hardened to the effects of HPM, but maintaining such shielding is difficult and probably not very cost effective. To validate that an attacker has a high probability of success against a particular system, many tests are required.

Finally, electromagnetic kills or upsets are very difficult to verify. If a communication or radar system is attacked, its failure to operate can be observed electromagnetically. Beyond that, confirmation of electromagnetic damage effects is very difficult. It is very likely that the success of such devices will have to be estimated based on lots of tests and certain risks accepted. Future research may develop active interrogation schemes that can assess the effects of an HPM attack but there are few such interrogation schemes currently available.

Particle Beams are the least developed of DEWs and no known systems test to determine operating parameters for a successful kill have been determined. It is highly likely that a similar level of target information will be required for the employment of particle beams as is required for high power lasers. Since particle beams do penetrate their targets, the interior designs may be necessary to identify aiming points and kill mechanisms. The effects of particle beams are better defined on a geometric configuration of materials than electromagnetic waves and many effects can be calculated from first principles if the materials and geometries are known.

Both electron beams and proton beams will produce a target return of electromagnetic radiation in the form of x-rays and gamma rays. Protons will also produce a return of neutrons. The intensity of these returns will vary with the target that is intercepted. Relative or spectral intensities may also provide some information on target materials. Whether these will be adequate for steering an invisible beam in space remains to be seen. Certainly lasers can be used to assist in the pointing and tracking problem.

A successful kill of a ballistic warhead by a particle beam will be difficult to identify unless enough energy is deposited to cause the target to self-explode. This may require a prohibitive amount of energy in the beam. If the goal is an electronic kill, any method developed for determining electronic kills for HPM weapons will be useful. Kills of aircraft or maneuvering systems in the atmosphere will be identified by the same anomalous behavior as has been identified for high power lasers.

6.2.1 Acquisition, Tracking, Pointing, and Fire Control

Directing the laser energy from the optics to the target requires a highly accurate acquisition, tracking, pointing, and fire control system. A laser weapon system, either space-based or ground-based, needs to locate the missile (acquisition), track its motion (tracking), determine the laser aim point and maintain the laser energy on the target (pointing), and finally swing to a new target (fire control). The accuracy for each component is stringent because of the great distances between the weapon and the targets.

The United States put considerable time and resources into both space and ground programs in acquisition, tracking, and pointing technologies. Space experiments are critical to any high-energy laser weapon system because they demonstrate the high-risk technologies and do so in the actual operational environment. However, the space programs in the 1980s suffered from high costs and the space shuttle Challenger accident.69 While many programs were terminated or had their scope reduced due to insufficient funding, two highly successful space experiments were completed in 1990. The Relay Mirror Experiment demonstrated the ability to engage in high accuracy pointing, laser beam stability, and long duration beam relays. This is a critical technology for any weapon architecture that requires relay mirrors in space. Another successful test was the Low Power Atmospheric Compensation Experiment that was conducted by the MIT Lincoln Laboratory, which demonstrated the feasibility of technologies that are designed to compensate for the atmospheric turbulence that distorts laser beams.

A number of the space experiments were canceled or redesigned as ground experiments. Ground experiments can be successfully conducted as long as the tests are not limited or degraded by the earth's gravity. Two ground experiments demonstrated the key technologies that are essential for the space weapon platform to maintain the laser beam on the target despite the large vibrations induced by the mechanical pumps of a high-energy chemical laser.70 The Rapid Retargeting/Precision Pointing simulator was designed to replicate the dynamic environment of large space structures. Using this technology, which is especially critical for a space-based laser, scientists tested methods to stabilize the laser beam, maintain its accuracy, and rapidly retarget. Within the constraints of a ground environment, the techniques developed should be applicable to space systems.

Another successful experiment was the Space Active Vibration Isolation project, which established a pointing stability of less than

100 nanoradians. This equates to four inches from a distance of 1000 kilometers. The Space Integrated Controls Experiment followed that program and further improved the pointing stability.72 To understand the technology necessary to control large structures, such as space mirrors, the Structure and Pointing Integrated Control

Experiment (SPICE) was developed to demonstrate the value of active, adaptive control of large optical structures. These tests, experiments, and demonstrations represent the current state-of-the-art in laser technology, which leads to the question of how to fit these technologies into architecture and how much further to push the technology.

6.3 Wavelength Effects

The wavelength of a laser sets some fundamental constraints on the optics that can be used with the laser. By far the most important is the Fraunhofer diffraction limit, which determines how small a spot the beam can form. In this case the spot size is measured as an angle (as viewed from the laser) that is proportional to the ratio of wavelength to the diameter of the focusing optics. The theoretical formula for the ideal case is [59];

$$\text{Spot Size} = 1.22 \text{ x } \frac{\text{wavelength}}{\text{optics diameter}} \qquad \text{Eq. 6-1}$$

This formula actually defines the first point at which the intensity falls to zero. There are a series of bright rings surrounding the control spot, falling off in intensity as the distance from the central spot increase. The formula is valid for a circular output mirror and a perfectly uniform laser beam, which does not exist in practice, but which does give a rough approximation for real lasers. It actually gives the sine of the angular spot size for small spots such as would be produced by a laser beam, which is virtually identical to the angle in radians. The formula is a fundamental one and comes from Donald H. Menzel [59].

This formula gives spot size in radians, an angular measure equal to the diameter of the spot divided by the distance to it. (One radian equals 57.3°.) Laser physicists usually talk in terms of spot size (sometimes sloppily called beam divergence, although in this sense it isn't exactly that) in radians. However, the formula can be altered to give spot size in meters:

$$\text{Spot Diameter (meter)} = \frac{1.22 \text{ x wavelength x target distance}}{\text{optics diameter}} \qquad \text{Eq. 6-2}$$

Note that in making calculations with either formula, it is essential that everything be measured in the same units. Thus, if wavelength starts in micrometers, target distance in kilometers, and optics diameter in meters, they would all have to be converted to meters before making the calculation. Spot diameter is important because it indicates onto how small an area on the target the laser's output can be concentrated. Dividing the area of the focal spot on the target into the laser power or energy gives the power or energy density at the target. Measurements of laser power or energy density on the target are useful in making rough approximations of the threshold for causing damage, but the actual mechanisms involved are quite complex and far beyond the scope of this book.

Another important factor is the beam "wander" or "jitter." That is, how precisely can the laser beam be kept on one spot on the target while it is depositing its lethal dose of energy? If the beam wanders all over the place, it will not stay at any one point long enough to do any damage. The usual assumption is that beam wander will have to be somewhat smaller than the spot size [58].

One suggestion to correct such wandering or jitter is coming from P. Sprangle, A. Ting, J. Peñano, R. Fischer of Plasma Physics Division of Naval Research Laboratory (NRL), and B. Hafizi of Icarus Research, Inc in their paper "High-Power Fiber Lasers for Directed-Energy Application". Their recommendation for compensating for Wandering or jittering of laser beam is approaches known as "Beam Wander and Tip-Tilt Compensation".

Introducing tip-tilt correction into the individual steering mirrors can reduce the overall laser spot size on target. Tip-tilt correction redirects the centroid's of the individual laser beams to cancel the effects of wander due to turbulence. This is accomplished by monitoring the intensity on target and redirecting the steering mirrors to minimize the spot size. Laser beam wander is a function of the scale size of the turbulence fluctuations. Turbulent eddies that are large compared to the laser beam diameter cause the laser beam centroid to be deflected and to wander in time due to transverse air flow. Eddies that are much smaller than the beam diameter causes spreading about the beam centroid and cannot be reduced by the use of tip-tilt compensation. The observed long time averaged laser spot size is a combination of beam wander and spreading about the centroid. In weak turbulence, the beam centroid wander represents a significant contribution to the laser beam radius. As the turbulence level increases, or for long propagation ranges, the beam wander contribution to the laser spot size becomes less important. In very strong turbulence, the laser beam breaks up into multiple beams making tip-tilt compensation ineffective. If the individual laser beams are separated by less than r_0 at the source, the wander of the centroids on the target will be correlated. In this case, it would be possible for beams to share a common tip-tilt correcting aperture, thus reducing the size and complexity of the system.

With this information in mind, you can calculate some very general requirements on a laser weapon system if you know the lethal power or energy density and the maximum range. For example, suppose that in the case of missile defense, it seems desirable to concentrate a laser power of about 5 million watts onto a spot about 1 m (about a yard) in diameter (a little over 6 million watts per square meter). If the target is 5000 km (3000 miles) away, in angular terms, the focal spot is 0.2 millionths of a radian (or 0.2 μrad in standard scientific terminology). That figure can be inserted into the equation that relates laser wavelength and optics diameter to spot size. Suppose, for example, the weapon system uses a space-based hydrogen fluoride chemical laser with a nominal wavelength of 2.8 μm (micrometers), or 0.0000028 m. Simple division shows that the output mirror must be 17 m (56 ft) in diameter. If that doesn't sound impressive enough, you should realize that the largest telescope in the United States, the 200-in. giant at Mount Palomar Observatory, has a main mirror only 5 m in diameter. The largest telescope mirror in the world is a 6-m one in the Soviet Union, which unofficial sources report hasn't been working very well. The largest mirror yet designed and built for use in space is the 2.4-m (8 ft) mirror for NASA's space telescope [60].

Use of a laser with higher power or shorter wavelength would allow use of a smaller mirror. If a 1.3-µm chemical oxygen iodine laser could be substituted for the hydrogen fluoride laser in the previous example, a mirror 8 m (26 ft) in diameter could produce a 1-m spot 5000 km (3000 miles) away. Increasing the laser's output power does not produce such dramatic reductions in required mirror size because damage depends on power density multiplied by illumination time, which increases faster with decreasing spot size than with increasing power. Thus, a 10-million-watt beam could be spread over twice as much *area* as a 5-million-watt beam, but as the area doubled, the spot diameter would increase only by the square root of two, a factor of 1.4. Thus, a 10-million-watt hydrogen fluoride laser beam could be focused onto a spot 1.4 m in diameter at a distance of 5000 km (3000 miles) with a mirror only 12 m (40 ft) in diameter, yielding the same power density as would be obtained when focusing a 5-million-watt laser over the same distance with a 17-m (56-ft) mirror onto a 1-m spot.

From a practical standpoint, shrinking the mirror diameter from 17 m (56 ft) to 12 m (40 ft) would be important. On the ground or in space, the weight of a massive mirror would present a problem. If weight was simply proportional to area (which in turn depends on the square of the diameter), reducing the diameter from 17 to 12 m would cut the weight in half. In practice, an even greater weight reduction would be possible, because the smaller-diameter mirror could be thinner and still have enough mechanical strength to maintain its shape [58].

These simple calculations demonstrate why the Pentagon is so interested in developing short-wavelength lasers. The prime allure of the ultraviolet is a wavelength about one-tenth that of the hydrogen fluoride laser, making it possible to use a mirror much smaller than needed for an iodine laser, although other considerations described below might weigh against picking the smallest possible mirror diameter [58].

It may be possible to put a laser weapon for use against missiles or satellites on the ground, but if the targets were in space, the focusing mirror would have to be there, too. Putting a large mirror into orbit is not going to be an easy job. Current proposals for space-based lasers envision either a 5million-watt chemical laser with a 4-m (13-ft) mirror or a more potent weapon using a 10-million-watt laser and a 10-m (33-ft) mirror. Mirror sizes would have to be the same to deliver the same power to the same size spot, with the same laser wavelength, even if the laser was on the ground. Military contractors seem to think the task is achievable. The Coming Glass Works, Perkin-Elmer Corp., Itek Corp., and Eastman Kodak have proposed a plan for a 4-m (13-ft) glass mirror [61]. The United Technologies Research Center has offered to build a 10-m (33-ft) lightweight mirror, using a graphite fiber reinforced glass matrix for the body of the mirror and vaporized silicon for the reflective coating.

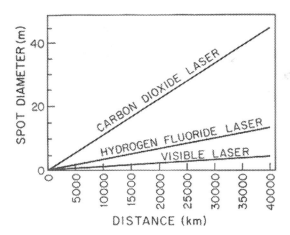

Figure 6-1: Laser spot size that would be pr at various ranges and wavelengths by a 30 m output mirror. The graphs shows spot diameter for the 10.6-μm carbon dioxide laser, the 2.8-μm hydrogen fluoride laser, and a hypothetical 0.5-μm visible laser, assuming that the figure of the mirror is accurate to within 1/50th of the laser wavelength. (Drawing by Arthur Giordani based on calculations by Wayne S. Jones, Lockheed Missiles and Space Co.)

The mirrors best able to stand up to high laser powers are made of solid metal typically honeycombed with holes through which coolant flows. The Department of Defense has spent millions of dollars developing ways to produce mirrors that absorb less than 1% of the incident laser light, and which I can efficiently conduct away what heat they do absorb. Much of the effort has gone to development of machines that use diamond-edged tools to cut mirror surfaces directly into metal blocks, vastly simplifying the traditional time-consuming process of making optics. Diamond turning, as the technique is called, also makes it possible to produce mirrors with surface shapes impossible to obtain by conventional grinding and polishing methods [58].

For more details on this subject please refer to the book by Jeff Hecht [58] "Beam Weapons, The Next Arms Race".

6.4 The Atmospheric Propagation Problem

Air looks much more transparent than it really is. In past decade researcher are working on a communication systems that relies on laser beams going through the air. New technologies in direct line of sight wireless communication systems are being developed at the University of Maryland. These are hybrid systems that use both free-space optical (FSO) communication links and radio frequency links (RF) [62]. In order to optimize these systems an understanding of the channel medium (the atmosphere) is requisite. The concern of the current research is the characterization of the effects of atmospheric turbulence on the propagation of electromagnetic waves at optical wavelengths.

One effect of atmospheric turbulence is that it scatters light. The current method of research into the characteristics of atmospheric turbulence is the analysis of this scattered light. It is this resultant scattered light that brings up two essential questions. What does the turbulence do to the light i.e. how does it scatter the light? What does the scattered light tell us about the atmospheric turbulence?

The answer to the first question is important for engineering applications like a FSO communication systems. Specifically our current research will look to optimize the receiver or aperture size for a FSO communication system. The answer to the second is important to the development of formal mathematical theories on the behavior or physics of the atmosphere.

The effects of atmospheric turbulence are easily seen by the propagation of the laser through the atmosphere. As can be seen on Figure 6-2 the turbulence induces intensity random fluctuations in the beam known as scintillation. This is an effect of the many random changes in the index of refraction along the path of beam propagation due to turbulence.

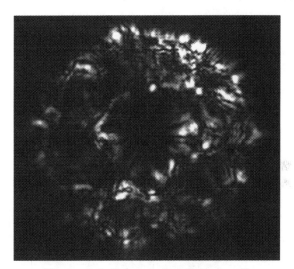

Figure 6-2: Screen shot of image [62]

Their current research will aid the development of these physical theories where they assumed that the atmosphere can be described as a moving fluid of air. As such it can be modeled by the Navier-Stokes equations (shown below) that describe the behavior of moving fluids [62].

$$\frac{\partial v}{\partial t}+(v\cdot\nabla)v=-\frac{1}{\rho}\nabla p+\upsilon\nabla^2 v \quad \nabla\cdot v=0$$

Navier – Stokes Equations (NSE)   Eq. 6-3

(Assuming incompressibility)

ρ is density, $\upsilon=\frac{\eta}{\rho}$ is called the kinematic viscosity. η is called the dynamic viscosity

These equations show that atmosphere can move as either as turbulent flow or laminar (non-turbulent) flow. Turbulence occurs when a fluid flow exceeds a critical Reynolds's number $R \equiv lu/\upsilon$ with l being a characteristic linear dimension, (traveled length of fluid, or hydraulic diameter when dealing with river systems) (m) while u is is the mean fluid velocity (SI units: m/s) which causes the non-linear term ($(v\cdot\nabla)v$) of the NSE to dominate which is characterized by the flow's chaotic behavior (as shown below).

$$\frac{(v\cdot\nabla)v}{\frac{\eta}{\rho}\nabla^2 v} \sim \frac{u^2/l}{\eta u/\rho l^2}=\frac{ul}{\upsilon}=R \qquad \text{Eq. 6-4}$$

The non-linear nature of the equations makes them difficult to with since there are no known solutions or families of solutions to the Navier-Stokes Equations. This forces one to look at other mathematical observations to take something meaningful from these equations. In low turbulence (when the non-linear term, $(v\cdot\nabla)v$, is much less than $\upsilon\nabla^2 v$) significant symmetries arise. These symmetries are space and time translation, Galilean transformation, parity, rotation, and scaling. In extreme turbulence, Kolmogorov predicted and proved that the symmetries of the Navier-Stokes Equations that exist in non-turbulent systems re-appear. The extreme complications of the Navier-Stokes equations, arising from the nonlinearity, force us to use statistical methods to characterize the behavior of a turbulent fluid as such the atmosphere. Fortunately, the symmetries give us insight into the statistics.

High energy lasers (HELs) have a number of directed energy (DE) applications [63] requiring high-intensity beams to be propagated long distances under a wide range of atmospheric conditions. The optimum wavelength for efficient HEL propagation depends on the atmospheric conditions and a number of inter-related physical processes which include: thermal blooming due to aerosol and molecular absorption [64], turbulence [65], aerosol and molecular scattering [66], thermal scattering due to heated aerosols, and aerosol heating and vaporization [67-71]. The relative importance of these processes depends on the parameters of the atmospheric environment which can vary significantly depending on location and time. The main objective that was discussed by Phillip Sprangle, Joseph Peñano and Bahman Hafizi [63] is about the optimum laser wavelength and power for efficient propagation in maritime, desert, rural and urban atmospheric environments. The theoretical/ numerical model used in this study includes the effects of aerosol and molecular scattering, aerosol heating and vaporization, thermal blooming due to aerosol and molecular absorption, atmospheric turbulence, and beam quality. These processes are modeled in a fully three-dimensional and time-dependent manner. It is found that aerosols, which consist of water, sea salt, organic matter, dust, soot, biomass smoke, urban pollutants, etc., are particularly important because they result in laser scattering, absorption and enhanced thermal blooming. In the water vapor transmission windows, the total absorption coefficient driving thermal blooming can be caused mainly by aerosols and not water vapor. In certain maritime environments the deleterious effects of aerosols can be reduced by vaporization. Aerosols which cannot be vaporized, such as those consisting of dust, soot, etc., can significantly increase thermal blooming. We show that moderate values of the laser beam quality parameter have little effect on the propagation efficiency. The laser power, averaged over dwell time, delivered to a distant target as a function of transmitted power is obtained for a number of wavelengths and atmospheric environments. The optimum wavelength and power are found for each atmospheric environment.

Atmospheric environments contain various types and concentrations of aerosols which can, for HEL beams, enhance thermal blooming and significantly affect the propagation efficiency. In general, aerosols consist of hygroscopic and non-hygroscopic particles of various sizes and chemical compositions. Hygroscopic aerosols are water-soluble and vary in size depending on the relative humidity [71]. Oceanic aerosols consist of sea salt, water, and organic material. Non-hygroscopic aerosols are composed of dust, soot, biomass smoke, and other carbon-based compounds. These aerosols typically have much larger absorption coefficients than water-based aerosols. While they are normally present in continental, rural and urban environments, dust aerosols can also be present in maritime environments hundreds of miles from shore [72].

Aerosols can absorb laser energy and, in the case of hygroscopic aerosols, the absorbed energy goes into both heating and vaporizing the aerosol. Heated aerosols conductively heat the surrounding air, resulting in an increase in thermal blooming of the HEL beam [73]. However, since aerosol scattering and absorption coefficients are strongly dependent on the aerosol radius, vaporizing the aerosol can improve the propagation efficiency. Non-hygroscopic aerosols (dust, soot, etc.), however, have large scattering and absorption coefficients and will not vaporize at the intensity levels anticipated in DE applications. These aerosols continually heat the surrounding air leading to significant thermal blooming. Water vapor absorption bands and those of carbon dioxide determine the atmospheric transmission windows in the infrared. Under a range of atmospheric conditions and laser wavelengths, aerosol absorption can exceed water vapor absorption and thus can be the dominant process for thermal blooming. For example, in a maritime environment at an operating wavelength of $\lambda = 1.045 \mu m$, the water vapor absorption coefficient is $\sim 3 \times 10^{-5} \text{km}^{-1}$ while the aerosol absorption [74] coefficient is often greater than 10^{-3}km^{-1}. In other water vapor transmission windows, i.e., 1.625 μm and 2.141 μm, the water vapor and aerosol absorption coefficients can be comparable. In addition to enhancing thermal blooming, aerosols can also significantly contribute to the total laser scattering coefficient [63].

Longer wavelength, such as microwaves, can penetrate through dust and precipitation because the particles in the air are much smaller than the wavelength. In some cases longer infrared wavelengths are transmitted much better than visible light because of the difference in their wavelengths [75].

Under typical atmospheric conditions the absorption of 10.6 μ radiation by various molecular species results in an absorption coefficient of approximately 1.5×10^{-6} cm^{-1} and leads to various nonlinear propagation problems [76-77]. For some lasers (e.g., the DF laser operating at 3.8 μ) the molecular absorption in the air is small (as low as 10^{-8} cm^{-1}) and the heating due to aerosols can dominate the heating of the air path. For a typical atmosphere this aerosol absorption corresponds to an attenuation coefficient of approximately 10^{-7} cm^{-1}, but could be higher if the aerosol concentration was unusually high [78]. In general, the nonlinear heating effects are more important than the linear power losses.

The natural heating effects of high energy laser beams could help to overcome some weather related transmission problems. A high energy carbon dioxide laser, for example, can bore its way through fog by heating the tiny water droplets that obscure vision enough to make them evaporate. Much the same could be done with clouds. Heavy rain would be harder, particularly in the realistic situation where the beam is being scanned quickly through rapidly falling rain. If the beam scans across the drops too quickly, it may only partly evaporate them before moving on to illuminate other drops.

Foul weather, dust, and smoke can do more than just block the beam from the high energy lasers. They can make it impossible to find targets visually or with infrared optical system, making it necessary to rely on microwave radar that can penetrate the obscuration. However, even if the high power beam could burn its way through, the limited resolution of microwave radars may not be able to pinpoint the target accurately enough for the laser beam to hit a vulnerable spot.

6.4.1 Laser Light Scattering and Intensity

In general, a laser beam is attenuated as it propagates through the atmosphere. In addition, the laser beam is often broadened, defocused, and may even be deflected (i.e. scattered) from its initial propagation direction. These atmospheric effects have far reaching consequences for the use of laser in optical communication, weaponry, target designation, ranging, remote sensing, and other applications that require transmission of laser beams through the atmosphere. In a tactical battlefield a new spectral light transport model for sand and other obstacles in the air should be studied and be mathematically analyzed and experimentally put it into test [84]. The model should employ a novel approach to simulated light interaction with particulate materials which yields both the spectral and spatial BRDF (Bidirectional Reflectance Distribution Function) responses of sand or other obstacles in the environment of battlefield which includes natural and man made media such as rain or fog and gun smoke. Furthermore, the parameters specifying the model should be based on the physical and mineralogical properties of sand and other obstacles of the concern. The model should be evaluated quantitatively, through comparisons with measured data. Good spectral reconstructions if any should be achieved for the reflectances of several real sand samples. Its potential applications include, but are not limited to, applied optics, remote sensing and image synthesis as well as weaponry.

Light scattering has provided an important method for characterizing macromolecules for at least three decades. However, the replacement of conventional light sources by lasers in recent years has qualitatively changed the field and has sparked renewed interest. Through the intense, coherent laser light and efficient spectrum analyzers and autocorrelators, experiments in the frequency and time domains can now be used to study molecular motion and other dynamical process. Classical light scattering studies are concerned with the measurement of the intensity of scattered light as a function of the scattering angle. In addition to this kind of study, laser light sources now permit spectral information (i.e. BRDF) to be obtained from the scattered light [85]. The latter type of experiment is often called Quasi-elastic Light Scattering (QLS), and the various forms of the experiment are known as Light Beating Spectroscopy (LBS), Intensity Fluctuation Spectroscopy (IFS), and Photon Correlation Spectroscopy (PCS). Related experiments in Laser Doppler Velocimetry (LDV) now permit very low rates of uniform motion to be measured. A special case of LDV is electrophoretic light scattering (ELS) where motilities are determined [85].

The attenuation and amount of beam alteration depend on the wavelength, output power, makeup of the atmosphere, and the day-to-day atmospheric conditions. When the output power is low, the effects are linear in behavior. That is, doubling the initial beam intensity results in a doubled intensity at every point along the beam's path. Absorption, scattering, and atmospheric turbulence are examples of linear effects. On the other hand, when the power is sufficiently high, new effects are observed that are characterized by nonlinear relationships. Some important nonlinear effects are thermal blooming, kinetic cooling, beam trapping, two-photon absorption, bleaching, and atmospheric breakdown, which, incidentally, fix an upper limit on the intensity that can be transmitted. In both cases the effects can be significant and may severely limit the usefulness of the beam. Many studies have been undertaken to define the different linear and nonlinear phenomena that can occur [83].

One parameter that is useful in determining the effectiveness of a Gaussian laser beam is the beam irradiance at the target. For a beam with output power P_0 and cross-sectional area A at the target, the peak irradiance I_p at the target is [83];

$$I_p = \frac{P_0 \tau}{A}$$

Eq. 6-5

where τ is the atmospheric transmittance. A major system design goal is to maximize I_p by minimizing the beam cross-sectional area A and maximizing the product $P_0 \tau$.

The propagation of a laser beam in a vacuum is governed by the diffraction theory, which tells us that no matter how parallel the beam may be initially, it will diverge and spaced as the beam propagates away from its source. Most laser beams have a Gaussian intensity profile in the transverse front. The beam radius w is defined as that transverse distance from the center of the beam (i.e., the beam axis) to the point where the intensity has fallen to 1/e² (0.13533) of its on-axis value (See Figure 6-3).

The two parameters of most interest in describing the propagation characteristic of a Gaussian beam are the beam radius $w(z)$ also known as spot size at any distance z from the beam waist and the radius of curvature of the phase front $R(z)$. These two parameters are given by;

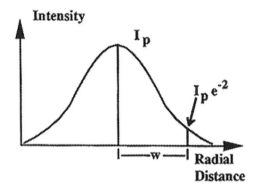

Figure 6-3: Intensity profile of Gaussian beam

$$w(z) = w_0\sqrt{1+\left(\frac{\lambda z}{\pi w_0^2}\right)^2} \qquad \text{Eq. 6-6}$$

and

$$R(z) = z\left[1+\left(\frac{\pi w_0^2}{\lambda z}\right)^2\right] \qquad \text{Eq. 6-7}$$

where w_0 is the radius at the beam waist (that part of the beam where the beam has its smallest diameter) and λ is the wavelength [83].

Like other beams, Gaussian beams diverge as they propagate through space. However, the intensity distribution remains Gaussian in every beam cross section. Only the width of the Gaussian profile increases as the beam propagates. At the beam waist ($z = 0$ and $R = \infty$), the phase front is a plane. For most practical lasers, the beam waist is located a short distance from the output mirror on the outside of the resonator (See Figure 6-4). As the Gaussian beam propagates away from the location of its waist, the beam's radius (or spot size) at first remains nearly constant but then begins to diverge linearly with distance at large distances from the waist. The smaller the spot size at the waist, the faster the beam diverges and the smaller the distance over which it stays collimated with a near constant diameter and a near planar wave front. The angle θ in Figure 6-4 is the beam divergence angle. It is given by

$$\theta = \frac{w(z)}{z} = \frac{\lambda}{\pi w_0} \text{ for } z \gg R_z = \frac{\pi w_0^2}{\lambda} \qquad \text{Eq. 6-8}$$

where R_z is the Rayleigh range. Equation 6-8 shows that the beam's cross-sectional area at distance z from the waist is

$$A = \pi \left[w(z) \right]^2 = \frac{\lambda^2 z^2}{\pi w_0^2} \qquad \text{Eq. 6-9}$$

From this we see that the beam's cross-sectional area can be reduced by selecting a shorter wavelength and by increasing the beam radius at the waist [83].

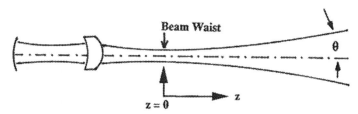

Figure 6-4: Gaussian beam with external waist at z=0

It is interesting to look at a few examples of the intensity of laser light. In a typical ruby laser, the concentration [86] of Cr^{+++} ions is about 2 X 10^{19} cm^{-3}, and population inversions are of the order of 3 X 10^{16} cm^{-3}. Crudely speaking, we can think of creating 3 X 10^{16} quanta/cm^3 in the lasing medium. Since we have arranged the laser so that the output is in a single direction, and since photons move with the speed of light, we obtain 3 X 10^{16} X 3 X 10^{10} = 9 X 10^{26} quanta/cm² sec from the laser. For ruby, the lasing wavelength is 6943 A°, and since the energy of each quanta is hv, one can readily calculate that the output is about 2.5 X 10^8 W/cm².

Let us compare this to the power that a hot body say the sun, emits at the same wavelength with a similar bandwidth. This can be calculated by the use of Planck's radiation law knowing that $\Delta E = hv$, where h is Plank's constant and v is radiation frequency [28]. This illustrated in Figure 6-5 and is the case for any light source, whether laser, flame, incandescent body, etc.

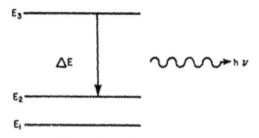

Figure 6-5: Energy levels

$$U_\omega = \frac{\hbar\omega^3}{\pi^2 c^3} \frac{1}{e^{\hbar\omega/kT}} \qquad \text{Eq. 6-10}$$

Where U_ω is the energy, per unit volume and per unit bandwidth, radiated by a blackbody at temperature T; k is Boltzmann's constant; c is the velocity of light in vacuum while $\omega = 2\pi v$ is angular velocity of photon and $\hbar = \dfrac{h}{2\pi}$ is reduced Planck's constant. The radiation leaves the blackbody source at rate c, so that the power radiated per unit area of the source, per unit bandwidth, is

$$I_\omega = \frac{cU_\omega}{4} = \frac{\hbar\omega^3}{\pi^2 c^2} \frac{1/4}{e^{\hbar\omega/kT} - 1} \qquad \text{Eq. 6-11}$$

If we use the sun's temperature of 6000 0K, and $\lambda = 6943\ \text{A}^0$,

$$I_{\omega} \approx 2 \text{ x } 10^{-5} \text{ erg/cm}^2$$

For the ruby laser, a typical line width is 3 Λ^0 , so $\Delta\omega \approx 1.2 \text{ x } 10^{12} s^{-1}$. Thus the power density at the source is

$$I \approx 2.5 \text{ x } 10^{12} \text{ erg/cm}^2\text{s} \approx 2.5 \text{ W/cm}^2$$

Thus the power density for comparable narrow-bandwidth, nearly single-frequency light is much greater at a laser source than at a conventional hot-body source, because laser light is coherent.

The propagation of laser light through the atmosphere poses a complex problem and it is discussed here. Suffice it to say that, as anyone who has driven on a foggy night certainly realizes, light is certainly scattered in the atmosphere. Lasers of high power density pose even more difficult propagation problems because the high intensity warms the air and creates a density change across the beam. This variation in density refracts the light and causes beam spreading, or "thermal blooming".

Consider briefly the propagation of laser light in free space or in vacuum. Under these ideal conditions, the only change in the power density is due to simple beam divergence. Since the typical laser emits light that is nearly unidirectional, the beam divergence is small. In fact, one feature of a laser is that the divergence is nearly at the diffraction limit, which is of the order of λ / a, where a is the diameter of the output aperture of the laser. For the ruby laser discussed above, this gives a divergence angle of [28].

$$\theta \approx \frac{6943 \text{ x } 10^{-8}}{1} \approx 7 \text{ x } 10^{-2} \text{ mrad}$$

for a 1·cm aperture. In practice, one needs to go to much trouble to realize this limit of divergence, but it has been done. More commonly, an "off-the-shelf" ruby laser might have a beam divergence of a few mrad.

The newcomer to lasers has usually heard about diffraction-limited beams and the consequent extreme directionality of laser light. He is usually surprised to discover that at long distances from the source these beams have power densities that vary as the reciprocal of the square of the distance, like all radiating sources. To see this, consider a source of power P W, diameter a, and divergence angle θ, as shown in Figure 6-6.

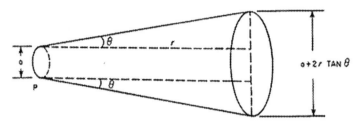

Figure 6-6: Simplified sketch of laser beam divergence

At distance r from the source, the power density is

$$I = \frac{P}{\frac{\pi}{4}(a + 2r \tan \theta)^2}$$

or, since θ is very small and $\tan \theta \approx \theta$,

$$I = \frac{P}{\frac{\pi}{4}(a + 2r\theta)^2}$$

or

$$I = \frac{P}{\frac{\pi a^2}{4}(1 + \frac{2r}{a}\theta)^2} \qquad \text{Eq. 6-12}$$

From this expression it is apparent that for large distance, such that $2r/a \gg 1$,

$$I = \frac{P}{\pi a^2 \cdot \dfrac{4r^2\theta^2}{4 \quad a^2}}$$

or

$$I = \frac{P}{\pi r^2 \theta^2}$$

Or, since $\theta \approx \lambda / a$

$$I = \frac{P}{\pi r^2} \frac{a^2}{\lambda^2}$$

For example, consider a 10-kW beam of 10.6 μm wavelength and 10 cm aperture at 1 mi (i.e., a high power CO_2 laser);

$$I = \frac{10^4 \times 10^2}{\pi (5280 \times 12 \times 2.54)^2 (10 \times 10^{-4})^2}$$

or

$$I \approx 12 \ \text{W/cm}^2$$

From Equation 6-12, if we substitute I_0, the power density at the source, for $P / (\pi a^2 / 4)$ and recall that $\theta \approx \lambda / a$,

$$I = I_0 \frac{1}{\left(1 + 2r\dfrac{\lambda}{a^2}\right)^2} \qquad \text{Eq. 6-13}$$

From this expression we can see that if r is small there is little change in power density emitted by the source. The distance at which this is true are referred to as "near-filed", and the fine details of the beam pattern, such as local variation in intensity, hot spots, etc., are preserved in the near field. It is apparent from Equation 6-13 that this near-field distance will be limited to r such that $I \approx I_0$, or

$$\frac{2r\lambda}{a^2} \ll 1$$

or

$$r_{near\ field} \ll a^2 / \lambda$$

For lasers with exceptionally good optics that have a Gaussian distribution of power density across the beam, the near field pattern will persist for distances on the order of a (a^2 / λ) [6,87,88].

As a final comment on power densities at distance from laser sources, let us use Equation 6-13 to calculate the distance at which the power density is halved [28]:

$$\frac{I}{I_0} = \frac{1}{2} = \frac{1}{\left(1 + \dfrac{2r\lambda}{a^2}\right)^2}$$

and

$$r_{1/2} = \frac{a^2}{2\lambda}(\sqrt{2} - 1)$$

For our illustration of a CO^2 laser with a 10-cm aperture, $r \approx 680\ \text{ft}$, or a little more than 0.1 mi. These calculations were done by J. T. Schriempf [28] and were reproduced here again.

6.5 Thermal Blooming Effects

High energy laser propagation in the atmosphere requires consideration of self-induced beam expansion due to thermal blooming and random distortion due to atmospheric turbulence. The thermal blooming is a result of interaction between the laser radiation and the propagation path. A small portion of the laser energy is absorbed by the atmosphere. This energy heats the air causing it to expand and form a distributed thermal lens along the path. The refractive index of the medium is decreased in the region of the beam where heating is the greatest, causing the beam to spread. Atmospheric turbulence is caused by random naturally occurring temperature gradients in the atmosphere.

Researchers are focusing on the design of beam control system for high energy lasers. In particular, some folks are concentrating to compares traditional phase conjugation and open loop techniques to a model based optimal correction technique which modified the laser power and focal length [79]. For light thermal blooming, phase conjugation is seen to be a reasonable control strategy. However, as the level of thermal blooming increases, phase conjugation performs increasingly worse. For moderate to heavy thermal blooming scenarios, the new technique is shown to increase peak intensity on target up to 50% more than traditional compensation methods. Considering a ground-based continuous wave laser operation in an environment with wind shows that in addition, the optimal correction technique is insensitive to errors in the model parameters. Assumption is that a tracking system provides target position and velocity. A reflection of the laser wave-front off the target is useful, but not required.

In case of Ground Based High-Energy Laser (GBL) a typical platform is consistent of the following elements which (i.e. the mirrors and separators), in order of an outgoing wave, are described below and the optical path is depicted in Figure 6-7 here;

1. **Deformable Mirror:** deforms the wave-front taking into account the wave-front received at the incoming and outgoing wave-front sensors.
2. **Beam Splitter:** Allows a small amount of the laser to be fed to the wave-front sensor while reflecting the rest onto the deformable mirror.
3. Outgoing Wave-front Sensor: Detects the wave-front error before the laser is reflected off any mirrors.
4. **Turning Mirror:** Reflects the beam.
5. Tilt Mirror: High bandwidth mirror which can point the beam in any direction, used to remove tilt errors from the wave-front.
6. **Beam Expansion:** Consists of a small convex mirror and a large concave mirror. It allows beam steering and focusing.
7. **Large Turning Mirror (Traverse):** Used for course pointing in combination with rotation of the whole beam expander. It has

limited orthogonal motion capability creating a traverse axis for better dynamic performance.

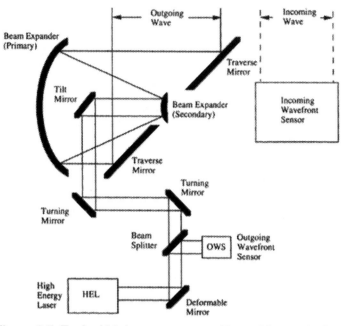

Figure 6-7: Typical high energy ground based laser platform

As we said before the purpose of a high energy laser beam system is to deliver maxim power to a target. Several atmospheric effects decrease the effectiveness of such mission for the given system. These effects include both linear and nonlinear terms (See section 6.3 in above). Diffraction, turbulence, jitter, and wander linearly decrease the intensity on target. If the nonlinear effects are ignored, any increase in intensity on target can be accomplished by increasing the laser power [72]. When the nonlinear effects of thermal blooming is included, increasing laser power will not always be beneficial and can even reduce the level of transmitted power. Figure 6-4 shows the performance of an open loop system by determining intensity on target as a function of laser power with and without blooming. As seen in Figure 6-8, it is clear that thermal blooming must be considered when evaluating this system if the laser is operating above 25×10^3 Watts. If thermal blooming is ignored in the design stage, the actual intensity on target will be a small fraction of what is expected.

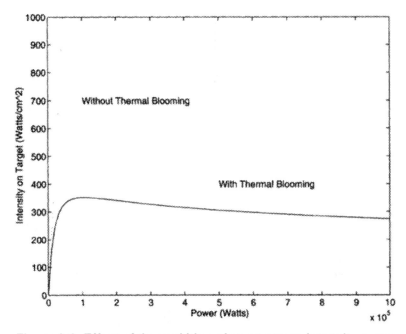

Figure 6-8: Effect of thermal blooming on power-intensity curve

Distortion caused by atmospheric turbulence is independent of the applied phase and phase conjugation has the possibility of significantly reducing wave-front distortion at the target. However, the atmospheric distortion caused by thermal blooming is a function of the applied phase. It is shown that phase conjugation techniques are not optimal and model-based controllers can improve the performance of direct6ed energy systems. It has been recognized for some time that phase conjugation methods are prone to instability. The phenomenon of Phase Compensation Instability, (PCI), has been studied extensively [80-81].

It is worth noting that thermal blooming produces a result that seemingly contradicts logic beyond a certain point, increasing the laser power can decrease the amount of laser energy delivering to target. This happens because the thermal distortions caused by the laser beam grow faster than the laser power. The more laser energy poured into the beam, the larger the percentage of energy that is bent away from the target. It is nature's reminder to the weapon system designers that bigger is not always better, and it sets an ultimate limit to the size of battlefield lasers. Note that this is not the case if the beam doesn't have to travel though atmosphere, so advocates of space-based laser weapons are free to propose laser as big as they like so long as they are not engaging in target during its boost phase from its launching platform. But the question is if they can build and deploy them to the orbit of their mission.

6.5.1 Mathematical Foundation of Thermal Blooming

Thermal blooming of high energy lasers is a beam-spreading effect that can significantly reduce the effectiveness of laser systems both as directed energy weapons and as remote powering devices. When a high energy laser propagates through a medium, a portion of the laser energy is absorbed by the medium. This absorbed power heats the medium causing it to expand, changing its index of refraction [79].

Thermal blooming is classified by the form of heat transfer that balances the absorbed power. The three cases are thermal conditions are;

1. Natural convection, and forced convection.
2. Thermal condition occurs where there is no relative motion between the beam and the medium and when no natural convective velocities are established. Natural convection results when the absorbed power causes gas heating, which establishes convection currents.
3. By far the most important continuous wave case is convection forced by wind and beam slewing.

A derivation of simple scaling laws for thermal blooming by J. Edward Wall [79] is defining basic nomenclature for adaptive optics and thermal blooming. The classical "bending into the wind" shape of a thermally bloomed wave was be pictured. Additionally, the important relationship between intensity and wave-front error is examined by him and he has introduced the representation of two-dimensional wave-fronts by Zernike polynomials.

Thermal blooming is a highly nonlinear phenomenon. A simple method for analyzing the effects of thermal blooming is to start with the general wave optics equations and find a perturbation solution [82]. The following equations completely specify steady-state thermal blooming in the ray optics limit. Further information and mathematical analysis can be found in a book by Hugo Weichel [83] where he has described mathematical analysis of laser beam propagation in the atmosphere.

6.6 Adaptive Beaming and Imaging in Turbulent Atmosphere

In order to deal with optical distortion that is caused by atmospheric turbulence and thermal blooming effects—corrective optics measurement, such as Adaptive Optical Systems is required. Due to dynamic nature and behavior of these effects and their continuous changes of their conditions, the corrective optics would have to be adjustable accordingly, or in the jargon of the field, "adaptive". The idea is to use the optics to adjust the wave-front leaving the laser beam weapon in a way that would compensate for the distortions that such beam encounters while going through atmosphere to engage with its designated target.

The extensive use of optical technologies for solving problems of information transfer, in form of a narrow-directional electromagnetic energy transport, and image formation in an outdoor atmosphere calls for the development of adaptive optical correction methods and devices. These methods call for an effective means of controlling the decrease in the efficiency of atmospheric optical systems caused by inhomogeneities in large-scale refractive indexes. These inhomogeneities are due to the turbulent mixing of atmospheric air masses and molecular and aerosol absorption in the channel of optical radiation propagation [89].

Ordinary transmissive optics is out of the question. The lens of the human eye is deformable or in sense "adoptive", but essentially all other transparent materials used as optical lenses are rigid. Solid transparent media can be damaged by high-power laser beams because they, like the air, absorb a small fraction of the optical energy they transmit. There is some research into the possibility of developing gaseous optics to make the required corrections, but it is far from clear if that concept can be made practical for the laser weaponry [58].

Wide practical application of Adaptive Optical Systems (AOS) has revealed a number of problems that call for the development of a theory of optical wave propagation under adaptive control conditions. A search for answers to these problems necessitates the development of detailed and adequate mathematical AOS models and the application of research methods such as numerical experiments that solve a system of differential equations describing optical wave propagation in the atmosphere.

Adaptive optical systems (AOS) that operate in real time allow one to

- Improve laser radiation focusing on a target, and hence increase the radiation intensity within the focal spot;
- Decrease the image blooming of astronomical and other objects m telescopes, increase image sharpness, and decrease the probability of object recognition errors; and
- Decrease the noise level and increase the data rate in optical communication systems.

Wide variety of research is going on to investigate using numerical experiments (models). Numerical experiments allow the maximum number of parameters to be considered to correctly model AOS and to investigate practically any significant radiative characteristic—the effective size of the light spot, the peak radiant intensity, the radiation power incident on the receiving aperture, the statistical characteristics of the radiant intensity and phase—in the context of a universal approach. A numerical experiment with applications to AOS allows one to predict the efficiency of various system configurations. Much time and considerable expense would be required to perform field experiment.

A method for numerical solution can be applied to two tasks:

1. High-power laser beam propagation in homogeneous media with absorption, and optical wave propagation through a random inhomogeneous turbulent atmosphere.

2. As high-power coherent laser beams propagate through a none-turbulent atmosphere, *Thermal Blooming* is one of the main factors causing distortion, along with turbulent fluctuations of the refractive index.

This nonlinear effect has the lowest energy threshold and arises as a result of absorption of part of the beam energy and the formation of the thermal inhomogeneities in the beam channel.

The longitudinal scale of variability for thermal inhomogeneities induced in the propagation channel of a high power laser beam (Thermal Blooming) is comparable to the diffraction length of the beam. In the interval Δz, the equation for the phase screen can be approximated by the product of step length Δz and the refractive index distribution at the center of the interval $[z_l, z_l + \Delta z]$ [89]. This is based on assumption of corresponding to propagation of a wave from the plane z_l.

$$\varphi_l(\vec{\rho}) = k \Delta z \delta n \left(\vec{\rho}, z_l + \frac{1}{2} \Delta z \right) + O(\Delta z^2) \qquad \text{Eq. 6-14}$$

Where;

$k = 2\pi / \lambda$:   is wave number.

$\vec{\rho}(x, y)$:   is the vector of coordinates in the beam cross section (the beam is directed along Oz axis).

$\delta n = (n-1) \ll 1$:   is the derivations of the refractive index from unity for $n_0 \approx 1$, with n_0 being vacuum refractive index

From equation 6-14, it follows that we have only to determine perturbations of the refractive index in some planes, the position of which are determined by the scheme of the splitting algorithm [89].

Heating of the medium that is caused by absorption of radiation energy includes variation of its density, which leads to a decrease in the refractive index related to the density ρ by the following law [90].

$$\delta n = K\rho \qquad \text{Eq. 6-15}$$

where K is a constant equal to two-thirds of the polarization factor of a molecule or gas atom.

In the isobaric approximation, the density of the medium is explicitly related to temperature by the ideal gas law, so variations of the refractive index can be expressed through temperature variations [89]:

$$\delta n \approx \frac{\partial n}{\partial T}(T - T_0) = n_T' \delta T \qquad \text{Eq. 6-16}$$

T_0 and T are corresponding to initial and final temperature respectively. The isobaric approximation is valid for the normal atmospheric conditions. Exceptions that should be taken under consideration are, fast scanning of a Continuous-Wave (CW) high-power beam when the beam speed with respect to the medium is greater than the sonic speed, and when the pulse duration τ_p is comparable with the acoustic time τ_s:

$$\tau_p = \tau_s = a/c_s \qquad \text{Eq. 6-17}$$

where a is the beam size and c_s is the sonic speed.

When the isobaric approximation is valid, the distribution of the refractive index in the beam cross section is determined by the heat balance, which is described by the heat transfer equation for the temperature field $T(x, y, z)$ [89]:

$$\frac{\partial T(x, y, z)}{\partial t} + \vec{V}_\perp \nabla T - \chi \Delta_\perp = \frac{\alpha}{\rho_0 C_p} I \qquad \text{Eq. 6-18}$$

where;

$\vec{V}_\perp = (V_x, V_y)$: is the transverse component of the beam velocity relative to the medium,

χ :	is heat conductivity,
ρ_0 :	is the specific density of the medium,
α :	is the absorption coefficient, and
C_p :	is the specific heat at constant pressure

Vladimir P. Lukin and Boris V. Fortes [89] have provided a solution for above equation and have argued when the isobaric approximation becomes invalid.

By creating an AOS that is smart enough with it's on board computer software system we can overcome thermal blooming effects for better laser weaponry system particularly dealing with Ground Based Laser (GBL), Air Born Laser (ABL) and Space Born Laser (SBL) in case of engagement with a target on ground (i.e. boost phase).

The most promising solution is to use a mirror in which the reflective surface is deformable, sometimes called a "rubber" mirror by engineers, although it really doesn't contain rubber. There are three basic types being developed. One is the segmented mirror in which there are many discrete segments, each of which is moved back and forth mechanically by a separate piston like device called an "actuator." Another is a mirror in which a reflective coating has been laid down on a base material that changes its shape when signals are applied to it. (In practice, the base material is generally a piezoelectric material, which changes size when an electrical voltage is applied to it. An array of electrodes applies different voltages to different parts of the mirror base) [58].

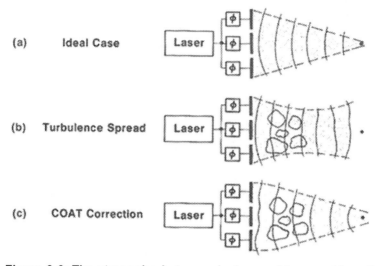

Figure 6-9: The atmospheric transmission problem, and how it can be overcome—at least in theory. In a vacuum a laser beam could be focused tightly onto a small spot (top picture (a)). In the atmosphere turbulence, thermal blooming, and other effects spread out the beam over a much larger area (middle (b)). By using adaptive optics to adjust the wave-front of the light emitted by the high-energy laser, the spreading can be reduced (bottom (c)). In these drawing, ϕ, indicates control systems that adjust the shape of the output mirror to control the laser wave-front; they are compensating for atmospheric effects only in the bottom drawing [91].

A third concept is similar in that the mirror has a continuous flexible surface, but in this case the precise contour of the surface is shaped by an array of individually controlled mechanical actuators lying beneath it [92]. All these concepts have been demonstrated, although not in the sizes necessary for practical weapon systems.

Performance requirements are stringent for high-energy laser applications. The mirror must be able to withstand the laser's high power, a need often met by forcing a liquid coolant through holes in the body of the mirror. Getting fine enough control over the wavefront of the beam requires many separate and ultra precise control elements in the mirror. A mirror 16 cm (6.5 in.) in diameter requires at least 60 separate actuators, and proportionately higher numbers are needed for larger mirrors. The 16-cm mirror, together with its mount, should hit the scales at about 1000 kg (2200 lb) and the 60 actuators should weigh no more than 800 kg (nearly 1800 lb) [93].

The shape of the optical surface must be precisely controlled. The mirror surface should be able to move back and forth over a total range of at least four times the laser wavelength. When the surface control is operating, the surface should be within one-twentieth of the laser wavelength of the ideal shape. As if that isn't enough, adjustments in mirror shape have to be made about 1000 times a second to keep up with fluctuations in the atmosphere. Because the optical tolerances depend directly on laser wavelength, they get tighter at shorter wavelengths. This helps to offset the advantage of being able to use smaller optics at such wavelengths.

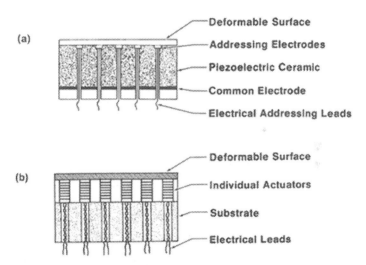

Figure 6-10: Two types of active mirrors shown in cross section to indicate how the surface is controlled. In the mirror at top the flexible surface layer rests on a block of piezoelectric ceramic, which changes its height when an electrical voltage is applied across it. Applying different voltages across different parts of the mirror alters its shape because the height of the piezoelectric material changes unevenly across the surface. In the mirror at bottom the flexible surface layer covers an array of piston like actuators, which move back and forth in response to electrical signals, thus change the shape of the mirror [91].

Adaptive optics can help compensate for effects other than atmospheric distortions that might defocus a laser beam. Some turbulence is inevitable in the laser itself, as gases flow rapidly through the laser cavity and react to release energy. Corrections applied through deformable mirrors can help in precisely tracking targets and in finely focusing the laser beam onto a distant target, although gross mechanical motion of the mirror would be needed to provide full compensation for anything beyond small movements [58].

6.6.1 Adaptive Optics

No matter how powerful a laser is, it will never reach its target without optical components. The optical components not only "direct" the beam through the laser to its target, but they also relay the laser energy and, when required, correct for any atmospheric turbulence that will distort the beam. The tremendous advances in optics have played a key role in convincing the Air Force that laser weapon systems can be produced. Without these successes by government laboratories and industry, high-energy laser weapons would be impossible.

The reason stars twinkle in the night sky is due to atmospheric turbulence, which also will distort and degrade any laser. This effect has especially severe effects for the shorter wavelength lasers, such as COIL. These systems require sophisticated optics in order to "pre-compensate" the laser beam for atmospheric turbulence.60 to pre-shape the laser beam; an adaptive optics technique is used. Over the past several years, the Air Force Research Laboratory, Phillips Research Site, and the Massachusetts Institute of Technology's Lincoln Laboratory have made significant strides in adaptive optics.

The principle behind adaptive optics is to use a deformable mirror to compensate for the distortion caused by the atmosphere. The system first sends out an artificial "star" created by a low power laser. When that laser beam is scattered by the atmosphere, the scattering radiation is reflected back and measured so that the system knows just how much the atmosphere is distorting the laser. By feeding this information into a complex control system, the deformable mirror, with its hundreds of small actuators positioned behind the mirror, alters the surface of the mirror to compensate for atmospheric distortion. Thus, a high-energy laser can be "pre-distorted" so it will regain its coherence as it passes through the atmosphere.

The Starfire Optical Range at the Phillips Research Site has successfully demonstrated the adaptive optics technique. It has a telescope with the primary mirror made of a lightweight honeycomb sandwich, which is polished to a precision of 21 nanometers, or approximately 3,000 times thinner than a human hair. To compensate for the distortion caused by gravity, the primary mirror has 56 computer-controlled actuators behind its front surface to maintain the surface figure. The 3.5-meter telescope adaptive optics system has a 941-actuator deformable mirror that is controlled by a complex computer system. What has been accomplished at the Starfire Optical Range represents possibly the most significant revolution in optical technology in the past ten years.

6.6.2 Deformable Mirror

Deformable mirror (DM) represents the most convenient tool for wave-front control and correction of optical aberrations. Deformable mirrors are used in combination with wave-front sensors and real-time control systems in adaptive optics. They are also finding a new use in femtosecond pulse shaping. The shape of the DM can be controlled with a speed that is appropriate for compensation of dynamic aberrations present in the optical system. In practice the DM shape should be changed much faster than the process to be corrected, as the correction process, even for a static aberration, may take several iterations. A DM usually has many degrees of freedom. Typically, these degrees of freedom are associated with the mechanical actuators and it can be roughly taken that one actuator corresponds to one degree of freedom.

6.6.2.1 Deformable Mirror Concepts

Segmented Concept: Mirrors are formed by independent flat mirror segments. Each segment can move a small distance back and forth to approximate the average value of the wave-front over the patch area. Normally these mirrors have little or zero cross-talk between actuators. Stepwise approximation works poorly for smooth continuous wave-fronts. Sharp edges of the segments and gaps between the segments contribute to light scattering, limiting the applications to those not sensitive to scattered light. Considerable improvement of the performance of the segmented mirror can be achieved by introduction of three degrees of freedom per segment: piston, tip and tilt. These mirrors require three times more actuators than piston segmented mirrors and they suffer from diffraction on the segment edges. This concept was used for fabrication of large segmented primary mirrors for the Keck telescopes.

Continuous Faceplate Concept: Mirrors with discrete actuators are formed by the front surface of a thin deformable membrane. The shape of the plate is controlled by a number of discrete actuators that are fixed to its back side. The shape of the mirror depends on the combination of forces applied to the faceplate, boundary conditions (the way the plate is fixed to the mirror) and the geometry and the material of the plate. These mirrors are often the most desirable implementation, as they allow smooth wave-front control with very large - up to several thousand - degrees of freedom.

MEMS Deformable: Mirror with 1020 actuators, from Boston Micromachines Corporation MEMS concept mirrors are fabricated using bulk and surface micromachining technologies. MEMS mirrors have a great potential to be cheap. They can break the high price threshold of conventional adaptive optics. MEMS mirrors typically have high response rates, high precision and have no hysteresis, unlike other types

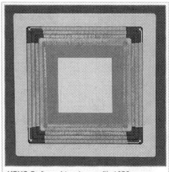

MEMS Deformable mirror with 1020 actuators, from Boston Micromachines Corporation

of deformable mirrors. Boston Micromachines Corporation is one example of a company that produces MEMS Deformable mirrors.

Membrane Concept: mirrors are formed by a thin conductive and reflective membrane stretched over a solid flat frame. The membrane can be deformed electrostatically by applying control voltages to electrostatic electrode actuators that can be positioned under or over the membrane. If there are any electrodes positioned over the membrane, they are transparent. It is possible to operate the mirror with only one group of electrodes positioned under the mirror. In this case a bias voltage is applied to all electrodes, to make the membrane initially spherical. The membrane can move back and forth with respect to the reference sphere.

Bimorph Concept: Mirrors are formed by two or more layers of different materials. One or more of (active) layers are fabricated from a piezoelectric or electrostrictive material. Electrode structure is patterned on the active layer to facilitate local response. The mirror is deformed when a voltage is applied to one or more of its electrodes, causing them to extend laterally, which results in local mirror curvature. Bimorph mirrors are rarely made with more than 100 electrodes.

Ferrofluid Concept: mirrors are liquid deformable mirrors made with a suspension of small (about 10 nm in diameter) ferromagnetic nanoparticles dispersed in a liquid carrier. In the presence of an external magnetic field, the ferromagnetic particles align with the field, the liquid becomes magnetized and its surface acquires a shape governed by the equilibrium between the magnetic, gravitational and surface tension forces. Using proper magnetic field geometries, any desired shape can be produced at the surface of the ferrofluid. This new concept offers a potential alternative for low-cost, high stroke and large number of actuators deformable mirrors.

6.6.2.2 Deformable Mirror Parameters

Number of Actuators: Determines the number of degrees of freedom (wave-front inflections) the mirror can correct. It is very common to compare an arbitrary DM to an ideal device that can perfectly reproduce wave-front modes in the form of Zernike polynomials. For predefined statistics of aberrations a deformable mirror with M actuators can be equivalent to an ideal Zernike corrector with N (usually N < M) degrees of freedom. For correction of the atmospheric turbulence, elimination of low-order Zernike terms usually results in significant improvement of the image quality, while further correction of the higher-order terms introduces less significant improvements. For strong and rapid wave-front error fluctuations such as shocks and wake turbulence typically encountered in high-speed aerodynamic flow fields, the number of actuators, actuator pitch and stroke determine the maximum wave-front gradients that can be compensated for.

Actuator Pitch: Is the distance between actuator centers. Deformable mirrors with large actuator pitch and large number of actuators are bulky and expensive.

Actuator Stroke: Is the maximum possible actuator displacement, typically in positive or negative excursions from some central null position. Stroke typically ranges from ±1 to ±10 micrometers. Free actuator stroke limits the maximum amplitude of the corrected wave-front, while the inter-actuator stroke limits the maximum amplitude and gradients of correctable higher-order aberrations.

Influence Function: is the characteristic shape corresponding to the mirror response to the action of a single actuator. Different types of deformable mirrors have different influence functions; moreover the influence functions can be different for different actuators of the same mirror. Influence function that covers the whole mirror surface is called a "modal" function, while localized response is called "zonal".

Actuator Coupling: shows how much the movement of one actuator will displace its neighbors. All "modal" mirrors have large cross-coupling, which in fact is good as it secures the high quality of correction of smooth low-order optical aberrations that usually have the highest statistical weight.

Response Time: shows how quickly the mirror will react to the control signal. Can vary from microseconds (MEMS mirrors) to tens of seconds for thermally controlled DM's.

Hysteresis and Creep: Are nonlinear actuation effects that decrease the precision of the response of the deformable mirror. For different concepts, the hysteresis can vary from zero (electrostatically-actuated mirrors) to tens of percent for mirrors with piezoelectric actuators. Hysteresis is a residual positional error from previous actuator position commands, and limits the mirror ability to work in a feed forward mode, outside of a feedback loop.

6.6.3 Large Optical Systems

In addition to adaptive optics, large mirrors, either on the ground or in space, are needed to expand and project the laser energy onto the missile. Several significant large optics programs were conducted in the late 1980s and early 1990s. The Large Optics Demonstration Experiment (LODE) established the ability to measure and corrects the outgoing wave front of high-energy lasers. The Large Advanced Mirror Program (LAMP) designed and fabricated a four-meter diameter lightweight, segmented mirror. This mirror consists of seven separate segments that are connected to a common bulkhead. The advantages of building a mirror in segments are to reduce the overall weight and fabricate larger mirrors. In addition, each segment can be repositioned with small actuator motors to slightly adjust the surface of the mirror. The program's finished mirror successfully achieved the required optical figure and surface quality for a space-based laser application.

6.6.4 What is Phase Conjugation in Optics

Phase conjugation is a fascinating phenomenon with very unusual characteristics and properties. It operates somewhat like holography, but it is a dynamic hologram, whose "holographic plate" is defined by interfering wave fronts in a nonlinear optical medium, rather than etched as a static pattern on a glass plate. In this section it is provided an intuitive explanation of the essential principles behind phase conjugation [94].

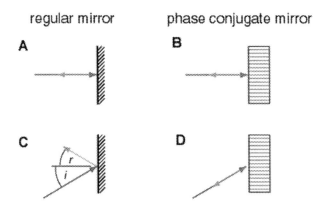

Figure 6-11: Image of regular and phase conjugate mirror

Let us begin with the properties of a phase conjugate mirror. A phase conjugate mirror is like a mirror, in that it reflects incident light back towards where it came from, but it does so in a different way than a regular mirror.

In a regular mirror, light that strikes the mirror normal to its surface, is reflected straight back the way it came (A). This is also true of a phase conjugate mirror (B). When the light strikes a normal mirror at an angle, it reflects back in the opposite direction, such that the angle of incidence is equal to the angle of reflection. (C).

In a phase conjugate mirror, on the other hand, light is always reflected straight back the way it came from, no matter what the angle of incidence. (D)

This difference in the manner of reflection has significant consequences. For example if we place an irregular distorting glass in the path of a beam of light, the parallel rays get bent in random directions, and after reflection from a normal mirror, each ray of light is bent even farther, and the beam is scattered.

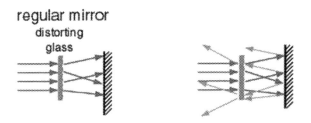

Figure 6-12: Image of regular mirror

With a phase conjugate mirror, on the other hand, each ray is reflected back in the direction it came from. This reflected conjugate wave therefore propagates backwards through the distorting medium, and essentially "un-does" the distortion, and returns to a coherent beam of parallel rays travelling in the opposite direction

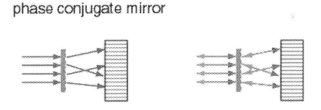

Figure 6-13: Image of phase conjugate mirror

6.6.4.1 How does the phase conjugate mirror DO that?

In linear optics, light waves pass through each other transparently, as if the other waves were not there, and the same is true of the ripples on a pond that also pass through each other totally unaffected after they cross. But almost any optical, or other wave phenomenon, will go non-linear if the amplitude is sufficiently high, and that is also true of water waves, to help our intuition. When waves in a ripple tank are driven too strongly, they lose their perfect sinusoidal shape, and form sharper peaks between wide valleys, like wind-driven waves on the ocean. A most extreme nonlinear wave is seen in breaking waves on the beach, whose towering crests carry with them a slug of moving water. Waves of this sort do not pass through each other transparently, but they collide and rebound energetically like colliding billiard balls. In reality, nonlinear waves exhibit both linear and nonlinear components, so that colliding waves will simultaneously pass mostly through each other unaffected, and at the same time some portion of those waves collide with, and rebound off each other, creating reflections in both directions. This concept of waves colliding and rebounding provides the key insight into understanding the otherwise mysterious phenomenon of phase conjugation. This anti-parallel rebounding of a ray of light in nonlinear optics, along with *Huygens's Principle* of wave propagation, are sufficient to explain some of the bizarre time-reversed reconstruction principles in phase conjugation, which is the principle that mirrors an observed property of perceptual reification.

6.6.4.2 Huygens's Principle

Huygens's principle states that a wave front is mathematically equivalent to a line of point sources all along that front, because the outward-radiating rays from adjacent point sources along the front eventually cancel by destructive interference, leaving only the component traveling in a direction normal to the local orientation of the front. This principle has an interesting spatial consequence, that if the flame front has a shape, whether curved convex or concave, or a zigzag or wavy line pattern, the shape of that wave front has a profound influence on the pattern of propagation of that front.

6.6.4.3 Two-Wave Mixing

The interactions between nonlinear waves is illustrated by the phenomenon of two-wave mixing, performed by projecting two laser beams to cross in the volume of a nonlinear optical medium. Figure 6-14 A shows two laser beams, B1 and B2 that intersect through some volumetric region of space. In the volume of their zone of intersection, a pattern of standing waves emerges in the form of parallel planes, oriented parallel to the bisector of the angle between the two beams, as shown in Figure 6-14 A. Figure 6-14 B shows in two dimensions how the wave fronts from the two beams intersect to produce high amplitude by constructive interference along the vertical lines in the figure, interleaved with planar nodes of low or zero amplitude in between, due to destructive interference.

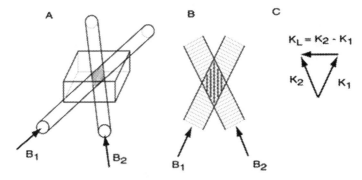

Figure 6-14: A: Two laser beams B1 and B2 that cross, create an
interference pattern in their zone of intersection.
B: Constructive interference creates a pattern
of high amplitude in parallel planes, parallel
to the angular bisector of the two beams,
with planes of low amplitude in between.
C: The wave vector diagram for the crossing beams,
including a new lattice vector K_L that corresponds to
the difference vector between the crossing beams

In linear optics this interference pattern is a transient phenomenon that has no effect on anything else. However if the crossing of laser beams occurs in the transparent volume of a nonlinear optical medium, as suggested by the rectangular block in Figure 16-14 A, and if the amplitude of the beams is sufficiently large, the interference pattern will cause a change in the refractive index of the nonlinear medium in the shape of those same parallel planes, due to the optical Kerr effect.

The alternating pattern of higher and lower refractive index in parallel planes behaves like a *Bragg diffractor.*

6.6.4.4 Bragg Diffraction

Bragg diffraction is distinct from regular diffraction by the fact that the diffracting element is not a two-dimensional grating of lines etched on a flat sheet, as in standard diffraction, but a solid volume containing parallel planes of alternating refractive index. Bragg diffraction was first observed in x-ray crystallography as a sharp peak of reflection at a particular angle of incidence to the crystal lattice planes. The crystal layers behave much like a stack of partially-silvered mirrors, each plane passing most of the light straight through undiminished, but reflecting a portion of that light like a mirror, with the angle of reflection equal to the angle of incidence.

However because of interference between reflections from successive layers at different depths, Bragg diffraction is stronger at those angles of incidence that promote constructive interference between reflected rays, but weakens or disappears altogether at other angles where the various reflected beams cancel by destructive interference. Maximal diffraction occurs at angles that meet the Bragg condition, that is,

$$2d \sin \theta = n\lambda$$

where θ is the angle of the incident ray to the plane of the reflecting surface, d is the distance between adjacent planes, λ is the wavelength of light, and n is an integer. In words, Bragg reflection occurs at angles of reflection where the path length difference between reflections from adjacent planes differs by an integer number of wavelengths.

6.6.4.5 Reciprocal Lattice Wave Vector Representation

The phase matching constraint enforced by the Bragg condition can be seen most easily in a Fourier space called the reciprocal lattice representation. Each beam is represented by a wave vector whose direction is normal to the wave fronts of the corresponding beam, and whose magnitude is proportional to the inverse of the wavelength, or spacing between successive wave fronts of the beam. This is a Fourier representation in that the magnitude of the wave vectors is proportional to the frequency of the corresponding wave. Mathematically, the magnitude k of the wave vector of a wave of wavelength l is given by

$$k = 2\pi / \lambda$$

The convenience of this representation is that the wave vectors of waves that are phase matched so as to be in a mutually constructive relationship, form closed polygons in this space, and this can be used to determine whether the Bragg condition is met.

Figure 6-14 C shows the wave vector representation for the crossing laser beams depicted in Figure 6-14 A. The wave vectors K_1 and K_2 are oriented parallel to their corresponding beams B_1 and B_2. The parallel planes of a Bragg diffractor, such as a crystal composed of parallel planes, can also be expressed as a wave vector because it behaves very much like a beam of coherent light to an incident beam that strikes it. As with wave vectors, the direction of this lattice vector K_L is normal to the planes of the grating, and the vector magnitude is proportional to the inverse of the spacing between lattice planes. Figure 6-15 A shows the nonlinear optical element replaced by a functionally equivalent crystal with lattice planes parallel to those of the standing wave. The vector diagram of Figure 6-14 C shows the lattice vector K_L that would be required for the phase matching relation dictated by the Bragg condition to hold. In terms of wave vectors in the reciprocal lattice representation, the Bragg condition holds when

$$K_1 + K_L = K_2$$

or equivalently,

$$K_2 - K_L = K_1$$

The lattice vector acts in opposite directions on K_1 and K_2, which is why it is added to one but subtracted from the other. Note how the lattice vector is oriented normal to the planes of the lattice, which are parallel to the angular bisector of the two beams, as required for the angle of incidence to equal the angle of reflection. For example if the lattice spacing were somewhat larger than that dictated by the Bragg condition, that would make the lattice vector shorter, and the three vectors would no longer form a closed triangle, and thus little or no Bragg refraction would be expected to occur with that crystal, that is, the light would pass through with little or no reflection. Bragg refraction could be restored, however, by re-aligning either or both beams to make their wave vectors meet the shorter lattice vector.

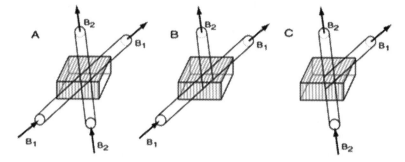

Figure 6-15: A: Nonlinear optical element replaced by functionally equivalent crystal with lattice planes parallel to the original standing waves and with the same spacing as the standing waves.

B: If beam B_2 were shut off, then beam B_1 together with the crystal would recreate B_2 by Bragg diffraction.

C: Conversely, if beam B_1 were shut off, then beam B_2 together with the crystal would recreate B_1 by Bragg diffraction

6.6.4.6 Magical Reification

The magic of nonlinear optics is that when laser beams cross in the volume of a nonlinear optical medium, as depicted in Figure 6-14 A, the wave vector of the resultant nonlinear standing wave pattern automatically takes on the configuration required by the Bragg condition, no matter what the angle of intersection of the two beams. So although Bragg reflection occurs off a crystal only for certain specific angles that meet the Bragg condition, laser beams that cross in a nonlinear optical medium create a standing wave whose lattice vector is automatically equal to the difference between the two crossing beams, or,

$$K_L = K_2 - K_1$$

This is a remarkable constructive or generative function of nonlinear optics, creating a whole new waveform out of whole cloth, equal to the difference between two parent wave forms. This magical act of creation can be understood as a property of the fundamental resonances in the nonlinear optical material set up by the passage of high amplitude laser beams. The laser beam sets up a resonance in the electrons that are attached to the molecules in the optical material, that makes them vibrate in sympathy with the passing wave. The difference in nonlinear optics is that this resonance takes energy to establish, as if the electron had a certain momentum to be overcome, or a capacitor that must absorb a certain charge, so that the optical material does not react instantaneously to the passing light, but with a certain energetic time lag, that borrows energy from the wave when the wave first turns on, and repays that energy debt when the wave is shut off again, like a capacitor discharging through a resistor, or a mass-and-spring system returning to center after wave passage. This is what makes nonlinear optics automatically balance the vector equation. If one wave vector deflects the electron this way, and another deflects it that way, the electron needs to return back to center before it can start the next cycle, and that returning back to center is what closes the wave vector diagram.

If the pattern of standing waves were somehow frozen as a fixed pattern of alternating refractive index, as in a layered crystal, as suggested in Figure 6-15 A, then this crystal would behave like a hologram that can restore the pattern of light if one of the input beams is removed. For example Figure 6-15 B shows beam B_1 refracted by the functionally equivalent crystal lattice to produce a reflected beam in the direction of the original beam B_2, and Figure 6-16 C shows beam B_2 refracted by the equivalent crystal lattice to recreate the original beam B_1. The reification in two-wave mixing has created a difference vector that has created a redundancy in the representation that allows either one of the input signals to be removed without loss of information.

If another analogy might be helpful, consider water flowing over sand, and creating little rippling dunes, and the rippling dunes in turn force the water to ripple over them, the flowing water and the rippling sand modulating each other by conforming to each other energetically. You can see the dunes eroding constantly from their flow-ward side, and building back up again on their leeward side, causing the little sand dunes to advance slowly to leeward, all in lock step with each other and with the corresponding ripples in the water. If you could instantly smooth the sand flat, but preserve the rippling pattern in the water flow, it would immediately re-establish the ripples in the sand, by allowing sand to accumulate in the stagnant parts of the flow. In fact, the rippling pattern would automatically re-establish itself naturally anyway, due to the fundamental dynamics of the water/sand interaction. Likewise, if the sand were frozen to a static plaster cast of the ripple pattern, that pattern would coerce any water flowing over it to conform to its pattern of ripples, which the water would happily comply with, if the ripples are of the right natural frequency.

The nonlinear standing wave establishes an energy coupling between the two intersecting waves, such that one wave can "pump" or amplify the other. For example if B1 is of higher amplitude than B_2, then the interference pattern between B_1 and B_2 reflects some of the energy of B_1 in the direction of B_2, as in Figure 6-15 A, whereas if B_2 is of higher amplitude than B1, some of the energy of B_2 is reflected in the direction of B1, as in Figure 6-15 B. In fact, whether the two beams are of equal amplitude or not, some portion of B_1 is always lost to B_2 through the crystal, while some portion of B_2 is lost to B_1, as suggested in Figure 6-15 A, so the net energy transfer always flows from the higher amplitude beam toward the lower. That is, the two waves are intimately coupled through the nonlinear standing wave, energy-wise, and this energy coupling is what allows phase conjugation to produce an amplified reflection.

6.6.4.7 Degenerate Four-Wave Mixing

To create a phase conjugate mirror we add a third probe beam, B_3, to intersect with the other two beams in the nonlinear optical element as shown in Figure 6-16 A. This creates a fourth signal beam B_4 which will eventually be our phase conjugate beam after one last modification. This configuration is known as degenerate four-wave mixing. (The word degenerate refers to the fact that the frequencies of all four beams are equal, as required for the simplest form of phase conjugation exemplified here) The direction of that fourth beam can be computed from the vector diagram shown in Figure 6-16 B, by the principle that the fourth beam will exactly cancel or balance the sum of the other three vectors, or,

$$K_1 + K_2 + K_3 + K_4 = 0$$

Again, this is dictated by the phase matching constraint, whereby the only waves that will emerge are those that reinforce each other constructively, and the reciprocal wave vector diagram helps identify the conditions under which that constraint is met. If the pumping beams K_1 and K_2 remain fixed, then whichever way the probe beam wave vector K_3 is directed from the point $(K_1 + K_2)$ in the vector diagram, the conjugate beam will always return back to the origin, as shown in Figure 6-16 B.

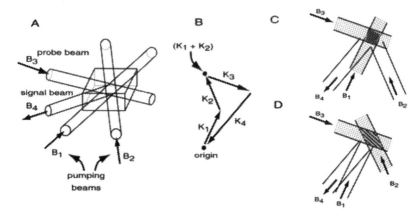

Figure 6-16: A: A third beam B$_3$ is directed into the intersection of the other beams, which produces a fourth beam B$_4$. The angle of that new beam can be calculated from the wave vector diagram as shown in

B. This can be seen intuitively as

C: an interference that forms between B$_3$ and B$_1$, followed by a reflection of B$_2$ by that pattern to create B$_4$, or alternatively it can be seen as

D: an interference between B$_3$ and B$_2$, followed by a reflection of B$_1$ by that interference pattern to create B$_3$.

There are two ways that this phenomenon can be understood intuitively. We can say that probe beam B$_3$ interferes with pumping beam B$_1$ to produce an interference pattern as shown in Figure 6-16 C along their angular bisector, then beam B$_2$ reflects off that interference pattern to produce the signal beam B$_4$ (angle of reflection equals angle of incidence) Alternatively we can say that the probe beam B$_3$ interferes with other pumping beam B$_2$ to produce an interference pattern as shown in Figure 6-16 D, then beam B$_1$ reflects off that interference pattern to produce the signal beam B$_4$. It is more accurate however to think of all four beams as interlocked in a four-way energy coupling consummated by the newly created signal beam that appears so as to balance the vector equation and maintain phase coherence between all four beams. In other words, both interference patterns of Figure 6-16 C and D co-exist simultaneously along with the original pattern of Figure 6-14 A, interlocking the four beams in a mutually interdependent energy relation.

6.6.4.8 Phase Conjugate Mirror

All we need to do to complete the phase conjugate mirror is to orient beams B_1 and B_2 anti-parallel to each other, so that in vector terms K_1 + K_2 = 0. This in turn means that K_3 + K_4 = 0, which means that the reflected beam B_4 must be the phase conjugate of the probe beam B_3. Figure 6-17 A shows the configuration required for phase conjugation. Pumping beams B_1 and B_2 are projected into the nonlinear optical element from opposite directions where they interfere to form a nonlinear standing wave. The probe beam B_3 can now be projected into the mirror from any direction, and this will produce the phase conjugate beam B_4 superimposed on B_3 but traveling in the opposite direction as a "time-reversed" reflection. The summation of B_3 and B_4 traveling in opposite directions converts the two waves into a standing wave that oscillates without propagation if they are of equal amplitude, otherwise there will be a net propagation in the direction of the higher amplitude beam. Figure 6-17 B shows the wave vector diagram showing how if K_1 + K_2 = 0, then K_3 + K_4 also equals 0 no matter what angle the probe beam enters the mirror, and thus B_4 must be the phase conjugate of B_3.

If the pumping beams are provided at high amplitude, then the energy built up in the nonlinear standing wave can spill over to the conjugate wave, creating an amplified reflection of the incoming wave back outward in the direction from whence it came. This is the phase conjugate mirror produced by degenerate four-wave mixing.

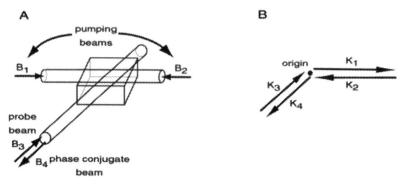

Figure 6-17. A: A phase conjugate mirror is produced by anti-
parallel pumping beams B_1 and B_2 that cross in
opposite directions in the nonlinear optical element.
When a third probe beam B_3 is projected into the
mirror from any direction, a phase conjugate beam
B_4 will appear as a time-reversed reflection of the
probe beam in the direction from whence it came.
B: The wave vector diagram shows how if K_1 +
K_2 = 0, then K_3 + K_4 also equals 0, and thus
B_4 must be the phase conjugate of B_3

6.6.4.1 Phase Conjugation and Optical Black Magic

Adaptive optics is more than simply deformable mirrors. A control
system is needed to determine how much to adjust the mirror's
shape. Extensive theoretical work has been done on the propagation
of high-energy laser beams through the atmosphere, but theory is
not enough. Some of the most important distortions are caused by
random atmospheric turbulence that theory cannot predict. The effects
influencing light along the path the beam is going to travel must be
measured, and that information must be converted into a control
signal. This means that the control system must receive light returning
along the beam path and analyze what has happened to it. This is by
no means an easy process, and the details are well beyond the scope
of this book [58].

After the control system has measured the effects that the beam will be subjected to, the type of compensation required must be determined. This process is called phase conjugation. It is a complex operation in which the measured effects of turbulence are used to create a laser wavefront that will undo what the turbulence did, making it possible to produce a tight focal spot on the target. The precise method by which phase conjugation works is too complex to describe here; suffice it to say that in theory the technique can be used to compensate for aberrations inside the laser and in the atmosphere. 21 The critical corrections are made by adjusting the relative phase of different parts of the laser beam-that is, by making parts of the laser beam slightly out of step with each other, instead of staying in the normal lockstep of the light waves in a laser beam. Interestingly, changes in the intensity pattern of the laser beam are less important in compensating for atmospheric effects than the more subtle phase shift [58].

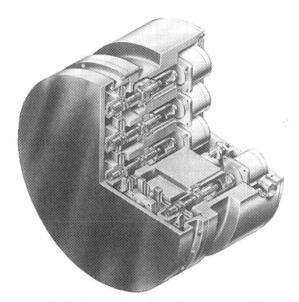

Figure 6-18: Cutaway view of a 19-actuator deformable mirror built by Rockwell International's Rocketdyne Division shows the complexity of adaptive optics. This mirror is 16 in. (40 cm) in diameter and weighs 100 lb (45 kg).

Beam distortions are not so serious in space, where there is no air to get in the way, but the tremendous distances involved to engage with target present. A massive amount of scientific manpower and defense money is going into development of adaptive optics. The topic is a common and hot one among scholar of this subject.

6.7 Target Effects

Once the beam reaches the target, it deposits part of its energy there. This involves a complex interaction between beam and target that depends strongly on the nature of the beam and property of the target, and which ultimately determines how much of the energy in the beam is transferred to the target. Only after the energy is transferred to the target can it do any damage.

No one is seriously thinking of using a laser beam to completely vaporize any military targets. Instead, a continuous laser beam would cause physical damage by heating a target until the beam melted through the skin and lethally damaged some internal components. The actual type of damage would depend on the target and where it was illuminated. Drilling a hole in a fuel tank could cause an explosion. Disabling the device called a "fuse", which triggers the explosion of a warhead, would prevent a bomb from exploding or alternatively might trigger a premature explosion of the warhead, in a place where it would not damage the intended target, but could cause considerable damage to other objects and people. Knocking out the control or guidance system could make a missile land far from its intended target [58].

A continuous laser beam can't do damage instantaneously. Heating the target to the required temperature would probably take a few seconds, depending on the laser power and the nature of the target; exact requirements are classified by the government, but can be estimated doing few mathematical analysis. The illumination time is long enough for the beam to wander off the target spot and let the heated area cool off. Techniques called "countermeasures", described in many related defense papers, could be used to reduce the amount of energy that the beam could deposit on the target. Other types of interactions could also help protect the target [58].

There is considerable interest in substituting a rapid series of short laser pulses for a continuous beam. As mentioned earlier, this might simplify the task of getting the beam through the air to its target. The abrupt heating and cooling could cause thermal shock, sufficient to shatter materials such as glass. A short, intense pulse could also rapidly evaporate a burst of material from the surface, generating a shock wave that would travel through the target and could cause mechanical damage. (Evaporation caused by a continuous beam would be more gradual and would not cause a shock wave.) The combination of thermal and mechanical damage and heating effects caused by a series of short, closely timed laser pulses does a better job of breaking through sheet metal of target than either heating or laser produced shock waves can do by themselves [58].

Physical damage is not the only way a laser beam can disable a target. The beam could also attack sensors that guide weapons to their targets, blinding or disabling them by other means. Particle beams, microwaves, and X rays have their own distinct ways of producing damages to target [58].

6.7.1 Measured Characteristic of Target both Optically and Thermally

The purpose of the measuring the characteristic of target is the absorptance of the target at the laser wavelength is needed for model calculations of the target's thermal response. Ideally, the absorptance should be known as a function of temperature. However, if this is not available, the initial absorptance at ambient temperature is still a vital input to the thermal model and high energy laser weaponry [95].

For accurate lethality estimates for a metal-skinned target, it is very desirable to know the target's absorptance at the laser wavelength and as a function of temperature. This can be done either with optical measurement approach that requires special equipment that is not generally available and is limited to power levels that would not contaminate the hardware with sample ejecta. In lethality testing at high power levels it is possible to get absorptance values in real time using simple thermocouple instrumentation as discussed below [95].

6.7.2 Target Absorptance Optical Approach

For opaque (optically dense) targets as can be assumed for standard cases, the absorptance $A(\theta)$ at a given incidence angle θ can be inferred from a measurement of total hemispherical reflectance $R(\theta)$ at that incidence angle;

$$A(\theta) = 1 - R(\theta)$$

Ther are a number of Government and Commercial laboratories that perform spectrally-resolved reflectance measurements. These give the *Directional Hemispherical Reflectance* (DHR) of a sample as a function of wavelength over a range of interest. The sample is positioned in an integrating sphere and is illuminated at a fixed incidence angle by a spectrally-resolved light source. This is due to the fact that absorptance of some materials is polarization-dependent, and, therefore, the light source should either be unpolarized or measurements should be made with orthogonal polarizations. For more information on polarization subject, reader should refer to Appendix F this book (Volume 2). Commercial and custom reflectometers have the capability of heating the sample in-situ to temperatures as high as 500 °C. Note that most laboratories restrict heating to temperature below the threshold for decomposition. Absolute measurement uncertainly is typically in the range of 0.01 to 0.02.

An alternative approach, illustrated in Figure 6-19, has been pioneered by the Air Force Research Laboratory. The instrument, in what is known as the Temperature-dependent Reflectance of Aerospace Materials (TRAM) facility, is a hemi-ellipsoidal gold-coated dome. The sample is heated by a laser whose wavelength is different from the wavelength of interest provided by the probe beam or weaponry beam. The sample is located at one of the foci of the hemi-ellipsoid and the entrance port of an integrating sphere is located at the other focal point.

In order for the integrating sphere detector to distinguish the probe beam signal from the heater beam, the probe beam is chopped at a relative high frequency (300 Hz) and a phase sensitive ('lock-in') amplifier is employed. Additionally, a filter having high reflectance at the heater laser wavelength is positioned in front of the detector.

A pyrometer or thermo-graphic imaging camera is employed to measure the sample's temperature as it is heated.

Note that for partially transparent materials, one must also measure their transmittance. Recent modifications to the TRAM instrument have permitted simultaneous measurements to be made of reflectance and transmittance as the sample is heated. However, this capability is still under development and not yet fully proven [95].

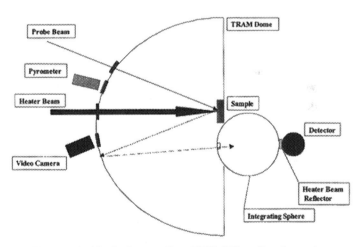

Figure 6-19: Schematic of TRAM reflectometer

6.7.3 Target Absorptance Thermal Approach

The thermal response of a metal plate may be used to estimate the target's absorptance as a function of temperature. Typically, the temperature of the rear surface is measured with attached thermocouples and/or by use of a thermographic imaging camera. In the latter case, the rear surface is coated with a high emittance, thermally stable black paint.

Under conditions where two-or three-dimensional heat conduction effects can be ignored, a closed form analytical solution has been found and it is shown in Section 6.6.4 below for the response of a finite thickness slab of material insulated in both faces to a constant uniform heat flux on one surface. This solution, which assumes constant thermal properties and no phase change is, is given by:

$$T(z,t) = T(z,0) + \frac{AIt}{\rho C_p L} + \frac{AIL}{k} \left\{ \frac{3(1-z/L)^2 - 1}{6} - \frac{2}{\pi^2} \sum_{n=1}^{\infty} \frac{(-1)^n}{n^2} \exp\left(-\kappa n^2 \pi^2 t / L^2\right) \cos\left(n\pi(1-z/L)\right) \right\}$$

Eq. 6-19

where the axial coordinate in the original formula has been replaced by $L - z$, and the heat flux is assumed to be the absorbed irradiance at $z = 0$. Of course, from initial temperature to melt, themophysical properties of most materials vary considerably, but for limited temperature changes, this assumption is reasonable if average values are used. The limitations are further discussed below. Note in the above equation that A is the absorptance, I is irradiance (W/cm²), t is time (sec), ρ is density (g/cm3), C_p is the specific heat (J/g °K), L is the slab thickness (cm), k is the thermal conductivity (W/cm °K), and κ is the thermal diffusitivity (cm²/Sec). The first term in the equation is the initial temperature and the second term in the equation is just the linear rise in average plate temperature. The summation in the bracket is a strong function of the axial Fourier number, $f_{Na} = \kappa t / L^2$, the ratio of the duration of the irradiance to the characteristic conduction time through the thickness L. For $f_{Na} > 0.3$, the summation is approximately zero and the first term in the bracket dominates; i.e., the temperature distribution develops a quasi-steady-state quadratic gradient superimposed on the average plate temperature. For small values of f_{Na}, the sum must be calculated to capture the transient; however, the sum converges rapidly with fewer than ten terms required for reasonable accuracy at $f_{Na} = 0.005$. The behavior of the bracketed term in Equation 6-19 is shown in Figure 6-20 below.

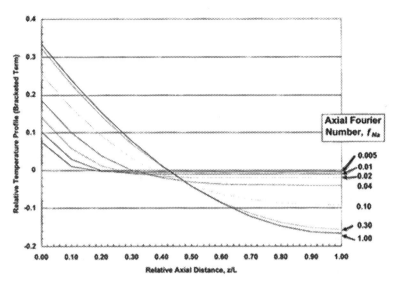

Figure 6-20: Relative axial temperature distribution in a heated finite plate as a function of axial Fourier number

The thermal diffusivity of a relative low thermal conductivity material such as steel approximately is 0.05 cm²/sec, and thickness values for many coupons are in the 0.1 to 0.3 cm range [95]. For an axial Fourier number of 0.3, the corresponding times are in the 0.06-0.54 sec range. This means that, for many cases of interest (exposure time greater than 0.5 sec at these thicknesses), Equation 6-19 may be reduced to a simpler form for analyzing plate heating,

$$T(z,t) = \frac{AIt}{\rho C_p L} + \frac{AIL}{k}\left\{\frac{3(1-z/L)^2 - 1}{6}\right\} \qquad \text{Eq. 6-20}$$

Evaluating this equation at $z = 0$ and $z = L$, the following two results are obtained:

$$T(0,t) = T_0(t) = \frac{AI}{\rho C_p L}\left[t + \frac{L^2}{3\kappa}\right] + T_0 \qquad \text{Eq. 6-21}$$

$$T(L,t) = T_L(t) = \frac{AI}{\rho C_p L}\left[t + \frac{L^2}{6\kappa}\right] + T_0 \qquad \text{Eq. 6-22}$$

where advantage has been taken of the relationship between thermal conductivity and diffusivity: $k = \rho C_p \kappa$. Taking the first derivative with respect to time of Equation 6-22, and rearranging, we arrive at:

$$A = \frac{\rho C_p L}{I} \frac{dT_L}{dt} \qquad \text{Eq. 6-23}$$

Thus, given knowledge of the density, specific heat, and local irradiance (opposite the location where the temperature is being measured), the absorptance can be determined from the slope of the rear surface's thermal response curve [95].

For most materials, the specific heat is temperature dependent. In addition, the irradiance may vary with time. Then Equation 6-23 can be conveniently evaluated using a spreadsheet that implements measured values for $C_p(T)$ and $I(t)$. Often the former are given by stepwise polynomial fits.

Note that this method of measuring absorptance is valid only up to the point where the target's front surface reaches its melting point. Also, the method must be applied under conditions where losses (convective, radiative, and lateral conductive) are small compared to the absorbed flux. Finally, the method should be applied when the beam's spatial irradiance profile is smooth with no local excursions about the mean greater than about 10% [95].

6.7.4 Mathematical Modeling of Thermal Approach

The heat flow in a finite or semi-infinite thin slab for One-Dimensional is governed by the Partial Differential Equation (PDE);

$$\frac{\partial u(z,t)}{\partial t} = c \frac{\partial^2 u(z,t)}{\partial z^2} \qquad \text{Eq. 6-24}$$

where c is a constant (called the diffusivity), and $u(z,t)$ is the temperature at position z and time t. The temperature over a cross-section at z is taken to be uniform. (See Figure 6-21)

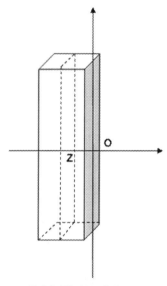

Figure 6-21: Finite slab geometry

Many different scenarios can arise in the solution of the heat equation; we will consider several to illustrate the various techniques involved.

Example-1: Solve the following heat transfer problem along with Boundary Condition (B.C.) and Initial Condition (I.C.) as follow (for simplicity of this analysis, we have assumed $c = 1$);

$$\frac{\partial^2 u(z,t)}{\partial z^2} = \frac{\partial u(z,t)}{\partial t} \qquad 0 < z < L \text{ and } t > 0$$

$$\begin{cases} (i) & u(z,0) = u_0 \qquad \text{Initial Condition} \\ (ii) & \dfrac{\partial u(0,t)}{\partial z} = 0 \\ & \qquad\qquad \text{Boundary Condition (i.e. now flow of heat over z=0} \\ (iii) & u(L,t) = u_1 \end{cases}$$

Solution: Taking the Laplace transform (See Appendix E and Equation E-38) over t of heat equation flow of above PDE gives;

$$\frac{d^2U}{dx^2} = sU - u_0$$

Then

$$U(z,s) = c_1 \cosh \sqrt{s}z + c_2 \sinh \sqrt{s}z + \frac{u_0}{s}$$

And by B.C. (ii), $c_2 = 0$, so that

$$U(z,s) = c_1 \cosh \sqrt{s}z + \frac{u_0}{s}$$

We find by B.C. (iii) that

$$U(L,s) = \frac{u_1}{s} = c_1 \cosh \sqrt{s}L + \frac{u_0}{s}$$

and so

$$c_1 = \frac{u_1 - u_0}{s \cosh \sqrt{s}L}$$

Therefore,

$$U(z,s) = \frac{(u_1 - u_0)\cosh \sqrt{s}z}{s \cosh \sqrt{s}L} + \frac{u_0}{s}$$

Taking the inverse Laplace Transform gives

$$u(z,t) = u_0 + (u_1 - u_0)\pounds^{-1}\left(\frac{\cosh \sqrt{s}z}{s \cosh \sqrt{s}L}\right)$$

$$= u_1 + \frac{4(u_1 - u_0)}{\pi} \sum_{n=1}^{\infty} \frac{(-1)^n}{(2n-1)} \exp\left(-(2n-1)^2 \pi^2 t / 4L^2\right)\cos\left(\frac{2n-1}{2L}\right)\pi z$$

This is analogous to Equation 6-19 except we have to replace $u(z,t)$ with $T(z,t)$, u_0 with $T(z,0)$ and u_1 with $T(L,t)$ as well as accounting for thermal conductivity or diffusivity c of Equation 6-24. Very similar solution is given by Carslaw and Jaeger [96] page 112 equation (3) and (4).

REFERENCES

1. Airborne Laser: Bullets of Light, Robert W. Duffner, Plenum Publishing Corporation, 1997, New York

2. Laser Weapons: The Dawn of a New Military Age, Major General Bengt Anderberg and Dr. Myron L. Wolbarsht, Plenum Publishing Corporation, 1992, New York.

3. Applications of High-Power Microwaves, Andrei V. Gaponov-Grekov and Victor L. Granatstein, Published by Artech House, Inc. Norwood, MA 1994.

4. Propagation of Intensive Laser Radiation in Clouds, Oleg A. Volkovitsky, Yuri S. Sedunov and Leonid P. Semenov, Volume 138, Published by AIAA, 1992 Washington DC.

5. The effects of Radiation on Electronic Systems, 2nd Edition, by George C. Meassenger and Milton S. Ash, Published by VNB, New York, NY 1992.

6. John F. Ready "Effects of High-Power Laser Radiation", Published by Academic Press, New York, NY 1971.

7. Effect of Laser Radiation on Absorbing Condensed Matter, Edited by V.B. Fedorov, Translated By Richard Moore, Proceeding of the Institute of General Physics Academy of Science of USSR, Series Editor: A.M. Prokhorov, Volume 13, Published by Nova Science, Commack, New York 1990.

8. Effects of Directed Energy Weapons, Philip E. Nielson, will be published.

9. Figure 2-1 has been adapted from Figure 3.13 in Eugene Hecht and Alfred Zajac, Optics, Addison-Wesley, 1976.

10. Laser Electronics, Cliffs Englewood, NJ Prentice-Hall, 1981.

11. Crokett, G., "Bi-directional Reflectivity Distribution Function (BRDF) Modeling to LRST: Maxwell-Beard, Phong, and Gaussian Models, Contract F04701-98-D-0100, CDRL A004," January, 1999.

12. Crokett, G., "Laser Range Safety Tools (LRST) Physics Reference" Logicon-RDA, Albuquerque, NM. Report AFRL-HE-BR-TR-2003, September 2003.

13. Larry C. Andrews and Ronald L. Phillips "Laser Beam Propagation through Random Media" 2nd Edition SPIE Press 2005.

14. Lasers, Ray Guns, & Light Cannons, Project from the Wizard's Workbench; Gordon McComb, McGraw-hill, 1997.

15. Charles Kittle, Introduction to Solid State Physics, Seventh Edition, John Wiley, 1996, New York, NY.

16. W.W. Duley 'Laser Processing and Analysis of Materials' Plenum Press1983, New York.

17. Hugo Weichel, "Laser Beam Propagation in the Atmosphere, SPIE, Optical Engineering Press, Bellingham 1990.

18. N. S. Kopeika, A system Engineering Approach to Imaging, SPIE Optical Engineering Press, Bellingham (1990).

19. L. A. Chernov, "Wave Propagation in a Random Medium, McGraw-Hill, New York, 1960, Translated by R. A. Silverman.

20. J. Crank, "The Mathematics of Diffusion", Second Edition, Oxford Science Publications, 1955.

21. A. V. Luikov, "Analytical Heat Diffusion Theory", Academic Press, New York and London, 1968.

22. David Holliday, Robert Resnick and Jearl Walker, "Fundamentals of Physics", 7th edition, John Wiley, 2005.

23. Matthew S Bigelow, Nick N Lepeshkin, Heedeuk Shin, Robert W Boyd, "Propagation of a smooth and discontinuous pulses through materials with very large or very small group velocities", Journal of Physics: Condensed Matter. 18, 3117-3126 (2006)

24. Brillouin, Léon. "Wave Propagation and Group Velocity". Academic Press Inc., New York (1960).

25. Bhag Singh Guru and Huseyin R. Hiziroglu, "Electromagnetic Field Theory Fundamentals", 2nd Edition, Cambridge University Press, 2004.

26. Carslaw, H. S. and J. C. Jaeger. 1959, Chapter 1 Page 11 and 89 in Conduction of Heat in Solids, 2nd edition, Oxford: Clarendon Press.

27. W. W. Duley, CO^2 Lasers: Effects and Applications, Published by Academic Press, New York, NY 1976.

28. J. T. Schriempf, Response of Materials to Laser Radiation: A short Course, NRL Report 7728, July 10, 1974. Naval Research Laboratory, Washington, D.C. 20375.

29. Kau-Fui Vincent Wong, 'Intermediate Heat Transfer' Marcel Dekker, Inc. New York. Basel, 2003.

30. Carlo Kopp, "The Electromagnetic Bomb: a Weapon of Electrical Mass Destruction", 1996

31. Samuel Glasstone "The Effects of Nuclear Weapons (Paperback)", Knowledge Publications (November 1, 2006).

32. James Benford, John A. Swegle and Ed Schamilogu, "High Power Microwaves" 2nd edition, Taylor & Francis, 2007.

33. J. F. Ready, *J. Appl. Phys.* **36**, 462, 1965.

34. R. E. Honig, *Appl. Phys. Lett.*, **3**, 8 (1963).

35. D. Lichtman and J. F. Ready, *Phys. Rev. Lett.*, 10, 342 (1963).

36. F. Giovi, L. A. Mackenzie and E. J. McKinney, *Appl. Phys. Lett.*, 3,25 (1963)

37. W. I. Linlor, *Appl. Phys. Lett.*, 3, 210 (1963)

38. N. G. Basov, S. Yu. Gus'kov, G.V. Danilova, N. N. Demchenko, N. V. Zmitrenko, V. Ya. Karpov, T. V. Mishchenko, V. B. Rozanov and A. A. Samarski, Sov. J. Quantum Electron., 15 No. 6 852 (1985).

39. J. H. Nuckolls, in 'Laser Program Annual Report 1979, UCRL-50021-79, Vol. 2, 2 (1980).

40. Yu. V. Afanasiev, E. G. Gamaly, S. Yu. Gus'kov, N. N. Demchenko, and V. B. Rozanov, Laser and Particle Beam, 6, Paert 1, 1 (1988).

41. A. M. Prokorov, V. I. Konov, "Laser Heating of Metals", The Adam Hilger Series on Optic and Optoelectronics, 1990.

42. John F. Ready, "Industrial Applications of Lasers", 2nd edition, Academic Press, 1997.

43. M. I. Cohen, *J. Franklin Institute* **283**, 271 (1967).

44. B. T. Barnes (1966), *J. Opt. Soc. Am.* **56**, 1546.

45. W. W. Duley, D. J. Semple, J. P. Morency, and M. Gravel (1979), *Opt. Laser Technol.* **11**, 281.

46. Wieting and J. L. De Rosa, *J. Appl. Phys*, **50**, 1071, 1979.

47. Wieting and J. T. Schriempf, *J. Appl. Phys.* **47**, 4009, 1976.

48. E. Sturmer and M Von Allmen, *J. Appl. Phys.* **49**, 5648, 1978.

49. J. Shewell, *Weld. Des. Fab.,* June, p. 100, 1977.

50. W. M. Steen and M. Eboo, *Met. Const.* **11**, 332, 1979.

51. Pirri, A. N., Root, R. G., and Wu, P. K. S. Plasma energy transfer to metal surfaces irradiated by pulsed lasers. AAIAJ, 16, 1296-1304, 1978.

52. Schulz W, Simon, G., and Vicanek, M. Ablation of opaque surfaces due to laser irradiation. J. Phys. D: Appl. Phys., 19, L173-L177, 1986.

53. Schellhorn, M. and von Bülow, H. CO_2 laser deep penetration welding - a comparative study to CO_2 laser welding. Paper presented at GLL 94, Friedrichshafen, 1994.

54. Solana, P., Kapadia, P. D., and Dowden, J. M. Surface depression and ablation for a translating weld pool in material processing: a mathematical model. J. Laser Applics., 12.2, 63-67, 2000.

55. Stratton, J A. Electromagnetic Theory. McGraw-Hill, New York:, 500-11, 1941.

56. John Michael Dowden, 'The Mathematics of Thermal Modeling, An Introduction to the Theory of Laser Material Processing', Chapman and Hall/CRC; first edition (May 24, 2001).

57. V. K. Konyukhov, I. V. Matrasov, A. M. Prokhorov, D. T. Shalunov, and N. N. Shirokov, *JETP Letters* **12**, 321 (1970).

58. Jeff Hecht, "Beam Weapons, The Next Arms Race", Plenum Publishing Corporation, 1984.

59. Donald H. Menzel, edited, *Fundamental Formulas of Physics*, Vol. 2 (Dover, New York, 1960), P. 416.

60. John N. Bahcall and Lyman Spitzer, Jr., "The space telescope", *Scientific American* **247** (1), 40-51 (July 1982).

61. "Senate directs Air Force to formulate laser plan", *Aviation Week & Space Technology*, May 25, 1981, pp. 52-55.

62. Michael Mendoza and William Jone, "Effects of Atmospheric Turbulence on Laser Propagation", University of Maryland, The Maryland Optics Group.

63. Phillip Sprangle, Joseph Peñano and Bahman Hafizi, "Optimum Wavelength and Power for Efficient Laser Propagation in Various Atmospheric Environments", Naval Research Laboratory, Plasma Division.

64. Smith, D.C., "High-Power Laser Propagation - Thermal Blooming," Proc. IEEE 65, 1679 (1977).

65. The Infrared and Electro-Optical Systems Handbook, vol. 2, edited by F.G. Smith, Environmental Research Institute of Michigan, Ann Arbor, MI, and SPIE Optical Engineering Press, Bellingham, WA (1993).

66. Measures, R.M., "Laser Remote Sensing, Fundamentals and Applications," Krieger Publishing, Malabar, FL (1992).
67. Williams, F. A, Int. J. Heat Mass Transfer. 8, 575 (1965).
68. Caledonia, G.E. and J.D. Teare, J. Heat Transfer 99, 281 (1977).
69. Armstrong, R.L., Appl. Optics **23**, 148 (1984); Armstrong, R.L., J. Appl. Phys. **56**, 2142 (1984); Armstrong, R.L., S.A.W. Gerstl and A. Zardecki, J. Opt. Soc. Am. A **2**, 1739 (1985).
70. Davies, S.C. and J.R. Brock, App. Optics 26, 786 (1987).
71. Hänel, G., Beiträge zur Physik der Atmosphäre 44, 137 (1971).
72. Reid, J.S., D.L. Westphal, R.M. Paulus, S. Tsay and A. van Eijk, "Preliminary Evaluation of the Impacts of Aerosol Particles on Laser Performance in the Coastal Marine Boundary Layer," Naval Research Laboratory, Monterey, CA 93943-5502, NRL/MR/7534—04-8803, Jun. 2004.
73. Brown R.T. and D.C. Smith, J. App. Phys. 46, 402 (1975).
74. Fulghum, S.F., and M.M. Tilleman, J. Opt. Soc. Am. B 8, 2401 (1991).
75. Albert V. Jelalian, "Laser and microwave radar", *Laser Focus* **17** (4), 88-94 (April 1981).
76. F. G. Gebhardt and D. C. Smith, IEEE J. Quantum Electron. **QE-7**, 63 (1971).
77. R. T. Brwon and D. C. Smith, " Aerosol-induced thermal blooming", J Appl. Phys., Vol. 46, No. 1, January 1975.
78. J. A. Hodges, Appl. Opt. **11**, 2304 (1972).
79. Joseph Edward Wall, III, "Adaptive Optics for High Energy Laser Systems", Partial Fulfillment of the Requirements for the Degree of Master of Science in Electrical Engineering and Computer Science, Massachusetts Institute of Technology, May 30, 1994.
80. D. Greenwood and C. Primmerman, "Adaptive Optics Research at Lincoln Laboratory", *Lincoln Laboratory Journal,* Vol. 5, No. 1, pp. 131-150, Spring 1992.
81. T. Karr, "Thermal Blooming Compensation Instabilities", *J. Opt. Soc. Am. A* Vol. 6, No. 7, pp. 1038-1048, July 1989.
82. M. Born and E. Wolf, " Principles of Optics", Pergamon Press, 1980.
83. Hugo Weichel, "Laser Beam Propagation in the Atmosphere", Tutorial Texts in Optical Engineering by SPIE, The International Society for Optical Engineering, 1990.

84. BradleyW. Kimmel and Gladimir V.G. Baranoski, "A novel approach for simulating light interaction with particulate materials: application to the modeling of sand spectral properties", 23 July 2007 / Vol. 15, No. 15 / OPTICS EXPRESS 9755.

85. Charles S. Johnson, Jr. and Don A. Gabriel, "Laser Light Scattering", Dover Publication, Copyright 1981 by CRC Press, Inc.

86. D. Ross, "Light Amplification and Oscillators", Academic Press, New York, 1969, p 72.

87. T. J. Wieting and J. T. Schriempf, "Report of NRL Progress", June, 1972, pp. 1-13.

88. A. M. Bonch Bruevich and Ya. A. Imas, *Zh. Tekh. Fiz.* 37, 1917 (1967): English transl.: *Sov. Phys.-Tech. Phys.* **12**, 1407 (1968).

89. Vladimir P. Lukin and Boris V. Fortes, "Adaptive Beaming and Imaging in the Turbulent Atmosphere", SPIE PRESS, 2002.

90. V. V. Vorob'iev, *Thermal Blooming of Laser Beams in the Atmosphere: Theory and Model Experiment,* Nauka, Moscow, 1978.

91. James E. Pearson, R. H. Freeman, and Harold C. Reynolds, Jr., "Adaptive Optics Techniques for Wavefront Correction", *Applied Optics and Optical Engineering,* Vol. VII (Academic Press, New York, 1979) pp. 246-340.

92. R. H. Freeman and James E. Pearson, "Deformable Mirror for all Seasons and Reasons", *Applied Optics* **21** (4), 580-588 (February 15, 1982).

93. *Ibid.,* p. 581.

94. http://sharp.bu.edu/~slehar/PhaseConjugate/PhaseConjugate.html

95. Joseph S. Accetta and David N. Loomis, "High Energy Laser (HEL) Lethality Data Collection Standards-Revision A", Directed Energy Professional Society, Albuquerque, New Mexico, www.DEPS.org.

96. H. S. Carslaw and J. G. Jaeger, "Conduction of Heat in Solid", 2nd Edition, Page 112, Published by Oxford at the Clarendon Press, 1959.

97. W. W. Duley, " UV Lasers: effects and applications in materials science", Cambridge University Press, 1st edition, 1996.

98. S. Barbrino, F. Grasso, G. Guerriera, F. Musumeci, A. Scordino and A. Triglia, 1982. *Appl. Phys.* **A29**, 77.

99. A. Roos, M. Bergkvist. and C. G. Ribbing, 1989. *Appl. Opt.* **28**, 1360.

100. G. Kinsman and W. W. Duley, 1993. *Appl. Opt.* **32**, 7462.

101. F. Wooten, "Optical Properties of Solids", Academic Press, New York, 1972.

102. J. B. Birks, "Photophysics of Aromatic Molecules", Wiley-Interscience, London, 1970.

103. A. Vertes, P. Juhasz, R. Gijbels, Z. Fresenius, *Anal. Chem.*, **1989**, 334, 682.

104. L. Balaze, R. Gijbels and A. Vertes, *Anal. Chem.*, **1991**, 63, 314.

105. Y. Kawmura, K. Toyoda, and M. Kawai, **1984**. *Appl. Phys. Lett.* **45**, 308.

106. Vertes, A.; Juhasz, P.; De Wolf, M.; Gijbels, R. *Int. J. Mass Spectrum Ion. Processes* 1989, 94, 63.

107. Vertes, A.; Juhasz, P.; De Wolf, M.; Gijbels, R. Scanning Mcrosc. 1988, 2, 1853.

108. Vertes, A.; Juhasz, P.; De Wolf, M.; Gijbels, R. Adv. A&s Spectrom. 1989, 77, 1638.

109. M. O. Oziski, "Boundar Value Problems of Heat Conduction", Published by Dover, 1968.

110. Dr. Carlo Kopp "High Power Microwave", http://www.globalsecurity.org/military/systems/munitions/hpm.htm.

111. Dr. Richard M. Roberds, "Introducing the Particle-Beam Weapon", http://www.airpower.maxwell.af.mil/airchronicles/aureview/1984/jul-aug/roberds.html.

APPENDIX A: DATA AND PLOTS OF THERMAL PARAMETERS OF DIFFERENT MATERIALS

One of the major goals of physics and so as ours in case of laser in particular and its interaction with materials is to understand the nature of light. Due to the complexity nature of the light this goal is very difficult to fully achieve but this complication means that light offers many opportunities for different applications including optical interferences and in our case response of materials to laser radiation and its interaction with matter and specifically metallic materials.

A-1 Thermal Conductivity Data

Plots of K versus T are given for aluminum, copper, chromium, cobalt, gold, iron, lead, molybdenum, nickel, platinum, rhodium, silver, tantalum, tin, titanium, tungsten, uranium, vanadium, zinc, zirconium, Armco iron, 302, 303, and 304 stainless steel, aluminum oxide, fused quartz, magnesium oxide, and titanium dioxide. K is in units of W / cm ^{0}C.

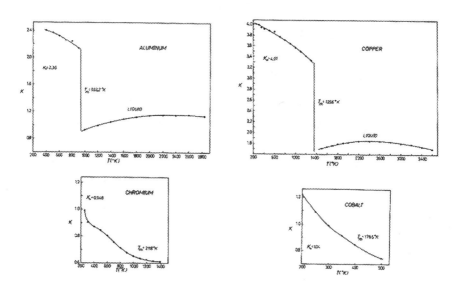

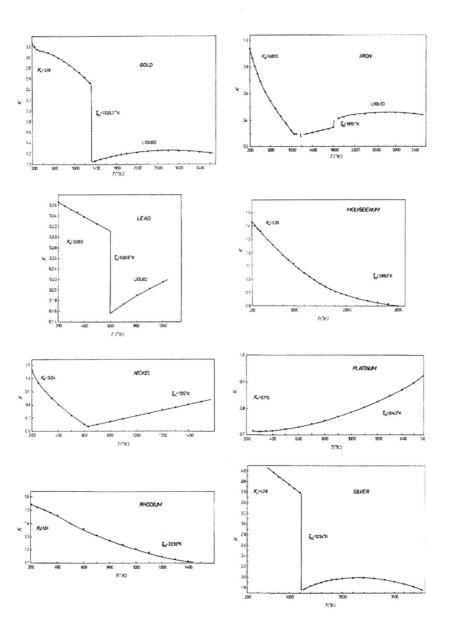

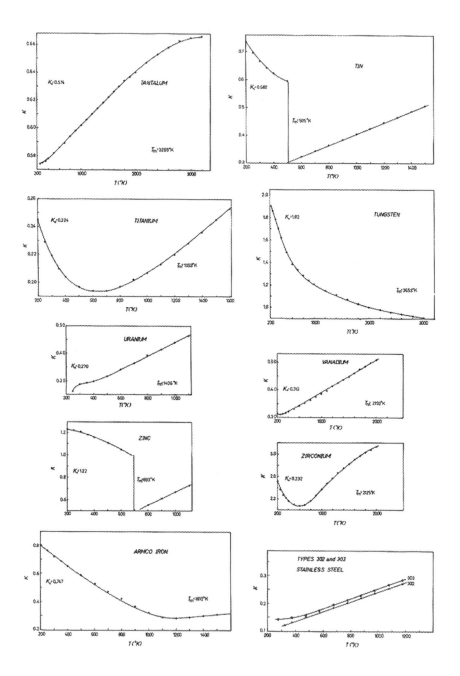

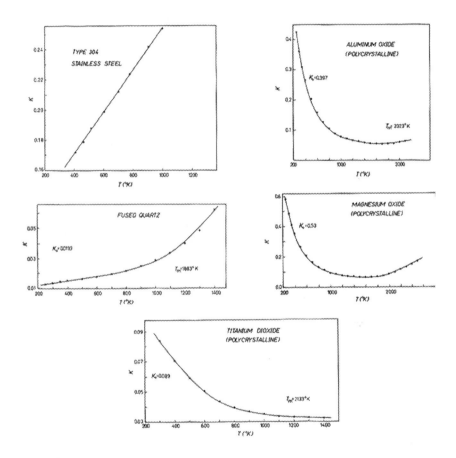

A-2 Heat Capacities

Plots of C_p versus T are given for aluminum, chromium, copper, gold, iron, lead, molybdenum, nickel, platinum, silver, tantalum, tin, titanium, tungsten, uranium, vanadium, zinc, zirconium, Armco iron, 304 stainless steel, aluminum oxide, magnesium oxide, fused quartz, and titanium dioxide. C_p is in units of J/g ^{0}C.

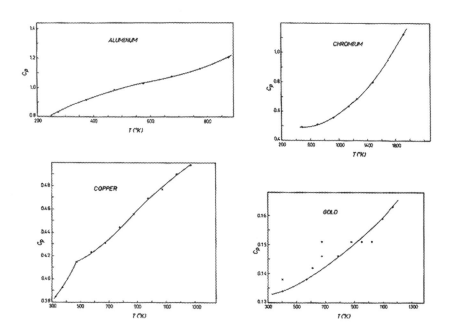

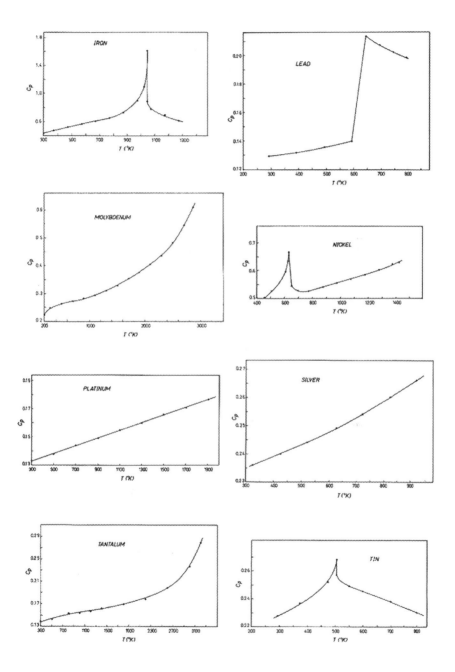

279

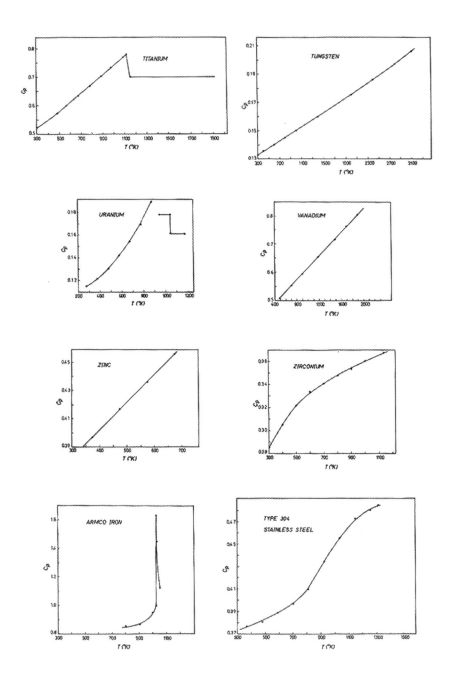

280

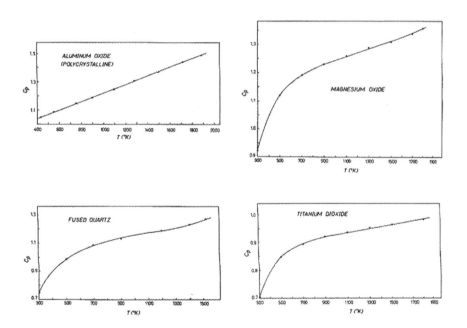

A-3 Thermal Diffusivity Data

Plots of κ versus T are given for aluminum, chromium, copper, gold, iron, lead, molybdenum, nickel, platinum, silver, tantalum, titanium, tungsten, uranium, vanadium, zinc, zirconium, 304 stainless steel, aluminum oxide, magnesium oxide, fused quartz, and titanium dioxide. κ in units of cm ^{2}/sec.

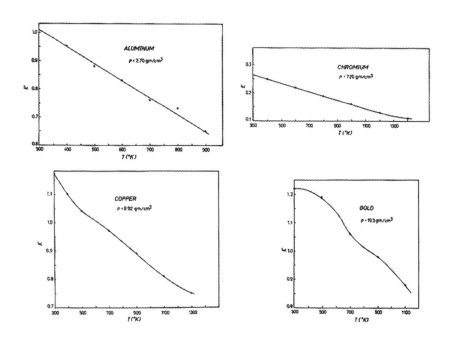

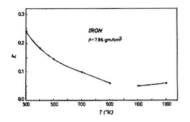

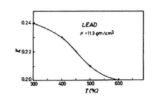

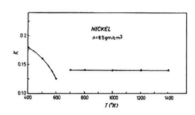

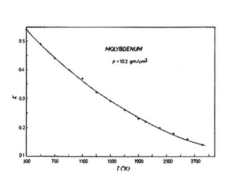

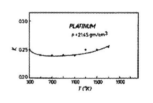

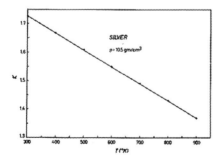

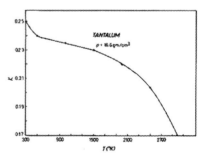

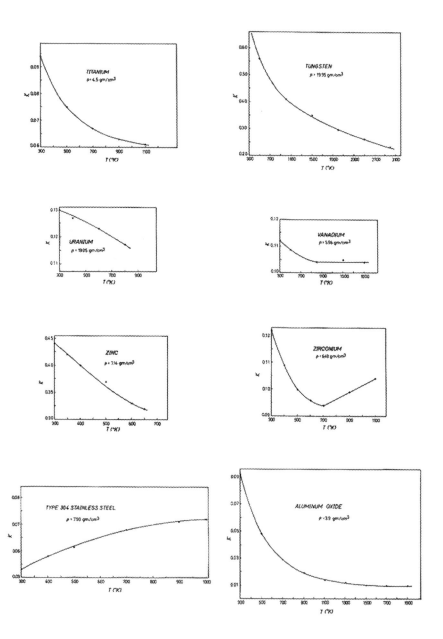

284

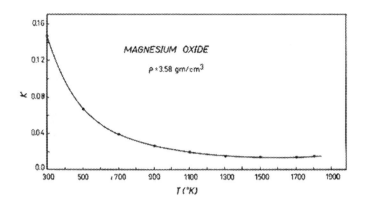

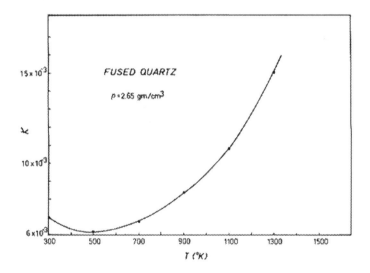

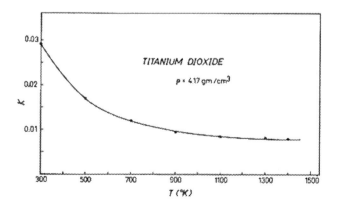

A-4 References

Additional references for more information for the readers that are interested to study further.

References:

Anisimov S. I. et al., 1971, Effects of High-power Radiation on Metals

Knudsen M., 1909 Ann. Phys., Lpz. 28 999

Finke B. R. and G. Simon, 1988, "On the gas kinetics of laser-induced evaporation of metals," *J. Phys. D: Appl. Phys.* 23 (1990) 67-74.

Knight, C. J., "Theoretical Modeling of Rapid Surface Vaporization with Back Pressure," *AIAA Journal*, Vol. 17., No. 5, May 1979.

Wenwu Zhang, Y. Lawrence Yao,"Modeling and Analysis of UV Laser Micro-machining of Copper," *ICALEO 2000*.

References:

J. Crank, *Free and moving boundary problems*. Clarendon Press, Oxford (1984)

N. Ramachandran, J. R. Gupta and Y. Jalunu, Theraml and fluid flow effects during solidification in a rectangular cavity. *Int. J. Heat Mass Transfer* 25, 187-194 (1982)

A. Gadgil and D. Gobin, Analysis of two dimensional melting in rectanguar enclosures in presence of convection, *J. Heat Transfer* 106, 20-26 (1984)

S. V. Partankar, *Numerical Heat Transfer and Fluid Flow*, Hemisphere, Washington, DC (1980)

V. R. Vollwe and C. Praksh, A fixed grid numerical modeling methodology for convection-diffusion mushy region phase-change problems. Int. J. Heat Mass Transfer., vol. 30, No. 8, pp.1709-1719, (1987).

Wenwu Zhang,Y. Lawrence Yao and Kai Chen, 2000, "Modeling and Analysis of UV Laser Micro-machining of Copper," ICALEO 2000.

References:

Suhas V. Patankar, 1980, Numerical Heat Transfer and Fluid Flow, McGraw, new York, 1980.

J. Mazumder, P.S. Mohanty and A. Kar, "Mathematical modelling of laser materials processing," 1996, *Int. J. of Materials and Product Technology*, Vol. 11, pp.193-252.

Frank, P. I. and David P. D., 1996, Fundamentals of Heat and Mass Transfer, John Wiley & Sons, Inc., 4th edition, New York.

Frank, M. W., 1999, Fluid Mechanics, WCB/McGraw-Hill, 4th edition, New York

References:

Aden, M., et al., 1992, "Laser-induced vaporization of a metal surface," J. Phys., D 25, pp. 57-65.

Dabby, F.W., and Paek, U.C., 1972, "High-intensity laser-induced vaporization and explosion of solid material," IEEE J. of Quantum Electronics, Vol. QE-8, No. 2, pp. 106-111.

Ho, J. R., et al., 1995, "Computational Model for the Heat Transfer and Gas Dynamics in the Pulsed Laser Evaporation of Metals," J. Appl. Phys., Vol. 78(7), pp. 4696-4709.

Kar, A., and Mazumder, 1994, "Mathematical model for laser ablation to generate nanoscale and submicometer-size particles," J. Physical Review E, Vol. 49(1), pp. 410-419.

Kezhun Li and Paul Sheng, 1995, "Computational model for laser cutting of steel plates," MED-Vol.2-1/MH-MH-Vol.3-1, Manufacturing Science and Engineering, ASME 1995, pp.3-14.

L. Cai and P. Sheng, 1996,"Analysis of laser evaporative and fusion cutting," Journal of Manufacturing Science and Engineering, May 1996, Vol.118, pp.225-234

Modest, M. F., 1996, "Three-dimensional, transient model for laser machining of ablating de-composing materials," Int. J. Heat Mass Transfer, Vol 39 (2), pp. 221-234.

Paek, U. C., and Gagliano, F. P., 1972, "Thermal analysis of laser drilling processes," IEEE J. of Quantum Electronics, Vol. QE-8, pp. 112-119.

Singh, R. K., and Narayan, J., 1990, "Pulsed-laser evaporation technique for deposition of thin films: physics and theoretical model," Phys. Rev. B 41(3), pp.8843-8859.

APPENDIX B: ACRONYMS AND DEFINITIONS

DOF

> The depth of focus is the distance over which the focused beam has about the same intensity; it is defined as the distance over which the focal spot size changes -5%~5%.

Electronic assembly

> A number of electronic components (i.e., "circuit elements", "discrete components", integrated circuits, etc.) connected together to perform (a) specific function(s), replaceable as an entity and normally capable of being disassembled.

Evaporative Laser Cutting

> Evaporative laser cutting is the laser cutting process that target material is ablated through direct vaporization; typical applications are laser cutting of low vaporization temperature and low thermal conduction materials.

Excimer Lasers

> Lasers which use the noble gas compounds for lasing. Excimer lasers generate laser light in ultraviolet to near-ultraviolet spectra, from 0.193 to 0.351 microns. Gas Laser A laser in which the active medium is gas. The gas can be composed of molecules (like CO^2), Atoms (like He-Ne), or ions (like Ar+).

Laser Fusion cutting

> Laser fusion cutting is laser cutting through melting and gas jet blowing.

Ground State

> Lowest energy level of an atom or molecule.

Heat Affected Zone

Heat affected zone is the region close to the laser irradiated area that obvious temperature change from original area happens, or obvious strain state change happens.

Hologram

An interference phenomena captured on a plate (or film). It can contain enormous amount of information and a 3 dimensional image can be constructed from it.

Knudesen layer

In laser processeing, strong evaporation occurs. The gas near the phase interface is not in translational equilibrium and the translational equilibrium is achieved within a few mean free paths by collisions between particles in a thin region. This region is called Knudsen layer

Laser

Laser is the acronym of Light Amplification by Stimulated Emission of Radiation. Laser is light of special properties, light is electromagnetic (EM) wave in visible range. Lasers, broadly speaking, are devices that generate or amplify light, just as transistors generate and amplify electronic signals at audio, radio or microwave frequencies. Here light must be understand broadly, since lasers have covered radiation at wavelengths ranging from infrared range to ultraviolet and even soft x-ray range.

Laser machining

Laser machining is material removal accomplished by laser material interaction, generally speaking, these processes include laser drilling, laser cutting and laser grooving, marking or scribing.

Laser Mode

Laser mode is the possible standing em waves in laser cavity.

Longitudinal (Axial) Modes

Axial standing em waves within the laser cavity.

Laser Resonator or Laser Cavity

The optical mirrors, <u>active medium</u> and pumping system form the <u>laser resonator</u>, which is also called Laser Cavity. Laser cavities can be divided into Stable Cavities and Unstable Cavities according to whether they make the oscillating beam converge into the cavity or spread out from the cavity.

Line-width

The line-width of laser is the width of laser beam frequency. Laser line-width is much narrower than normal light.

Liquid Laser

Lasers which use large organic dye molecules as the active lasing medium.

M^2 of the beam

M^2 is a beam quality index that measures the difference between an actual beam and the Gaussian beam.

Matrix

A substantially continuous phase that fills the space between particles, whiskers or fibers.

Marangoni Mechanism

Liquid surface force due to temperature gradient (thermal) or composition gradient (chemical)

Microcircuit

A "monolithic integrated circuit" or "multichip integrated circuit" containing an arithmetic logic unit (ALU) capable of executing a series of general purpose instructions from an external storage. N.B.1: The "microprocessor microcircuit" normally does not contain integral user-accessible storage, although storage present on-the-chip may be used in performing its logic function. N.B.2: This definition includes chip sets which are designed to operate together to provide the function of a "microprocessor microcircuit".

Multichip

A "integrated circuit" where two or more "monolithic integrated circuits" bonded to a common "substrate".

Mode Locking

A method to create very short laser pulses. It makes the phase difference of many modes (frequencies) in the laser cavity fixed, or locked, thus very narrow pulses (in time) are created.

Mushy region

Phase changes happen over a temperature region in general, thus solid and liquid state coexist during phase changes. The region of this mixture of solid and liquid is called Mushy region.

Photon

The minimum quantity of light energy that can be exchanged is called a light quantum or photon.

Polarized Light

If the light has a dominant direction of the E vector, we say the light is polarized. Natural light is not polarized, while laser beam is polarized. Polarization can be created and adjusted by polarizer.

Population Inversion

Normally the number of atoms at high energy level(E1) is less than those in low energy level(E1), $N2(E2) < N1(E1)$. If $N2>N1$, we say population inversion exists, which is a necessary condition for lasing.

Pumping

The process to raise atoms from lower level to upper level is called pumping.

Q-Switching

A method to create laser pulses. It modulates the Q (Quality) of laser cavity to build population inversion first, then release the accumulated energy suddenly, in this way high energy pulses can be created.

Recombination Radiation

In semiconductors, when the electrons combine with the holes, photons are emitted, this is called Recombination **Radiation Semiconductor Lasers** are based on this mechanism.

Resolution

The least increment of a measuring device; on digital instruments, the least significant bit. (Reference: ANSI B-89.1.12)

Solid State Laser

A laser in which the active medium is in solid state (usually not including semiconductor lasers).

Semiconductor Lasers

Lasers which use semiconductor as active medium. The majority of semiconductor materials are based on a combination of elements in the third group of the Periodic Table (such as Al, Ga, In) and the fifth group (such as N, P, As, Sb) hence referred to as the III-V compounds.

Spontaneous Radiation

According to quantum mechanics, the electrons of atoms can take different energy states, say E1, E2, E3, etc., E1<E2<E3<.... Lower energy level is more stable than higher energy levels, so electrons at high energy levels tend to decay to low energy levels, the energy difference between the two levels can be given out as electromagnetic radiation. This process is called Spontaneous Radiation.

Stable Cavity and Unstable Cavity

Cavities can be identified as stable or unstable according to whether they make the oscillating beam converge into the cavity or spread out of the cavity, if converge it is stable, if spread out, it is unstable.

Stimulated Absorption

When the atoms at lower energy levels absorb the incident energy with corresponding frequency, they jump to upper level states, this is called Stimulated Absorption.

Stimulated Emission

Under the action of the incident electromagnetic field with the corresponding frequency, the atoms at upper level have a certain possibility to jump to the corresponding lower levels, emitting electromagnetic waves or photons with the same frequency, direction and phase with the incident waves. This process is called Stimulated Emission.

Substrate

A sheet of base material with or without an interconnection pattern and on which or within which "discrete components" or integrated circuits or both can be located.

Super-alloy

Nickel-, cobalt- or iron-base alloys having strengths superior to any alloys in the AISI 300 series at temperatures over 922 K (649° C) under severe environmental and operating conditions.

TEM Mode

Transverse Electromagnetic Mode (TEM) of laser beam is called TEM mode. Three index are used to indicate the TEM modes. TEMplq, p is the number of radial zero fields, l is the number of angular zero fields, q is the number of longitudinal fields.

YAG

yttrium/aluminum garnet

Ultra-short Pulsed Laser

Laser whose pulse duration time is very short, below 1 ns, usually in the fs scale.

INDEX